Research Meth
for Complexity
Theory in Applied
Linguistics

SECOND LANGUAGE ACQUISITION

Series Editors: **Professor David Singleton**, *University of Pannonia, Hungary* and Fellow Emeritus, *Trinity College, Dublin, Ireland* and **Associate Professor Simone E. Pfenninger**, *University of Salzburg, Austria*

This series brings together titles dealing with a variety of aspects of language acquisition and processing in situations where a language or languages other than the native language is involved. Second language is thus interpreted in its broadest possible sense. The volumes included in the series all offer in their different ways, on the one hand, exposition and discussion of empirical findings and, on the other, some degree of theoretical reflection. In this latter connection, no particular theoretical stance is privileged in the series; nor is any relevant perspective – sociolinguistic, psycholinguistic, neurolinguistic, etc. – deemed out of place. The intended readership of the series includes final-year undergraduates working on second language acquisition projects, postgraduate students involved in second language acquisition research, and researchers, teachers and policymakers in general whose interests include a second language acquisition component.

All books in this series are externally peer-reviewed.

Full details of all the books in this series and of all our other publications can be found on http://www.multilingual-matters.com, or by writing to Multilingual Matters, St Nicholas House, 31-34 High Street, Bristol BS1 2AW, UK.

SECOND LANGUAGE ACQUISITION: 137

Research Methods for Complexity Theory in Applied Linguistics

Phil Hiver and Ali H. Al-Hoorie

MULTILINGUAL MATTERS
Bristol • Blue Ridge Summit

DOI https://doi.org/10.21832/HIVER5747
Library of Congress Cataloging in Publication Data
A catalog record for this book is available from the Library of Congress.
Names: Hiver, Phil, 1984- author. | Al-Hoorie, Ali H., 1982- author.
Title: Research Methods for Complexity Theory in Applied Linguistics/Phil Hiver and Ali H. Al-Hoorie.
Description: Blue Ridge Summit: 2019. | Series: Second Language Acquisition: 137 | Includes bibliographical references and index. | Summary: "This accessible guide to Complex Dynamic Systems Theory (CDST) research presents practical methods and templates for how applied linguistics researchers can design and conduct research using the CDST framework and equips readers with the knowledge to ensure compatibility between empirical research designs and the theoretical tenets of complexity"— Provided by publisher.
Identifiers: LCCN 2019021985 | ISBN 9781788925747 (hardback) | ISBN 9781788925730 (paperback) | ISBN 9781788925778 (kindle edition) | ISBN 9781788925761 (epub) | ISBN 9781788925754 (pdf)
Subjects: LCSH: Language and languages—Study and teaching. | Second language acquisition—Study and teaching. | System theory.
Classification: LCC P53 .H565 2019 | DDC 401/.93—dc23
LC record available at https://lccn.loc.gov/2019021985

British Library Cataloguing in Publication Data
A catalogue entry for this book is available from the British Library.

ISBN-13: 978-1-78892-574-7 (hbk)
ISBN-13: 978-1-78892-573-0 (pbk)

Multilingual Matters
UK: St Nicholas House, 31-34 High Street, Bristol BS1 2AW, UK.
USA: NBN, Blue Ridge Summit, PA, USA.

Website: www.multilingual-matters.com
Twitter: Multi_Ling_Mat
Facebook: https://www.facebook.com/multilingualmatters
Blog: www.channelviewpublications.wordpress.com

The policy of Multilingual Matters/Channel View Publications is to use papers that are natural, renewable and recyclable products, made from wood grown in sustainable forests. In the manufacturing process of our books, and to further support our policy, preference is given to printers that have FSC and PEFC Chain of Custody certification. The FSC and/or PEFC logos will appear on those books where full certification has been granted to the printer concerned.

Typeset by Deanta Global Publishing Services, Chennai, India.
Printed and bound in the UK by Short Run Press Ltd.
Printed and bound in the US by NBN.

Contents

Part 4: The Future of CDST Methodology

Foreword: Taking the Next Step

It was only five years ago, in 2014, that I had an opportunity to speak at the University of Nottingham at the invitation of Professor Zoltán Dörnyei. On that occasion (the Motivational Dynamics Conference), Professor Dörnyei introduced me to two of his graduate students – Phil Hiver and Ali Al-Hoorie. He told me that the two were excellent students and that they were interested in complexity theory. It was clear to me then, not only from the strong endorsement by Professor Dörnyei, but also by the depth with which the students and I engaged in discussions of complexity theory (one of which took place on an excursion to Sherwood Forest!), that these were two gifted scholars. Well, time has passed, and Professor Hiver and Professor Al-Hoorie are no longer graduate students, but academics in their own universities. They have had a productive collaboration in the intervening years, and happily, they have joined forces once again to produce this volume. I am grateful that they have done so.

This is an important book. Complexity theory has ushered in a new way of thinking, challenging some basic conceptions about how scientific inquiry should be conducted. No longer can we be content with Newtonian reductionism, a Laplacian clockwork universe with its deterministic predictability and the use of statistics to generalize from the behavior of population samples to individuals. Closer to our academic interests, this new way of thinking has called into question conventional ideas about language and its learning/development. For instance, language has been seen as composed of a static system of rules, and second language acquisition has been depicted as taking place when learners move from speaking a fixed homogeneous native language to one which increasingly conforms to a uniform target language. This earlier perspective is in sharp contrast with what complexity theory affords.

With complexity theory, or complex dynamic systems theory (CDST, as it is called when applied to second language development), the shape that language takes is deferred, always in process, ever-emerging dynamically from interaction. It is helpful to conceive of language as displaying 'patterns in the flux', like an eddy in a mountain stream, where the water droplets are continually flowing through while the pattern endures.

CDST posits a poststructural ecological view, in which the spatiotemporal context is seen as playing an integral role in affecting development. For this reason, it is counterproductive to separate the learner from the learning process. Individual differences are truly person-oriented, even phenomenological, and mutable. Variability in intra- and inter-individual performance is ubiquitous. Equifinality, *autopoiesis*, self-organization, interconnectedness, co-adaptation, transdisciplinarity – all are core, foundational features of open complex systems.

Clearly, I have provided only a partial and an abbreviated account of the new ontology that CDST has introduced. For some, this new way of thinking has yielded rich descriptions of complex systems, including those in second language development. Indeed, much early inquiry was directed at determining if the characteristics of complex systems applied to phenomena of interest to applied linguists. The result of these investigations has powerfully informed theorizing and philosophical explorations, and it has inspired significant new insights into the nature of language and its learning/development. Additionally, Lynne Cameron and I suggested 'complexity thought modelling', i.e. ways to think in terms of complex systems as a lead-in to actual data collection or to conducting an intervention. Hiver and Al-Hoorie extended this basic modeling approach by proposing a 'dynamic ensemble', nine considerations intended to inform research design – both approaches valuable for conveying what a different way of thinking would entail for empirical investigations.

Still, if the value of CDST is to be fully realized, researchers need to take the next step beyond describing and theorizing change in dynamic systems; they need to conduct research and adduce evidence, informed by CDST. Some researchers have already done so, but methodological options have not always been apparent. Indeed, it has not been immediately obvious how to go about studying processes of change, particularly when the relation among the factors in focus wax and wane in their influence with the passing of time and when the particular spatiotemporal context in which the complex system is embedded is so influential. Yet, we applied linguists know that our problem orientation means that we have a responsibility to go beyond the unique time and place of a study and to posit a connection between events that were studied and those that were not.

What this book gives us is a rich array of research methods in order to begin to make that connection. It provides an invaluable guide for how to go about designing and implementing research consistent with CDST. It does so by taking into consideration what readers are likely to bring to their reading, providing accessible descriptions of each method, one per chapter, illustrating each method with an example study and linking each to a set of research questions and annotated readings. The book concludes with a helpful glossary and provides further resources.

Interpretations of CDST can sometimes be superficial, merely pointing out the shared attributes between complex systems and language; that is certainly how many of us began. In this, their latest contribution, Hiver and Al-Hoorie display a depth of understanding of the fundamental CDST concepts, and they take us beyond description to research designs that are sensitive to a complex and dynamic reality. Further, the volume is impressive for how the authors deal in a sophisticated and nuanced way with demanding issues (from a CDST point of view), such as causality and generalizability.

I also appreciate the anecdotes that make this text eminently readable, such as learning that Sir Ronald Fisher's poor eyesight meant that he had to rely on his imagination when it came to mathematics, which allowed him to visualize math geometrically and be the first to lay the foundation for modern statistics. The authors' comments at other times are amusing, but I don't want to be a spoiler by relaying them here.

Another quality I appreciate in this book is that while it does not walk away from controversy (e.g. the current preference for, and debate over, mixed methods), it thoroughly engages in the issue, and thus it is not immediately dismissive of particular positions. This restraint is not always evident in applied linguistics, but one in which civility does not reflect weakness, but rather indicates a commitment to a deeper, less divisive understanding. As an illustration, the authors conclude a discussion of this particular controversy by wisely counseling that research methods should be integrated rather than mixed.

The potential to deliver robust findings, consistently and convincingly, through powerful analytical tools is a most welcome next step in the evolution of CDST in service to furthering our understanding of second language development. Taking the next step to a problem-oriented approach to scientific inquiry means that this book, a model of clarity, is fully consonant with the best of what is on offer from applied linguistics. For me personally, I derive a great deal of comfort from knowing that the important and profound work of a CDST-inspired understanding of second language development is in good hands and that it will continue.

Diane Larsen-Freeman
Professor Emerita, University of Michigan
May 2019

Dedicated to Zoltán Dörnyei

supervisor
mentor
friend

Part 1

Introduction to Complexity Theory

1 Introduction

Complexity is part of the world, but it shouldn't be puzzling: we can accept it if we believe that this is the way things must be [and] explore the nature of complexity, relish its depth, richness, and beauty, [and] at the same time... fight against unnecessary complications.

Norman (2011: 4)

Over the past several years, complexity and dynamic systems theory (CDST) has captured the imagination of many in the field of applied linguistics. By way of illustration, consider that Larsen-Freeman's (1997) first proposal that applied linguistics issues could profit by being viewed explicitly in complexity terms is now listed as among the most influential articles in the field (de Bot, 2015). Similarly, Larsen-Freeman and Cameron's (2008a) comprehensive, prize-winning, field-specific overview of CDST has also been ranked among the most impactful books in applied linguistics (de Bot, 2015). We must admit that we find this explosion of interest in CDST unsurprising. After all, applied linguistics is a broad and inclusive field with a distinct flavor of hybridity – what some refer to as interdisciplinarity – and has always been characterized by an openness to outside influences (Chapelle, 2014). A general intellectual reorientation around complexity theory has swept through the social disciplines more broadly, providing evidence that many of the major issues of our time are complex and systemic and must be approached with a corresponding shift in perception (Capra & Luisi, 2014). Applied linguistics, too, has now 'gone complex', and the fact that complexity has emerged as an influence on applied linguists' thinking in important ways is perhaps to be expected and welcomed.

Newcomers to such ideas may wonder, however, why adopt a CDST framing at all? What does CDST enable us to accomplish that we would not otherwise be able to get at, do, see and talk about in applied linguistics research (see e.g. Ortega & Han, 2017)? For starters, complexity is an empirical reality of the human and social world. The place of CDST in

21st-century applied linguistics, for us, is oriented by a claim that Edgar Morin has made in his work:

> Fragmented thinking makes us unable to connect parts and wholes, to deal with change, the unexpected and the uncertain in response to the continuing acquisition of new information. We need, instead, a radical capacity to reconnect subjects that are disjointed and compartmentalized, to think about their complexity, their totality.... We must learn to navigate on a sea of uncertainties. (Morin, 2001: 1–3)

CDST, in this sense, allows the ideas and issues that applied linguists grapple with, both by design and as a matter of course, to be more closely understood in ways that better approximate their dynamic and situated realities (see e.g. Larsen-Freeman & Cameron, 2008a).

As recent work (e.g. Larsen-Freeman, 2017) synthesizing current strands of applied linguistics that have been informed by CDST shows, CDST has continued to permeate questions throughout language development/acquisition (de Bot, 2008; Ellis & Larsen-Freeman, 2009; Verspoor *et al.*, 2008), language attrition (Schmid *et al.*, 2013), language change (Cooper, 1999; Kretzschmar, 2015), language ecology (Cowley, 2011; Kramsch & Whiteside, 2008), language evolution (Ke & Holland, 2006; Mufwene *et al.*, 2017), language policy and planning (Hogan-Brun & Hogan, 2013; Hult, 2010a; Larsen-Freeman, 2018b), language pedagogy (Kostoulas *et al.*, 2018; Mercer, 2013, 2016), lingua franca English (Baird *et al.*, 2014; Bouchard, 2018; Larsen-Freeman, 2018a), linguistic landscapes (Soler-Carbonnell, 2016), bilingualism and multilingualism (Herdina & Jessner, 2002; Todeva, 2009), sociolinguistics (Bastardas-Boada, 2013; Blommaert, 2014), educational linguistics (Hult, 2010b), conversation analysis (Seedhouse, 2010), communication studies (Massip-Bonet & Bastardas-Boada, 2013; Massip-Bonet *et al.*, 2019) and countless other areas of applied linguistics.

At the same time, applied linguistics has always had an explicit orientation to practical concerns in the real world. Its application is in relation to events, spatiotemporal settings and people for which knowledge of language and its use are key to resolving dilemmas of one sort or another (Davies & Elder, 2004). Complexity is equally grounded in the phenomenological reality of the social world, and in countless conversations with other applied linguists we have heard time and again that such a perspective makes good intellectual sense given its ability to capture the inherent situated and dynamic reality of such phenomena of interest. Equally often, however, we have heard that despite close resonances between CDST and scholars' thematic areas of expertise, the methods for 'doing' CDST and researching such issues using insights from CDST remain elusive (cf. Lowie, 2017; MacIntyre *et al.*, 2015). This is perhaps surprising, given what is now clear to us: CDST is grounded in a problem-focused orientation to research methodology and calls for approaches to doing science that emerge from the needs of inquiry (Morin, 2008). Clearly, the main hurdle to empirical scholarship informed by complexity theory has been applied linguists' uncertainty regarding what designing and conducting actual CDST research entails (e.g. MacIntyre *et al.*, 2017). The result is a distinct lack of consensus regarding which phenomena or questions merit examination, how systematic investigation should be structured and conducted (e.g. with regard to instrumentation and data collection) and how the results of this research should be analyzed and interpreted (e.g. Ellis, 2018).

How We Came to Write This Book

In an intensely emotional recount of the intellectual challenges of grappling with new concepts for which scientists' language and way of thinking at the time were inadequate, Nobel Prize winner Werner Heisenberg (1901–1976) recalls that

> I remember discussions with [Niels] Bohr which went through many hours till very late at night and ended almost in despair; and when at the end of the discussion I went alone for a walk in the neighboring park I repeated to myself again and again the question: Can nature possibly be so absurd as it seemed to us in these... experiments? (Heisenberg, 1958: 42)

It took these physicists an extended period of time to accept that complexity and the seeming paradoxes it encompassed were essential to understanding the way things exist in nature. Once they did, however, they began to ask more precise and insightful questions and discover explanations for these seeming contradictions which shaped one of the most exciting periods of modern science (Capra & Luisi, 2014).

Though less dramatic, our own experience with complexity theory has been marked by a similar struggle as the intellectual challenge these quantum physicists encountered – navigating, in a sense, on Morin's (2001) 'sea of uncertainties'. We both began our scholarly apprenticeship and research careers in applied linguistics with an interest in people – that is, we developed a fascination with how individuals' (i.e. learners and teachers) thoughts and actions in settings of second and foreign language (L2) learning and instruction contribute to their meaningful participation and ongoing development in those environments and how such psychosocial aspects of L2 learning lead to intentional effort, engagement and persistence on the part of those individuals. Of course, in our desire to understand the ways and means by which individuals actively devote effort and attention to L2 learning opportunities, we saw little choice but to foreground the interdependencies between the many cognitive, affective and behavioral factors at the individual level as well as between individuals and their environment. This natural development was encouraged by the thinking and influence of our mentors in the field (Dörnyei, 2008, 2017; Larsen-Freeman, 2012; Mercer, 2011; Verspoor *et al.*, 2011). Our work, like theirs, sought to place an explicit focus on language in contexts of learning, teaching and use, and called direct attention to the dynamic nature of these phenomena. However, this project was anything but straightforward.

We discovered firsthand that one of the pre-eminent challenges of doing applied linguistics research from this dynamic and situated perspective is, with a handful of notable exceptions (e.g. Larsen-Freeman & Cameron, 2008b; Verspoor *et al.*, 2011), very little methodological guidance exists for those intending to design and conduct research informed by complexity theory. Even in the social sciences more broadly, the sources on complexity research that exist are framed conceptually (see e.g. Mitleton-Kelly *et al.*, 2018) – this disconnect is somewhat similar to trying to learn to drive a car by referencing an explanation of drive-by-wire and throttle-by-wire mechanisms instead of taking a practice drive. This is not a scenario we would wish on anyone. As we have written elsewhere, we discovered almost immediately that scholarly work stops short of the level of practical application necessary to ensure compatibility between empirical research designs and the theoretical tenets of complexity (Hiver & Al-Hoorie, 2016). In response to this, we expanded the scope of our search for such methodological guidance. We read voraciously on complexity and research methods – as just one example, the 12,000-page *Encyclopedia of Complexity and Systems Science* (Meyers, 2009) became our bedtime reading. This early experience of exploring Lyapunov functions, Feigenbaum constants and Mandelbrot set algorithms was informative and it convinced us of several things.

Primarily, we became convinced, like our mentors, that uncritically importing mathematical methods wholesale from complexity science would be of limited productivity, given that the objects of interest in applied linguistics sometimes differ radically from those in the natural sciences, and because the social sciences do not have the sort of data that the physical sciences use to model complexity mathematically (Dörnyei *et al.*, 2015; Larsen-Freeman & Cameron, 2008b; Verspoor *et al.*, 2011). However, we were equally convinced that the existing templates and methods of analysis already well-established in empirical complexity research in other human and social domains hold considerable promise for studying complex dynamic phenomena in the field of applied linguistics. As we hope to show in Parts 2 and 3 of this book, both quantitative and qualitative methodologies play a vital role in CDST research. Complexity's philosophy of science does not suggest a mutually exclusive approach, and advocating an either/or choice is neither defensible nor pragmatic for the range of phenomena that necessitate investigation. The value of qualitative methods is that they allow finely grained observations of situated developmental processes, and, as we also hope to show, advanced quantitative techniques that value variation, interconnectedness and change do exist.

Having said this, we should not be naïve to the fact that the introduction of any 'new' research approach frequently leads to two different reactions from the research community: the inclination to reject the approach as 'too risky' (i.e. too difficult to learn and apply), or as 'nothing new'. Here, we draw inspiration from Lisa Feldman Barrett (2017) who writes:

> Scientific revolutions are difficult. At the beginning, new paradigms raise more questions than they answer. They may explain existing anomalies or redefine lingering questions out of existence, but they also introduce a new set of questions that can be answered only with new experimental and computational techniques. This is a feature, not a bug.... A new paradigm barely gets started before it is criticized for not providing all the answers. But progress in science is often not answering old questions but asking better ones. The value of a new approach is never based on answering the questions of the old approach. (Barrett, 2017: 14)

We hope to encourage active engagement with these methods and ideas, first, by reassuring readers that the methods for doing CDST research in applied linguistics that we have included in this book, though not exhaustive by any means, are in widespread use by social complexivists and have a firm methodological basis and examples, albeit outside of applied linguistics. In a sense then, we applied linguists are not 'going it alone'. Instead, by adopting these methods we are joining a vibrant community of like-minded researchers fascinated with the situated and dynamic nature of the human and social world. Second to this, each of these methods has a unique flavor as they explicitly address certain criteria or corresponding requirements for CDST research. We feel that, similar to a broader pivot in applied linguistics research methods to address issues of precision and rigor in empirical research, this innovation should be welcomed. In fact, several methods that are in widespread use across applied linguistics seem ill-suited to studying its complex and dynamic realities and situating these phenomena firmly in context. Clearly, an expansion of the available methods is needed. Our field is, therefore, following other social and human disciplines that also seek to understand complexity by routinely innovating with existing methods and borrowing compatible methods from neighboring fields. Our field is also catching up with advances in the methodological reform movement, including open instrumentation and material, open data, preregistration and replication. These initiatives can enrich the CDST research agenda.

Thus, we set out to write a book containing the research guidance that we would have liked to have when we set out to adopt this perspective in our own work. However, our point has never been to advance an agenda or provide a set of definitive answers, but rather to join a stimulating conversation with others that will make possible a different kind of practice in research. In the end, we have found this process to be one that closely mirrors the principles of self-organization and emergence. Although we certainly began with an initial picture of what kind of book we wanted this to be, how we arrived there was close to what Edgar Morin refers to as a *chemin faisant* (i.e. path-making) process in which the progress towards our goal was inherently exploratory and became much less bounded than at the outset. This is apropos to the focus of the volume, and we would not have wanted it any other way.

Organization of the Book

This book consists of four parts, each addressing a different angle of the main topic. Coming immediately after this general introduction, Chapter 2 sets out to introduce the conceptual apparatus and terminology of complexity theory. This is not intended to be a comprehensive overview of complexity science, as our main mission is to link CDST to research methods on which applied linguists can draw. However, some background context is appropriate to situate the methods we review and introduce their empirical *modus operandi*. This is the purpose of Chapter 2. We discuss the meaning and origins of complexity and systems thinking for research, and touch on several key principles and points of reference to begin to understand and operate within a CDST paradigm. Newcomers to CDST will find that the information presented in Chapter 2 can bring them up to speed relatively rapidly, while those familiar with CDST may also find that it sharpens their thinking on the enterprise of CDST research.

Chapter 3 takes a step forward from this background knowledge and examines the philosophical and methodological issues (e.g. generalizability, causality) that arise when researching the complex and dynamic social world. We do this by drawing a distinction between dealing with complexity empirically and doing so in a way that is more paradigmatic in nature. In addition, we discuss how the complex realist view of the world treads a middle way between realism and relativism, and informs a problem-driven approach to CDST research by relying on a pragmatic balance of methods determined by the object of inquiry. We then examine what some of the key tasks of CDST research might be and consider what these might mean for a transdisciplinary programme of applied linguistics research.

Starting from Part 2, we move from theory to methods in earnest. Our aim in the 14 chapters that make up Parts 2 (qualitative) and 3 (quantitative) is to provide a conceptual introduction to a range of methods for CDST research. Readers will discover that we do not provide as much detail as can be found in a typical book-length treatment of a single method. Put differently, our purpose is not to explain which button to click in a given software package for a given method – although we do refer the reader to further texts that provide this information. Instead, our primary goal in each chapter is to offer an informative *conceptual introduction* to the method in question. Our ultimate aim is to provide an overview of the available tools to help an applied linguist decide which of these available methods is most relevant to their topic of interest or most appropriate for their research questions. Once the reader picks a method, we then provide a guide to more in-depth information on actually applying it.

Each chapter deals with a different method. Each chapter starts by introducing the method, a variety of research questions it can address and some of its technical features. To make the discussion less abstract, all chapters also include an 'Example Study' section that provides an overview of a published study utilizing the method in question, so that the reader will have a more concrete example of how the method is used in practice. The example study has been chosen to model best practices in the respective method, and interested readers can examine the full study for a more detailed illustration. These example studies, despite the title of the book, sometimes come from outside of the field of applied linguistics. In these cases, we chose to include example studies from the social sciences more broadly and exemplify the methods introduced with them for a particular reason: we selected these examples deliberately because the method ranges from relatively uncommon to more or less non-existent in applied linguistics – which is, after all, the whole point of introducing them into applied linguistics – or we have found existing applied linguistics examples insufficiently transparent to be used as a pedagogical example for introducing these methods to the uninitiated reader. Each chapter ends with a list of annotated readings for readers who would like to pursue further learning about a particular method. This list contains both introductory and more advanced readings in order to cater for a wider audience.

Finally, Part 4 offers a sense of what the future of CDST research in applied linguistics might look like when expanded to incorporate mixed and multi-method research designs. Chapter 18 presents our initial thinking on several dimensions around which such forward-thinking programmes of CDST research can be organized, and how such an expansion of research designs that integrate qualitative/quantitative, group-based/individual and falsificatory/exploratory research designs can help push forward methods for CDST research in applied linguistics. We then wrap up the entire volume with a helpful glossary of CDST terminology used in earlier sections of the book, primarily chapters in Part 1, and introduce some excellent online and offline sources and databases related to CDST and CDST research. Our hope is that interested readers will continue their exploration of CDST and its contribution to applied linguistics research through these resources.

This book can be read in different ways by different readers. For those who are already conversant with complexity theory, Chapter 2 may be skipped or merely skimmed through. It is there for those looking for an introductory guide to complexity theory, its conceptual tools and its terminology. Readers wishing for just such a primer on CDST are encouraged to begin with Chapter 2, and then progress to the chapters either in Part 2 or Part 3, depending on the methodological orientation with which they most identify. Chapter 3 establishes our take on what the CDST frame of reference means for the enterprise of empirical research. We are convinced this background knowledge can lead to a more profound understanding of the CDST paradigm's potential, and realize also that this sort of intellectual deep-dive is an acquired aspect of any intellectual journey. Readers who find that these ideas leave them with a feeling of vertigo, are encouraged to return gradually to Chapter 3 as they sort out the type of research questions they would like to investigate and the method(s) they find appropriate for researching them. This will allow readers to approach this coming to terms with the philosophical underpinnings of CDST at their own pace, reduce unnecessary ambiguity in the process and ultimately lead them to a broader understanding of how their research can be informed by CDST.

For readers with a well-defined topic or thematic area of research wishing to dive straight into methods, the chapters in Parts 2 and 3 will be their immediate point of entry. These parts of the book are about how to do CDST research, and the 14 chapters are a guide to applying CDST empirically in research designs and methods. The first seven of these chapters present qualitative methods while the latter seven introduce quantitative methods. This distinction, which we must admit is slightly arbitrary and not essential for CDST research, will be useful for researchers who self-identify with a certain approach to research and are comfortable with one or the other of these modes of scientific inquiry. While we have chosen to keep this organizational scheme for Parts 2 and 3, we extend this in Part 4 with a chapter exploring mixed methods and the future of CDST research. Through this chapter, we hope it will also become obvious that many CDST research methods draw on both qualitative and quantitative data, at both individual and group levels, and can serve an exploratory or falsificatory function depending on how they are applied. In the best sense, CDST research has something for everyone.

This book, then, is about the relevancies of CDST for applied linguistics research. However you approach it, we invite you to read on and join us as researchers and as applied linguists in this exciting step of putting CDST into practice. Have fun!

References

Baird, R., Baker, W. and Kitazawa, M. (2014) The complexity of ELF. *Journal of English as a Lingua Franca* 3, 171–196.

Barrett, L.F. (2017) The theory of constructed emotion: An active inference account of interoception and categorization. *Social Cognitive and Affective Neuroscience* 12 (1), 1–23.

Bastardas-Boada, A. (2013) Language policy and planning as an interdisciplinary field: Towards a complexity approach. *Current Issues in Language Planning* 14 (3–4), 363–381.

Blommaert, J. (2014) From mobility to complexity in sociolinguistic theory and method. *Tilburg Papers in Culture Studies*, 103.

Bouchard, J. (2018) On language, culture, and controversies. *Asian Englishes* 20 (3), 268–278.

Capra, F. and Luisi, P.L. (2014) *The Systems View of Life*. Cambridge: Cambridge University Press.

Chapelle, C. (ed.) (2014) *The Encyclopedia of Applied Linguistics*. New York: Wiley.

Cooper, D. (1999) *Linguistic Attractors: The Cognitive Dynamics of Language Acquisition and Change*. Amsterdam/Philadelphia, PA: John Benjamins.

Cowley, S.J. (ed.) (2011) *Distributed Language*. Amsterdam/Philadelphia, PA: John Benjamins.

Davies, A. and Elder, C. (eds) (2004) *The Handbook of Applied Linguistics*. Oxford: Blackwell.

de Bot, K. (2008) Introduction: Second language development as a dynamic process. *The Modern Language Journal* 92, 166–178.

de Bot, K. (2015) *A History of Applied Linguistics: From 1980 to the Present*. New York: Routledge.

Dörnyei, Z. (2008, March) Are Individual Differences Really Individual? Plenary given at the meeting of the American Association for Applied Linguistics, Washington, DC.

Dörnyei, Z. (2017) Conceptualizing learner characteristics in a complex, dynamic world. In L. Ortega and Z. Han (eds) *Complexity Theory and Language Development: In Celebration of Diane Larsen-Freeman* (pp. 79–96). Philadelphia, PA/Amsterdam: John Benjamins.

Dörnyei, Z., MacIntyre, P.D. and Henry, A. (eds) (2015) *Motivational Dynamics in Language Learning*. Bristol: Multilingual Matters.

Ellis, N.C. and Larsen-Freeman, D. (eds) (2009) *Language as a Complex Adaptive System*. Boston, MA: Wiley-Blackwell.

Ellis, R. (2018, October) Oral Corrective Feedback in SLA: Taking a Holistic Perspective. Plenary given at the 2018 meeting of the Second Language Research Forum, Montreal, Canada.

Heisenberg, W. (1958) *Physics and Philosophy*. New York: Harper.

Herdina, P. and Jessner, U. (2002) *A Dynamic Model of Multilingualism*. Clevedon: Multilingual Matters.

Hiver, P. and Al-Hoorie, A.H. (2016) A 'dynamic ensemble' for second language research: Putting complexity theory into practice. *The Modern Language Journal* 100, 741–756.

Hogan-Brun, G. and Hogan, S.J. (2013) Language planning and complexity: A conversation. *Current Issues in Language Planning* 14 (3–4), 490–496.

Hult, F. (2010a) Analysis of language policy discourses across the scales of space and time. *International Journal of the Sociology of Language* 202, 7–24.

Hult, F. (2010b) The complexity turn in educational linguistics. *Language, Culture and Curriculum* 23, 173–177.

Ke, J. and Holland, J.H. (2006) Language origin from an emergentist perspective. *Applied Linguistics* 27, 691–716.

Kostoulas, A., Stelma, J., Mercer, S., Cameron, L. and Dawson, S. (2018) Complex systems theory as a shared discourse space for TESOL. *TESOL Journal* 9 (2), 246–260.

Kramsch, C. and Whiteside, A. (2008) Language ecology in multilingual settings: Towards a theory of symbolic competence. *Applied Linguistics* 29, 645–671.

Kretzschmar, W. (2015) *Language and Complex Systems*. Cambridge: Cambridge Press.

Larsen-Freeman, D. (1997) Chaos/complexity science and second language acquisition. *Applied Linguistics* 18, 141–165.

Larsen-Freeman, D. (2012) Complex, dynamic systems: A new transdisciplinary theme for applied linguistics? *Language Teaching* 45, 202–214.

Larsen-Freeman, D. (2017) Complexity theory: The lessons continue. In L. Ortega and Z.H. Han (eds) *Complexity Theory and Language Development: In Celebration of Diane Larsen-Freeman* (pp. 11–50). Amsterdam/Philadelphia, PA: John Benjamins.

Larsen-Freeman, D. (2018a) Complexity and ELF. In J. Jenkins, W. Baker and M. Dewey (eds) *The Routledge Handbook of English as a Lingua Franca* (pp. 51–60). New York: Routledge.

Larsen-Freeman, D. (2018b) Resonances: Second language development and language planning and policy from a complexity theory perspective. In F. Hult, T. Kupisch and M. Siiner (eds) *Bridging Language Acquisition and Language Policy* (pp. 203–217). New York: Springer.

Larsen-Freeman, D. and Cameron, L. (2008a) *Complex Systems and Applied Linguistics*. Oxford: Oxford University Press.

Larsen-Freeman, D. and Cameron, L. (2008b) Research methodology on language development from a complex systems perspective. *The Modern Language Journal* 92, 200–213.

Lowie, W. (2017) Lost in state space? Methodological considerations in complex dynamic theory approaches to second language development research. In L. Ortega and Z.H. Han (eds) *Complexity Theory and Language Development: In Celebration of Diane Larsen-Freeman* (pp. 123–141). Amsterdam/Philadelphia, PA: John Benjamins.

MacIntyre, P.D., Dörnyei, Z. and Henry, A. (2015) Hot enough to be cool: The promise of dynamic systems research. In Z. Dörnyei, P.D. MacIntyre and A. Henry (eds) *Motivational Dynamics in Language Learning* (pp. 419–429). Bristol: Multilingual Matters.

MacIntyre, P.D., MacKay, E., Ross, J. and Abel, E. (2017) The emerging need for methods appropriate to study dynamic systems: Individual differences in motivational dynamics. In L. Ortega and Z.H. Han (eds) *Complexity Theory and Language Development: In Celebration of Diane Larsen-Freeman* (pp. 97–122). Amsterdam/Philadelphia, PA: John Benjamins.

Massip-Bonet, À. and Bastardas-Boada, A. (eds) (2013) *Complexity Perspectives on Language, Communication, and Society*. New York: Springer.

Massip-Bonet, À., Bel-Enguix, G. and Bastardas-Boada, A. (eds) (2019) *Complexity Applications in Language and Communication Sciences*. Cham: Springer.

Mercer, S. (2011) The self as a complex dynamic system. *Studies in Second Language Learning and Teaching* 1, 57–82.

Mercer, S. (2013) Towards a complexity-informed pedagogy for language learning. *Revista Brasileira de Linguistica Aplicada* 13 (2), 375–398.

Mercer, S. (2016) Complexity, language learning and the language classroom. In G. Hall (ed.) *The Routledge Handbook of English Language Teaching* (pp. 473–485). New York: Routledge.

Meyers, R. (ed.) (2009) *Encyclopedia of Complexity and Systems Science*. New York: Springer.

Mitleton-Kelly, E., Paraskevas, A. and Day, C. (eds) (2018) *Handbook of Research Methods in Complexity Science: Theory and Applications*. Cheltenham: Edward Elgar.

Morin, E. (2001) *Seven Complex Lessons in Education for the Future*. Paris: United Nations Educational, Scientific and Cultural Organization.

Morin, E. (2008) *On Complexity*. Cresskill, NJ: Hampton Press.

Mufwene, S.S., Coupé, C. and Pellegrino, F. (eds) (2017) *Complexity in Language: Developmental and Evolutionary Perspectives*. Cambridge: Cambridge University Press.

Norman, D.A. (2011) *Living with Complexity*. Cambridge, MA: MIT Press.

Ortega, L. and Han, Z.H. (eds) (2017) *Complexity Theory and Language Development: In Celebration of Diane Larsen-Freeman*. Amsterdam/Philadelphia, PA: John Benjamins.

Schmid, M.S., Köpke, B. and de Bot, K. (2013) Language attrition as complex, non-linear development. *International Journal of Bilingualism* 17, 675–683.

Seedhouse, P. (2010) Locusts, snowflakes, and recasts: Complexity theory and spoken interaction. *Classroom Discourse* 1, 4–24.

Soler-Carbonnell, J. (2016) Complexity perspectives on linguistic landscapes: A scalar analysis. *Linguistic Landscape* 2 (1), 1–25.

Todeva, E. (2009) Multilingualism as a kaleidoscopic experience: The mini-universes within. In E. Todeva and J. Cenoz (eds) *The Multiple Realities of Multilingualism* (pp. 53–74). Berlin: Mouton de Gruyter.

Verspoor, M., Lowie, W. and van Dijk, M. (2008) Variability in L2 development from a dynamic systems perspective. *The Modern Language Journal* 92, 214–231.

Verspoor, M., de Bot, K. and Lowie, W. (eds) (2011) *A Dynamic Approach to Second Language Development: Methods and Techniques*. Amsterdam/Philadelphia, PA: John Benjamins.

2 What is Complexity Theory?

I hope you will abandon the urge to simplify everything, to look for formulas and easy answers, and begin to think multidimensionally, to glory in the mystery and paradoxes of life, not to be dismayed by the multitude of causes and consequences that are inherent in each experience—but to appreciate the fact that life is complex.

Peck (1993: 14)

Complexity: Woven Together

Complexity is a characteristic of the human and social world (Human, 2015). Despite this near truism, it remains a challenge to define complexity succinctly or to describe what is complex. Surely, one might assume that there is a general preference for simplicity, and yet in work looking at the historical significance of the term *complexity*, some (e.g. Morowitz, 1996) suggest that over time many of the phenomena researchers wish to investigate, in particular those related to the human experience or the social realm, have become too complex for the simple tools that exist with which to study them. Others go a step further and argue that human civilizations are locked in 'a complexity race' (Nowotny, 2005: 20): Our daily manipulation and intervention in the human and social world seems to result in ever more complexity, while researchers and scientists simultaneously seek new methods to reduce the increasing levels of complexity that result. So what does complexity in the context of the human and social world refer to then? The quality of phenomena that these examples refer to is far more than the converse of simple – it refers instead to the relations between things (Morin, 2008).

The word complexity originates from the Latin *cum plectere* or *complexus*. These mean, quite literally, what is woven together. One of the first to use the term in this technical sense related to science and scientific inquiry was the physicist and information scientist Warren Weaver (1894–1978) in his 1948 paper published in the *American Scientist* (Davis & Sumara, 2006). As a noun, a *complex* refers to a whole that comprises a number of parts, especially parts that are interconnected in a fabric of relations. Complexity, then, refers to the idea that the quality of existence for many things is intricately interwoven, consisting of various parts formed in combination, united together and unknowable except as a whole (Alhadeff-Jones, 2008).

We should very quickly, however, clear up one possible source of confusion between the terms *complex* and *complicated*. These terms are frequently, but also mistakenly, used interchangeably. Complicated denotes something quantitatively different from simplicity; complexity, however, refers to a qualitative difference (Reitsma, 2003). And, unlike the complex, what is complicated *is* fundamentally knowable by breaking it down into its component parts. For example, a complicated mechanical clock may have many parts big and small, such as a perpetual calendar, a chronograph, a moonphase or a repeating chime. In the field of horology, these complications built into a timepiece are a source of genuine bragging rights. What is more, the complicated tasks of assembling or repairing the mechanical timepiece and its many complications may involve many steps in sequence, both familiar and unfamiliar or requiring more or less skill. However, this ultra-complicated clock will never be anything other than what it is. At the global level of 'clockhood', for lack of a better word, we will never see a clock undergo a qualitative change into something new or different. In other words, a complete and accurate picture of what is complicated can be taken from the attributes of its internal parts (Byrne & Callaghan, 2014). If we could find a way to carefully dismantle and reassemble it, the complicated system would work in exactly the same, predictable way.

Complicated things, ideas or issues may involve many elements that exist or occur together. Flying a plane and extracting a brain tumor are genuinely complicated tasks: they require 'engineer-designed blueprints, step-by-step algorithms, well-trained staff, and... computer software running carefully calibrated equipment' (Cuban, 2010). Change that is introduced into complicated structures is highly mechanical: it involves laying out a detailed design of what is to be changed at the most minute level possible, determining step-by-step procedures to implement the change from the top down and overcome any roadblocks. Unlike this extreme reduction, what is complex is part of a whole that is not analytically tractable from its components, and in combination has greater capacities than just the sum of its parts. 'The important point is that in complexity and dynamic systems theory (CDST), complex is the sense of exhibiting emergent behavior that cannot be anticipated from the behavior of its components' (Diane Larsen-Freeman, personal communication, 16 December 2018).

An example that encapsulates these characteristics well is a society (Sawyer, 2005). In a society, the interrelated individuals and structures as well as the spatiotemporal relations between them produce the entity we refer to by this name and allow this complex unit to perform a collective function. The interactions of components are not fixed and clearly defined, but are vibrant, messy, adaptive and dynamic. Adapting to change and dealing with conflict is natural, not an aberration. Given its complex nature, building understanding of a society is not possible simply by examining its internal parts and their functions. Much more is required to understand the interdependencies and the adaptive dynamics that give coherence to the thing we term a 'society'. Though not reducible to its parts, all is not lost. As Cilliers (2005: 263) argues, 'we cannot know complex things completely, [but] this does not imply that we can know nothing about complex systems, or that the knowledge claims we make about them have to be... weak. We can make strong claims, but... we have to be modest about them'.

To offer a domain-specific example, consider the increasingly preferred view of language as complex and adaptive in nature – something genuinely irreducible (Ellis & Larsen-Freeman, 2009; Kretzschmar, 2015). This systems view of language provides a divergent lens that questions many of the dichotomies prevalent in other non-complex systems perspectives, such as the distinction between language as an abstract representation and direct experience with the language, between learning and use, or between performance and competence (Larsen-Freeman & Cameron, 2008). Instead, languages – like most human phenomena – cannot be usefully separated from their inherent social function or the agents (i.e. individuals) who use them to interact through time (Beckner *et al.*, 2009). While other perspectives may see the nature of language as something close to how we have defined 'complicated', when language is characterized as 'complex' the possibilities are truly novel. Language, thought of in this way, exists both in individuals and in communities, is constrained by the social structures of interaction and is in constant change and adaptation (Douglas Fir Group, 2016). As the Five Graces group concludes in pioneering just such a view, '[c]ognition, consciousness, experience, embodiment, brain, self, human interaction, society, culture, and history are all inextricably intertwined' (Beckner *et al.*, 2009: 18).

In this chapter, we will begin with a brief overview of the origins of these ideas that together form complexity thinking in the social sciences, and how these crystalized more formally in CDST. However, because we have a very pragmatic intent with this book, namely to present CDST as an appropriate mode of thought for doing research, this chapter is not a journey to the heart of complexity, and in its pages we do not intend to offer a comprehensive summary or review of complexity. Having said that, it is still likely that some newcomers to CDST may find Chapters 2 and 3 rather dense with information. We assure the reader that this is not characteristic of the rest of the book, which is practically oriented.

To frame the issues that are of significance for research, we continue by surveying the core ideas and principles from CDST that inform this approach to planning and carrying out research, and discuss how these conceptual tools enable applied linguists to structure and conduct research in ways that are consistent with complexity theory. We provide just the orientation necessary to prime our reader for the following parts of this volume where we look at how such principles are reflected in research designs and methods for studying all that is interrelated and dynamic.

The Origins of Complexity Thinking in the Social Sphere

Humans, their behavior and their interactions are the primary objects of interest in social science. Different intellectual traditions have different understandings of the social world, and yet looking at human behavior and interaction in all of its richness is not something from which social scientists have shied away (Byrne, 2011). A complexity-rich discourse in the contemporary human and social sciences can be traced back to Adam Smith's (1723–1790) 'invisible hand' that describes the unintended consequences of some social actions, the reflections of Edmund Burke (1729–1797) on the politics of his time, and in the contrasting writings of Ralph Waldo Emerson (1808–1882) and Karl Marx (1818–1883), both of whom highlighted how seeming contradictions in social systems were in fact what sustained social order (Urry, 2003). Compatible notions are apparent throughout the work of the English philosopher Herbert Spencer (1820–1903), and are also evident in Émile Durkheim's (1858–1917) holistic conception of social facts and Vilfredo Pareto's (1848–1923) notions of political economy. With some historical awareness, we can now look back in recognition of these scholars' contribution that provided the foundation for complexity thinking to germinate over generations of intellectual thought.

Although at the time complexity theory had not yet been expressed explicitly, its ideas loosely parallel the scholarly work of Kurt Lewin and George Mead from the 1930s. Prominent social researchers from the second half of the 20th century represent additional examples of ideas that were not formally associated with complexity but still functioned based on such an understanding of the world, including Anthony Giddens' structuration theory, Talcott Parsons' discussion of the cognitive complex, Jürgen Habermas's theory of communicative action, Albert Bandura's reciprocal causation model and Urie Bronfenbrenner's ecological systems theory (see e.g. reviews in Eve *et al.* [1997]). Even more remarkable, however, since the middle of the 20th century the human and social disciplines have contributed at least as much to theorizing complexity as they have drawn on its insights (Capra & Luisi, 2014).

The more direct predecessors of contemporary complexity science are cybernetics, general systems theory and system dynamics, all of which emerged in the early to mid-20th century. Perhaps not surprisingly, complexity has now become a foundation for scientific inquiry in domains such as physics, applied mathematics, computer science, meteorology and neuroscience (Abraham, 2011). Because its roots are in these physical and mathematical sciences, borrowing insights and ideas from complexity may appear to some as inherently incompatible with the social phenomena most applied linguists are concerned with and even the existing theoretical frameworks that are used to conceptualize these phenomena (Lantolf, 2016).

While it is often acknowledged that social science represents a parallel reality to the natural sciences (Byrne & Ragin, 2009), the contemporary shift toward using complex-systemic understandings as the foundation for human and social inquiry suggests that there is a gradual realization in these disciplines that the human and social domains, at their core, reflect and are characterized by the very principles that make up complexity (Capra & Luisi, 2014). In fact, as some reviews show, the disciplinary influence of complexity has firmly extended to include prominent areas in the social sciences particularly within sociology and anthropology (e.g. politics, health, economics, psychology and management). A more general point can be made to address this issue of compatibility, and it is the fact that there are many instances when the human and social sciences have taken their inspiration from developments in the physical sciences or actually developed parallel insights independently from those domains (Horn, 2008; Ridley, 2015), to the degree that these have become net contributors to the fields initially drawn from and now firmly situate these insights within their discipline-specific knowledge base.

For instance, the philosopher Edgar Morin (1921–), famous for first drawing a distinction between general and restricted complexity, has remained active well into his nineties by applying his thinking across disciplines, while Gregory Bateson (1904–1980), an anthropologist by training, spent the final decade of his life pulling together various systems theories and developing a meta-science of epistemology. Other substantial contributions to applied complexity have been made by contemporary human or social scholars – to highlight just a few – in areas of philosophy of science by Roy Bhaskar, John Urry, Willis Overton and Paul Cilliers; in systems and complexity thinking by David Byrne, Francis Heylighen, Robert Axelrod and Derek Cabrera; and in methodology by Charles Ragin, Albert-László Barabási, Peter Checkland and Brian Castellani. Centers and institutes dedicated to the study of human and social complexity now exist at pre-eminent universities across the globe; academic journals, conferences and associations for complex dynamic systems in the human and social domains have been around for the better part of two decades. Complexity, clearly, is no longer – if it ever truly was – the domain of the physical and mathematical sciences (e.g. Koopmans, 2019).

Complexity and what it offers for the enterprise of research has been described as 'a pioneering break from a moribund Newtonian worldview' (Manson, 2001: 412) – in our own experience we have found it to be no less. Let us now examine the assumptions underlying this theoretical perspective and look at how it enables its users to think about the social world and investigate phenomena of interest.

From Complexity Thinking to Complexity Theory

Early in the year 2000, the prominent physicist Stephen Hawking commented, 'I think the next century will be the century of complexity'. His remark, made in reference to the emergent paradigmatic reorientation that is rapidly becoming part of mainstream intellectual culture, was strikingly prescient given that as a coherent realm of ideas complexity has only come together over the past several decades (Davis & Sumara, 2006). 'Complexity theory' (also complexity science) is an umbrella term that covers mutually intelligible and complementary foci such as chaos theory (mathematics), nonlinear dynamical systems theory (mathematics), synergetics (physics), complex adaptive systems (physics), dissipative structures (chemistry), autopoietic systems (biology) and emergentism (philosophy).

Complexity, as a broad orientation to scientific inquiry, has no shortage of terminology attached to fairly specific technical meanings, for instance 'self-organized criticality' or 'hysteresis' (these and other terms are defined in the Glossary toward the end of this book). These domain-general terms, nonetheless, refer to phenomena in which many subfields in the aforementioned social sciences share an interest. Consequently, exploiting this shared scientific lexicon may help the field of applied linguistics to increase cross-disciplinary communication and lessen mutual distances (Larsen-Freeman, 2017). Within applied linguistics specifically, use of the hybrid term 'complex/dynamic systems theory' or CDST has become widespread. For purposes of clarity, we adopt this term throughout the remainder of this book when we refer specifically to the field of applied linguistics.

Over the past few decades, many scholars have worked to clarify the ways in which complexity is appropriate and useful for social inquiry (Byrne & Callaghan, 2014). Looking to the other social and human disciplines that draw on complexity enables us to see how these fields and their scholars have addressed the potential of this poststructural ecological theory (Larsen-Freeman, 2017). Here are a few of the ways in which these scholars have suggested complexity functions:

- as an interpretive paradigm for understanding the social world (Byrne, 1998);
- as a methodological frame of reference (Byrne, 2005);
- as a worldview or scientific understanding (Cilliers, 2005);
- as a transdisciplinary discourse (Klein, 2004);
- as principles that constitute a habit of thought (Kuhn, 2008);

- as an approach to describing and explaining change (Mason, 2008);
- as a unified conceptual framework for understanding social phenomena (Urry, 2005);
- as a conceptual toolbox (Walby, 2007).

The common thread that ties all these understandings of complexity together is that complexity is not articulated in such a way that it could be termed a theory *per se* (Manson, 2001). Our reader may wonder then, 'if not a theory, what is complexity?' The wide range of functions has led some scholars to adopt the more accurate term *meta-theory* (Larsen-Freeman, 2013, 2015; Overton, 2013) – a set of coherent principles of reality (i.e. ontological ideas) and principles of knowing (i.e. epistemological ideas) that, for applied linguists, underpin and contextualize object theories (i.e. theories of language, language use and language development/learning) consistent with these principles.

Overton (2015: 166) remarks that meta-theories such as CDST 'capture concepts whose scope is broader than any particular theory, and which form the essential conceptual core within which scientific theory and observation function'. Furthermore, while object theories are provisional, and their predictions must constantly be evaluated against observation of new evidence, the CDST meta-theory pertains to notions of what phenomena, questions and aspects of social and human inquiry are 'meaningful and meaningless, acceptable and unacceptable, central and peripheral' for a field (Overton, 2007: 154). As such, CDST has unique potential to move beyond discipline-specific approaches to address common problems – what some have termed 'transdisciplinarity' (Montuori, 2013).

The CDST meta-theory groups together a set of relational principles (Overton, 2007, 2013), namely that certain phenomena (a) involve multiple interconnected parts (b) changing together (c) through dynamic, nonlinear processes that (d) lead to emergent patterns over time (Holland, 2012). Complexity as a meta-theory represents a set of powerful intellectual tools and concepts capable of informing diverse theories. It does this by providing researchers with 'effective ways to organize the world, logical structures to arrange their topics of study, [and] scaffolds to assemble the models they construct' (Castellani & Hafferty, 2009: 34). CDST, then, is a meta-theory for investigating the nature of, and the reasons for, dynamic change and emergent outcomes in the social world (Morin, 1992, 2008). It provides an ontological position for understanding the social sphere in complex and dynamic terms. Its conceptual tools serve as a rigorous epistemological aid to thinking and theorizing, and what is especially important for our purposes is that they function as the necessary intellectual blueprint for conducting and evaluating research about the human and social world.

We turn now to the important conceptual tools and ideas that are 'baked in' to a complexity mindset for research.

Complex Systems: Relational Units of Analysis

Francis Heylighen (1960–) has famously noted that several basic principles underlie most complexivists' work, including the work of researchers outside the human and social sciences. The most important of these is known as the *relational principle*, which states that phenomena (e.g. objects, processes) do not exist on their own, but only in relation to other phenomena. The word *system* derives from the Greek *syn histanai* meaning 'to place together'. This is why understanding things systemically literally means putting them into a context and establishing the nature of their relationships. This meaning also illustrates the importance in CDST research of thinking, first and foremost, how parts of the whole relate to each other. Thus, a main tool that comes with CDST is a distinctive relational unit of analysis – a complex dynamic system. *Complex* references the multiple interdependent elements that make up the system, a state of affairs sometimes described as complete interconnectedness (Straussfogel & Von Schilling, 2009). These systems, defined and understood relationally, are the fundamental unit of analysis in research that adopts this perspective (Byrne, 2002).

The unit(s) of analysis that CDST gives us – phenomenologically real complex systems situated in context – are as 'dynamic' as the human and social world (Larsen-Freeman, 2016a). This dynamism is reflected in the change that characterizes individual elements as well as in system-wide behavior (van Geert, 2009). System outcomes and processes arise from a web of relationships that continually grow, change and adapt to new situations. The behavior of a system, what much of CDST research aims to explain, emerges from system components and their relationships on multiple levels – this illustrates the importance of relational units in research (Lerner & Overton, 2008).

As we have done elsewhere (Hiver & Larsen-Freeman, 2020), we must caution against conceiving of 'system' as implying 'the existence of a discrete entity when in fact none exists' (Osberg & Biesta, 2010: 597). Here, we also need to foreground that a system is not a thing, and when applied to issues in our field, it is certainly not fixed. A system is a relational entity 'produced by a set of components that interact in particular ways to produce some overall state or form at a particular point in time. Systems differ from sets, aggregates, or collections, in that belonging to the system affects the properties of the components' (Larsen-Freeman & Cameron, 2008: 26). Thus, rather than an object-based understanding of the field, from this relational perspective, it is complex dynamic systems that reflect the ontological assumptions and defining characteristics of applied linguistics issues (see also Overton & Lerner, 2014).

Of course, operationalizing systems can at first appear to be an abstract exercise for the newcomer to CDST (see also Mercer, 2013). However, the truth of the matter is that 'there is nothing metaphysical about complex systems' (Cilliers, 2000: 31). For this reason, we feel the most tractable approach is to operationalize a system as something that has concrete phenomenological validity. This view, that systems are real entities that reflect the operation of actual causal mechanisms, is consistent with the notion in social complexity of a *case* as a complex system (Uprichard, 2013). From this systems perspective, individuals, groups and interactions are all suitable units of analysis (i.e. cases), but components, abstract variables and other artefacts are less so. Later in this chapter, we return to the idea of a case as an appropriate unit of analysis for research purposes, and why we feel that in CDST research the method does not always define the case.

At the same time, the study of human and social systems always implicates agency, whether this is individual or distributed (Al-Hoorie, 2015), and we are not alone in this thinking (see e.g. Kelso [2016] and Larsen-Freeman [2019] for more comprehensive treatment of this topic). The centrality of agency to human and social systems makes it necessary to include within any system's boundaries an agent, or agents, capable of exercising intentional action that contributes causally, though not deterministically, to the outcomes and processes of change that arise from that system under investigation (Juarrero, 1999). Complex systems that may form the basis for research (Hiver & Al-Hoorie, 2016):

- consist of a number of heterogeneous elements or components situated in context;
- these components, at least one of which is an agent, interact with each other at multiple levels;
- over time, the components change as a result of their interactions with other components;
- the effects of these interactions result in the system exhibiting system-wide and macro-level patterns of behavior.

To illustrate, consider an example offered by Larsen-Freeman and Cameron (2008: 37): A speech community is made up of varying social groups, individuals and their language resources embedded in a field of action; through conversation dynamics and the ongoing negotiation of understanding, discourse patterns and participation take shape modifying the nature of those social groups, individuals and their language resources; in the complex system of the speech community, unique global patterns that emerge through time may range from specific constructions (e.g. lexical bundles, idioms, memes), to discourse events (e.g. encounters, instances of use) and even specific languages (e.g. creoles).

We would suggest that all CDST research proposing to study such relational units articulate how these necessary criteria apply to the units chosen in order to ensure that these units correspond with the characteristics of complex systems (see Chapter 3 for further discussion on such considerations). Operationalizing the units of analysis this way allows researchers to conceptualize relevant phenomena more organically as a relational and soft-assembled system – that is, constrained more by contextual affordances and material demands – rather than reductionistically (Kloos & Van Orden, 2009). Doing so also allows researchers to value the particularity and heterogeneity of individuals that might otherwise be discounted in a study of the aggregate (Larsen-Freeman, 2019; Lowie & Verspoor, 2019). CDST is a systems theory, and such complex systems in context can be considered the paradigmatic object of interest.

Perceptive readers, however, may have noticed a twist. Adopting complex systems as the basic unit of analysis raises what Larsen-Freeman (2017) has termed 'the boundary problem', which can be summarized this way: if everything is connected to everything else in a complex and dynamic way, how can a representation of a complex system be reached, and how can researchers delineate the systems of interest from context and from other systems without drawing lines that break up what is being explained? One way to address this problem in doing complexity research would be to think in terms of what Larsen-Freeman (2017), citing the work of Richard Lewontin, has called 'functional wholes' (Lewontin, 1998). That is, instead of drawing arbitrary boundaries for systems or for units of analysis, scholars remain concerned first and foremost with explaining phenomena, and any parts, processes or boundaries that are examined in the research design depend on what is being explained.

The example often given is that the appropriate unit of analysis for explaining the fine motor skills of grasping a pencil differs substantially from the appropriate unit of analysis to explain the swing of a tennis racquet. Examples of units of analysis that are closer to home include the individual language user acting in context as a unit of analysis for studying developmental processes and outcomes (Larsen-Freeman, 2016b), interactional collectives of language users in linguistic communities as a unit of analysis for exploring emergent patterns in discourse and meaning-making, and systems of language components interacting through time as a unit of analysis for patterns of language use and language change (Kretzschmar, 2015). Thus, when examining complex systems that range in scope from the macro to the more micro, specifying the phenomenological boundaries of that unit of analysis is crucial as it allows the researcher to focus more explicitly on a narrower band of phenomena (Harvey, 2009; Ragin, 2009).

The study of complex systems also entails a focus on processes of change, an idea we expand on at length later in this chapter. How complex systems adapt to their environment in order to maintain their functioning over time is in fact a question with relevance to nearly every field (O'Sullivan, 2009). In studying such issues and gaining greater understanding of such complex and dynamic occurrences and phenomena, the complex macro-behaviors, dynamic micro-interactions within the system and the emergence of new patterns of behavior are all of great interest (Hiver & Al-Hoorie, 2016). It is true that applied linguistics phenomena operate at different levels and are broad enough to warrant multiple ways into any topical area. Several examples that come to mind include a focus on the structure of interdependent relations, a focus on relational dynamics, a focus on trajectories of change and self-organized processes or a focus on emergent outcomes. Of course, relational systems also have constituent parts, and one basic approach to research might be to describe these parts and their connections. As Hilpert and Marchand (2018: 2) suggest, system components can take 'material, conceptual, or semiotic forms such as individual students, and teachers, and technological objects; motivation, behavioral, affective, epistemological and cognitive variables; or words, text, symbols, and discourses' (see also Marchand & Hilpert, 2018). Such descriptive and component-dominant research can serve to '(a) examine a single element from the center of a CS [complex system] and study its dynamic, time-intensive behavior; (b) define a natural boundary for a CS and study the underlying, relation intensive structure; and (c) choose several critical elements from a CS and study their dynamic, time-relation intensive interactions' (Hilpert & Marchand, 2018: 8). However, as we have observed elsewhere (Hiver & Al-Hoorie, 2016), it is fundamental for a CDST perspective to adopt relational units given that these systems describe and provide coherence to the complex, dynamic and emergent processes that shape applied linguistics phenomena at multiple levels.

What follows are some detailed CDST characteristics and principles crucial for understanding the behavior of complex systems. These not only inform the ways in which researchers can think about the social world and its phenomena, but they also provide new parameters for how to conduct research within social science.

The CDST Conceptual Toolkit for Researchers

Time and sensitive dependence on initial conditions

One of the most important shifts in adopting a CDST perspective for research is that time matters (de Bot, 2015; Lemke, 2000). This gift of time entails refocusing attention more explicitly on developmental processes than products. This is a message that has begun to gain prominence in studies of language use and language development (e.g. Fogal, 2019a; Lowie et al., 2014; Lowie & Verspoor, 2015; Polat & Kim, 2014; Schmid et al., 2013). A primary way of employing time in understanding processes and outcomes is that each and every system has a history

(De Villiers-Botha & Cilliers, 2010). History and context have a critical role to play in making sense of where systems end up and how they got there. And, in complex systems such as social institutions, language communities or classrooms where many different components and factors interact over time, small differences in some factors at an early point in time can have a substantial impact on the eventual outcome – a notion popularized through the term 'butterfly effect' (Kauffman, 1995). This highlights the nonlinear quality of complex systems: A small discrepancy in one component at one time can lead to large differences in a later state, and a slight difference in the initial conditions can have major implications for future behavior (Prigogine & Stengers, 1984). An example of this can be seen in the way that the experiences of newcomers to a social and linguistic community may diverge as time passes. For instance, in the speech community we used as an example earlier in this chapter, some newcomers may integrate and come to establish mutual dependencies with those already part of the speech community while other individuals may remain relatively isolated despite the same opportunities for participation. At a further point in time, this may result in more refined levels of proficiency and higher degrees of participation for those integrating closely in the linguistic community.

Another intriguing aspect of sensitive dependence on initial conditions is that initial conditions allow systems to evolve rules over time. Systems opt for the strongest rules (i.e. those that are most plausible and salient in the systems' experience) as they adapt – adaptation is a kind of self-organization – and incorporate those that allow the systems to perform or develop optimally. Think here of human interactions and how they draw on some fairly straightforward but often competing principles such as reciprocity and self-interest. These rules can shape the actions of the components and by extension the self-organized outcome of the system (Holland, 1992). Thus, even in systems that initially appear to be identical, the rules that develop to guide the subsequent adaptation may diverge significantly (Holland, 2012). This is evidence of the rich interdependence of all the components in the system and further illustrates how small differences in initial inputs can become overwhelming differences in output over time (Kelso, 1995). Initial conditions are rarely a central feature of more conventional research paradigms, but they become a critical part of researching complex systems as they 'form the system's landscape and influence the trajectory of the system as it changes' (Larsen-Freeman & Cameron, 2008: 230).

Adaptation to the environment and other systems

Very little in the human and social world is fixed. Change is everywhere. For this reason, a particular added value of CDST for research and its explicit focus on time (Elman, 2003) is an emphasis on processes of adaptive development. In domains of language use and development, such processes of adaptive change have come to be explicitly investigated by numerous scholars (Baba & Nitta, 2014; Fogal, 2019b; Lenzing, 2015; Lowie & Verspoor, 2011; Verspoor *et al.*, 2008, 2012). Systems constantly reorganize their internal working parts to adapt themselves to the problems posed by their surroundings or by other systems (Juarrero, 1999). This is known as co-adaptation (Larsen-Freeman, 2010), and can be illustrated for instance through the example of language users' intelligibility, which might see a speaker adapt their volume, pitch, diction, tone of voice and use of paralinguistic features in response to acoustic conditions, their purpose for communication and cues from their interlocutor. As the latter change from moment to moment, so too will the former. By evolving indefinitely over time, systems attempt to optimize interactions with their surroundings and with other systems (Nowak *et al.*, 2005). This adaptation progresses without a predetermined, fixed goal (Rose *et al.*, 2013). Instead, systems are said to iterate so that they may return to the same state repeatedly as they continue to move and change (Kelso, 2002).

In addition to constantly changing their internal parts while adapting, systems also initiate change in the environment, and this nonlinear adaptivity that effects change in context in turn influences systems' ongoing behavior (Prigogine & Stengers, 1984). This reciprocity is a prime characteristic of systems. In addition to such gradual and sustained changes, systems often change in much more forceful ways. An example of this type of change is a *bifurcation*, or a developmental change in the state space that occurs when a small adjustment to system parameters results in a major phase shift or a qualitatively different outcome for a complex system. Classic examples of such phase shifts can be seen in the physical world when molecular changes in water that relate to the temperature 'parameter' cause it to turn to ice (a phase shift) or to steam (another phase shift). Yet another instance can be found in the natural gait of a horse, where increasing the speed 'parameter' will turn a horse's walk to a trot, then to a canter and finally to a gallop. Systems bifurcate in ways that lead to greater equilibrium for the system in its environment (i.e. period-halving bifurcations) or that result in greater variability and complexity (i.e. period-doubling bifurcations). Through this sustained adaptation and creative change, systems are capable of producing a rich repertoire of behaviors, and this 'moving target' (Holland, 1992: 18) can therefore be challenging to understand and control.

There is yet another feature that contributes still more complexity to these systems: through adapting to their environment and to other systems they come to anticipate. In seeking to adapt to changing circumstances and other systems they encounter, the parts develop rules that anticipate the consequences of certain responses (Holland, 1995, 2006). This emergent ability to anticipate is one of the least-understood features of systems, yet it is also one of the most empirically compelling. As a real-life example, in 2014 Google's subsidiary DeepMind created a deep learning program AlphaGo, which started with a large database of human Go (a complex board game of spatial logic) games and a learning algorithm. Using this large database to learn from previously played human Go games, AlphaGo was soon able to anticipate the range of possible human moves in particular game-play scenarios and before long routinely beat champion human players. Because a temporal view of human and social phenomena is part and parcel of CDST, research that is informed by this perspective will, by necessity, place a heavy emphasis on development and adaptive processes. We say more on this issue in following chapters.

Feedback and self-organized criticality

As we have mentioned, complex systems do not remain passive to changing events but rather adapt to and anticipate an ever-changing environment, and in turn initiate change to that environment. This precise quality gives systems their reputation as nonlinear and feedback sensitive (Gell-Mann, 1994). In CDST terms, *feedback* refers to instances when the system's output loops back as input and influences change (Davis & Sumara, 2006). Two-way flows of feedback in language use are a central part of any interaction event (e.g. Seedhouse, 2010). Such feedback loops are so important to CDST that they have been called the central 'nervous system' of complex systems (Newman, 2009: 4638).

Although feedback often originates internally from interaction between the system's components, it can also originate from an external source such as the environment or another dynamic system. One example of such feedback loops from the natural sphere is the human body's mechanism for thermoregulation. The human body is able to maintain a relatively constant internal temperature of 37 degrees in conditions of high physical exertion and extreme temperatures by constantly adjusting its energy use and optimizing blood flow to the muscles. *Negative feedback*, or self-maintaining feedback, is the most common type found in systems; its role is simply to dampen system change or adaptation (O'Sullivan, 2009). Negative feedback maintains a system within a certain set of parameters to enable its stable functioning. For example, in instances of language contact and conflict in multilingual communities that appear to be headed towards glottophagia (i.e. an occurrence in which a major language or dialect absorbs or replaces minority ones), stakeholders and policymakers can intervene to reverse these effects through strategic initiatives (see also Kretzschmar, 2015). This negative feedback impacts the systems by restoring equilibrium and bringing its behavior back in line. However, a system governed only by negative feedback is by definition 'dead' and not adaptive (Banzhaf, 2009).

Positive feedback, or self-augmenting feedback, on the other hand is a state of affairs in which *A* produces more of *B* which in turn produces more of *A*. Such positive feedback reinforces a system's adaptive changes along the developmental path on which it is already moving. Doing so amplifies change in the system that can spread to a system-wide pattern – referred to as *loop gain*. In extreme cases these iterative patterns of feedback with each repetition may lock-in the system to path dependence (Lewis, 2005). Positive feedback can also create unstable patterns that may reach points of criticality in the system (Straussfogel & Von Schilling, 2009). A field-specific example can be seen in how trends in language education have pushed the age of onset for instruction ever earlier; in many settings this results in formal policies being put in place to accommodate such trends more widely, to which the education sector responds with even more extreme and unsustainable tendencies (see also Larsen-Freeman & Tedick, 2016; Mercer, 2016).

Self-organized criticality takes place when systems reach the between (i.e. critical) transition point of two phases of stability or equilibrium. For this reason, self-organized criticality is closely related to phase shifts (see above). The result of a system reaching this critical value is often a dramatic change into a qualitatively different phase or state (Bak, 1996). Our previous example of water at its freezing point – and at its boiling point – is a critical system. To keep water in a partially frozen state requires active control of the temperature. If water is near the critical temperature, a small deviation tends to move the system into one phase (i.e. solid) or the other (i.e. liquid). A snapshot of self-organized criticality in spoken interaction, which itself is a back and forth between negative feedback and positive feedback as interlocutors negotiate meaning, can also illustrate this concept: too much negative feedback will shut the interaction down and lead to an impasse between interlocutors, while too much positive feedback can result in overt conflict with one interlocutor dominating the interaction, or both interlocutors competing for space in the interactive event space.

Finally, a complex system is never perfectly adapted to its environment because the adaptive processes of the system will themselves change the environment so that constant optimizing of the system through adaptation is part of its dynamic pulse (Nowak *et al.*, 2010). Continuing with the example of a speech community from earlier, not only do the system components change as a result of their interaction with other components, but the here and now in which this system is embedded is also modified as a result of its adaptive dynamics. Seen in this way, feedback offers an appropriate way of keeping systems' changing relationships and dynamic processes at the center of a research design or project.

Openness to context

It will be clear at this point that systems not only continuously interact with their environment or surroundings, but are themselves also an integral part of the context in which they exist (Ushioda, 2015).

A classic example here is social and linguistic groups and how their purpose, most often, exists in relation to certain times, places and larger social settings (see also Kretzschmar, 2015). Any complex system is, by definition, an open synthesis of many small parts interacting with one another and adapting to the larger context in which it is situated. All social and human systems possess or establish functional boundaries that situate them within their environment and demarcate where their constitutive components start or stop (Eoyang, 2004). Earlier in this chapter, we made the case for the importance of establishing and casing such boundaries in an empirically and phenomenologically meaningful way. To add important conceptual detail to those points, we could say that rather than cutting off the system from the rest of the environment, these boundaries remain open and allow the system to remain adaptive and robust.

For instance, although a social group has certain assumptions or formalized guidelines for what constitutes in-group members and non-members, most groups also have provision built in to them for how individuals wishing to do so may join or leave the group. The adaptive system-environment or co-adaptive system to system behavior that is made possible through the openness of complex systems' boundaries is an important way that these units actively try to turn their experiences to their advantage (Eoyang, 2003).

These open boundaries connect a system with its environment and to other systems through a notion known as *coupling*. In the absence of a coupling relationship, very little adaptation between the system and its environment will take place. And without this transfer of energy, resources or information, system-wide adaptive patterns of self-organization are unlikely to occur as there is no impetus to change (Juarrero, 1999). Systems' openness and coupling to the environment give rise to outcomes that can be explained once observed, but not deterministically predicted *a priori*, and this has important implications for designing and carrying out research (Reitsma, 2003).

Soft-assembly

Most research in the social sciences is grounded in the assumption that adaptation and development are based on rule-driven mechanisms that are hard assembled (Thelen & Smith, 1994). The idea behind this is that 'what works' is expected to do so fairly reliably across time and place. Hard-assembled mechanisms are independent of the immediate context in which the system is nested; they apply across multiple contexts, are discovered independent of performance and exist offline in some form of inactive, absolute state (Larsen-Freeman, 2015). In contrast, soft-assembled mechanisms emerge, they are contextually constrained and they involve a particular adaptation of the system to its environment (van Geert, 2009). This means that CDST research is concerned with determining what works, for whom, in which contexts and under what circumstances.

A characteristic feature of many systems is their remarkable flexibility or adaptiveness and their tendency to compensate for varying contexts and environmental situations (Kloos & Van Orden, 2009). Soft-assembly is temporary, takes place in real time and involves only tools and structures that are currently available and necessary. Soft-assembled mechanisms come into existence and are only realized within the immediate context of a situation or task (Thelen, 2005). Clearly, the context or environment in which a system is embedded cannot be seen as merely one factor to be considered when interpreting the system's behavior (Larsen-Freeman & Cameron, 2008). Instead, contextual factors must be seen as actual parameters or dimensions of the system itself (Goldstein, 2011a). To exemplify this using the notion of intelligibility from earlier in the chapter, one's purpose for communication, salient cues from their interlocutor and spatiotemporal conditions of the interaction, etc. – all of which can be seen as salient contextual elements – will help determine how a speaker adapts their volume, pitch, diction, tone of voice and use of paralinguistic features.

In Chapter 3, we discuss the stance that CDST researchers take regarding the core enterprise of research. Here, however, what we can say is that the importance of soft-assembly for CDST research does not mean that it is radically idiosyncratic. Elucidating causation is still a central part of scientific CDST inquiry (Byrne, 2009). Ultimately, in CDST research, it is the who, where (i.e. in what settings), how (i.e. under what conditions) and when that helps to determine what works.

Understanding Complex Dynamic Behavior

Earlier in this chapter, we suggested that complex systems are the units of analysis for CDST research; we can go even further and say that cases are the methodological equivalent of complex systems. This resonates well with much of social complexity as many of the methods used by social complexivists are case-based research methods. This also does not lock us in by any means to a certain way of collecting and analyzing data – a case-based approach encompasses both high-N and low-N, and quantitative and qualitative methods. However, while studying such cases and their relations with other cases can be fascinating, this is only half of the picture. Dynamic processes of change and emergent outcomes in such systems are arguably as interesting as systems themselves (Goldstein, 1999, 2000). In fact, systems only exist spatiotemporally, and the process of being and becoming are what give systems their meaning. This means that a 'state' or 'outcome' should be understood as a way of looking at a system's temporal, and dynamic, state of being. For instance, when we ask what a system is do*ing*, we are talking about an unfolding pattern of existence. This is what we mean by system 'behavior'.

The term *dynamics* has its origins in the Greek *dynamikos* (van Geert, 1998) meaning 'powerful'. This is apt because often the most empirically compelling thing about systems is their process of development and the forces acting to bring about this ongoing and nonlinear change. Forces at play in system behavior are also the central concern in much of applied linguistics research. As Larsen-Freeman and Cameron (2008: 229) propose, 'many of the phenomena of interest to applied linguists can be seen as complex systems' with powerful processes underlying them. Not only would we argue that such phenomena should be articulated as systems explicitly, we see their processes of becoming as even more compelling than their states of being. From this way of thinking 'understanding change in language use, language development, and language learning is central' to applied linguists' concerns (Larsen-Freeman & Cameron, 2008: 229).

Dynamic change is so important to understanding systems and to framing research using insights from CDST that we dedicate this section of the chapter to exploring three major ingredients of dynamic behavior – how it comes about (i.e. self-organization), where it unfolds (i.e. state space and attractor states) and the patterns it results in (i.e. emergence). These are necessary points of reference for investigating how change takes place.

Self-organization and emergence

In order to describe how the elements of a complex system interact and use the resulting system dynamics to move through a developmental trajectory, the notion of self-organization is important. When systems adapt their internal structure or their overall aggregate function in response to external circumstances through a process independent from overt direction, instruction or programming, this demonstrates *self-organization* (Dekker *et al.*, 2011). Haken (2009: 8927) described self-organization in his early work on synergetics as 'the spontaneous formation of spatial, temporal... or functional structures'. What he was describing was the global cooperation of elements in a system as they self-stabilize and self-regulate. Self-organization, which Kauffman (1995: 71) calls 'order for free', may sound like an oxymoron, but it is in fact the most common form of order-building and a primary driver of growth and change (Goldstein, 2000; Howe & Lewis, 2005). The notion of such order for free can be illustrated by how daily life unfolds: Many things in life tend to sort themselves out even better, given the right conditions and gradually over time, than if those involved had deliberately tried to force a solution.

We have argued that self-organization is a process, across time, through which systems acquire their structure and their functions without interference (see also Gershenson, 2007). The process of self-organization is often understood as one of pattern formation because of its ties to emergence. We elaborate further on this link later. However, self-organization technically does not have a specific end goal or external target apart from optimizing the system's own ongoing existence (Deacon, 2012; Rose *et al.*, 2013). In this sense, the entire process is non-teleological, oriented not to completion or an end-goal, but toward a purposeful and intrinsically directed, or 'immanent', teleology (Weber & Varela, 2002). Self-organization, for example, results in greater coordination and often increases a system's complexity. As a consequence, self-maintenance is an important function of systems that are self-organizing. Self-organization is a process that is at the very heart of the behavior of systems, so much so that it is easy to take for granted the clearly recognizable patterns it leads to in the lived world (Banzhaf, 2009). Let us look at the way it leads to such patterns.

An interesting feature of systems is that while they can lose their equilibrium, the result of it all can be the creation of new order. A system in flux is potentially, therefore, a system undergoing a process of transformation. And, as they self-organize through time, systems display new patterns or synchronies that could not have been anticipated by looking at their component parts one by one (Goldstein, 1999). It was the philosopher C.D. Broad (1887–1971) in the early 1920s who first coined the term 'emergent properties' for those properties that emerge at a certain level of complexity but do not exist at lower levels (Capra & Luisi, 2014). Wholes display novel patterns that do not necessarily follow from the parts. Think, for example, how in-depth knowledge of automobile parts and how to drive a car would provide almost no insight into the traffic patterns that emerge during rush hour. In the domains of speech and language use, we would similarly expect language learners who arrive at an appropriate mastery of pronunciation in a given language to need something more and at another level entirely than simply a precise knowledge of that language's phonological representation through its phonetic symbols.

Emergence, across space, occurs when a system shows qualitatively new behaviors on a higher level (i.e. the system level) of description which could not have been predicted from the interactions of components at the lower level. Self-organization, then, refers to the spontaneous pattern formation and change in systems, and can be seen as a robust general process that leads to emergent outcomes (Goldstein, 2000, 2011a) – a kind of bottom-up causation. These new coordinated patterns of existence or behavior are able to affect the lower level of the system components and influence them in a way that stabilizes the newly emergent behavior.

In this way, the coherent structures forming at the higher level of the system exert top-down causation.

State space and attractor states

Social phenomena are unmistakably varied, but one surprising outcome of complexity is that it is the norm rather than the exception to see stable patterns emerge in the world. These stable tendencies for systems are called *attractor states* (aka attractors) (Hiver, 2015). An attractor state is a critical value, pattern, solution or outcome toward which a system settles down or approaches over time (Newman, 2009). Attractor states are essential in understanding emergent outcomes. The evocative topographical metaphor CDST uses to capture where dynamic behavior unfolds and which patterned outcomes can exist for a system is the *state space* or landscape (Larsen-Freeman & Cameron, 2008). This landscape is an N-dimensional space of total possible outcome configurations that a system can be found in at any given time. In other words, it provides a more or less comprehensive idea of all the phenomenological outcomes for the system.

A patterned outcome (i.e. attractor state) that results from self-organization represents a pocket of stability for the system, and it can emerge without anyone purposely directing or engineering it into existence (van Geert, 2008). This closely mirrors phenomena across the field of applied linguistics (e.g. in language policy and use, in language development) where dynamic collections of variables spontaneously self-organize into attractor states that represent higher-order patterns of equilibrium (Larsen-Freeman & Cameron, 2008). We might think here of how second language (L2) learning events on smaller timescales involving teachers and learners add up to coherent wholes of activity that we term 'comprehension', 'development' or 'transfer of learning'. Of course, the states that the system settles in over time do not have to be described numerically. These outcomes are, among other things, often categorical, conceptual or phenomenological outcomes (Goldstein, 2011b).

A board game can provide an illustrative analogy of what the state space and attractor states represent. The state space for the board game is the total potential placements or configurations that can be found for the game being played. Gameplay consists of moving pieces around the board from configuration to configuration based on the rules of the game, and the attractor states of the game are the typical placement patterns of pieces on the board. There are a finite number of possible attractor states for a given system (De Wolf & Holvoet, 2005), and identifying these can reduce much of the unpredictability of complex systems' functioning and allow researchers to make informed choices about how to interact with emergent outcomes. An additional aspect of salient outcome patterns are the unique *signature dynamics* (Dörnyei, 2014), or the developmental mechanisms within a system that allow a researcher to offer a parsimonious account of the gameplay that has led that system to produce those configurations. An example from our board game would be unraveling the turn-by-turn moves and strategies that resulted in one player gaining the upper hand or winning altogether.

Attractor states are preferred states of equilibrium that a system evolves toward or approaches over time in the landscape or 'gameboard' of the social and human world. However, these do not actually exert a pulling force of attraction in the way that a magnet does (Haken, 2006). The term 'attractor' is simply a convenient way to describe the behavior of a complex system as it moves toward some, and away from other, critical values (Holland, 1995, 2012). An attractor state allows us to describe what position or state of being a system is in right now or how it is currently acting, and the outcome or pattern it has fallen into through self-organization (Thelen & Bates, 2003).

The number of such patterned outcomes (i.e. attractor states) observable in the human and social world is finite, but as we have said these novel emergent outcomes at the system level cannot be inferred or explained from the discrete interactions of system components alone. To take an example of group behavior, a collection of individuals is the system and we might observe the self-organization that occurs through distributed interactions and resulting changes in the group's intensity of emotions. When we imagine the total possible configurations in a landscape of group phenomena, we see various possibilities such as a crowd, a demonstration, a community, an audience, even a mob. Each of these has particular emergent characteristics. In the case of group behavior, individual components manage to acquire collective properties that transcend the individual parts (Holland, 2012). In a group, this can lead the system to settle into patterns of conformity, isolation, groupthink, activism or other patterns entirely.

Attractors represent outcomes or states of dynamic equilibrium into which a system stabilizes. While outcomes account for what a system is doing now and the state in which it has stabilized, it is the adaptive changes that provide a temporal narrative for the process of how and why the system got to where it is, and the places it may be going to. Specific mechanisms of change – or signature dynamics as we have previously called them – produce a particular time signal or trajectory of change over time in the state space that is essential for understanding the causal complexities of system development or change (Mackenzie, 2005). And, just as the emergent patterns for a system are not unlimited, the trajectories to those outcomes are more or less finite.

Attractor states are generally thought to come about through interactions among the system's components (Banzhaf, 2009). They can also be created spontaneously if system parameters pass certain critical values. Attractor states may also emerge when a change in a system parameter causes the system to split into divergent paths of behavior (i.e. it bifurcates) and to move toward entirely new attractors. Finally, values borrowed from the system parameters themselves can become attractor states if they are consistent enough to achieve the critical mass to be 'engraved' in the state space (Nowak *et al.*, 2005: 361).

The simplest type of attractor state is a *fixed-point attractor state*. The fixed point of this state refers to a unique point of equilibrium in which the system tends to settle over time (Haken, 2006). An example of a fixed-point attractor might be the bottom center position of an unpushed pendulum, the position in which it tends to settle over time. In reality, because of the immense complexity of life, systems that only tend to settle into a single fixed-point attractor state are rarer than one might expect (Byrne, 1998, 2002). *Periodic attractor states* are one step up in complexity because they provide more possibilities for variations in system behavior than fixed-point attractor states. A periodic attractor state, also known as a limit-cycle attractor state, represents two or more values that the system cycles back and forth between in a periodic loop. An example of this would be a pushed pendulum that swings up and down and up again. Patterns emerge when events or behaviors repeat themselves at regular intervals (Abraham & Shaw, 1992). *Strange attractor states*, also known as chaotic attractor states, are the most complex of all. They represent values that a system tends to approach over time but never quite reaches (Strogatz, 2003). An example of a strange attractor might be weather patterns that form from day to day. The motion of a system in a strange attractor state is called 'chaotic' – but only in the mathematical sense – because the dynamics trace a somewhat erratic or irregular pattern that never quite repeats itself, although these systems do, in fact, show complex forms of organization that can be understood after the fact (Gleick, 2008).

Pulling it together: Accounting for self-organization and emergence in practice

Recall once more that for a phenomenon to be termed emergent it should generally be unpredictable from a lower-level description. This is why even detailed knowledge of a complex system's components and how they interact often does not provide researchers with the understanding needed to predict the patterns that will result from their interaction (Johnson, 2009). At the very lowest level, the phenomenon usually does not exist at all or exists only in trace amounts: It is irreducible. This does not mean, however, that such dynamism cannot be accounted for by CDST researchers. One descriptive model of self-organization comes from Lewis's (2005) work in psychological dynamics and it is broadly illustrative of how the self-organization process unfolds in human and social systems. In this four-phase heuristic model of self-organization, the first two phases are concerned with behavior and interaction of system components on the local level, while the two latter phases shift up to a whole-system, global level (Jost *et al.*, 2010).

First, self-organization can only proceed if there is a trigger such as a significant *perturbation* that nudges a system out of an existing attractor state (Kiel & Elliott, 1996). A perturbation originates through the interaction of systems with their environment or with other systems and causes a system disturbance similar to the ripples caused by a pebble thrown into still water. Instability is the generic mechanism that underlies most self-organized pattern formation, and this is because individual elements in a system adjust and reorder themselves in response to changing conditions (Kelso, 1995). An important consideration here is the nonlinear relationship between the size of a perturbation and the size of its effect (Kra, 2009). Large forces may lead to relatively little impact on a system if the system is in a deep attractor state, whereas other relatively minor glitches can have a sustained impact (Straussfogel & Von Schilling, 2009). Disturbances in a system can follow two possible paths: through amplifying they increase in strength to destabilize a system, or they can be subdued when subject to a damping force (Boschetti *et al.*, 2011).

During the process of self-organization, behavior can be observed in which the system actively tries to turn what is happening to its advantage (Manson, 2001). This is when system components interact in a way that develops intelligently (Reitsma, 2003). The technical term for element-to-element interactional linking is *coupling* (Dooley, 1997). Coupling involves an exchange of energy or information in ongoing feedback loops. These allow new system-wide patterns of behavior to emerge (Haken, 2009). As we mentioned earlier in this chapter, feedback loops are a two-way flow of energy or information necessary for the system to experience growth and change (Newman, 2009). Positive feedback reinforces the local perturbations until they push the entire system toward certain new attractor states, while negative feedback reins in change and returns the system to its original attractor (O'Sullivan, 2009). Although self-organization at times appears to be random, there are in fact many systematic variations that steer the path of the emerging stability (Goldstein, 2011a, 2011b). These are termed *control parameters* (aka driving parameters) as a reminder that nothing is haphazard, and that there are pre-existing parameters that a system must stick to and rules by which its components play (Gorochowski *et al.*, 2011). Some common examples of control parameters that can act as motors of change in systems range from temperature, velocity, pressure or density in physical systems, to proximity, scarcity, frequency or novelty in human and social systems.

Shifting now to the higher system-level of self-organization, the result of a system continuing to realign its internal structure is that it crosses a threshold where there is enough coherence and structure for the system to begin to reconfigure itself toward a new *attractor basin* – the set of conditions that allow a system to evolve to an attractor state (van Geert, 2009). This return to stability takes place through the emergence of new higher-order patterns (Kiel & Elliot, 1996). Because these changes and new patterns in the system come about spontaneously, they are said to have emerged (Kauffman, 1995). When the outcome pattern of the system that emerges through this realignment is different in some of its main qualities from what was started with, this new state is termed a major *phase shift* (aka phase change) (Boschetti *et al.*, 2011). Examples of these system-level, qualitative changes include the examples of shifting states of matter (solid, liquid, gas) and gaits of a horse (walk, trot, canter and gallop). The key to understanding changes such as these is that they are the emergent result of a system's adaptive self-organization, and do not rely on any one component or on any linear process (Juarrero, 1999).

Once the newly emergent pattern is firmly consolidated system-wide – i.e. the system settles into its new attractor state – the emergent outcome begins to influence and determine future cycles of self-organization (Abraham & Shaw, 1992). In other words, it develops into an *order parameter*. Order parameters (aka constraint parameters) spread and restrict the future behavior of a system (Haken, 2009) helping to keep the new attractor state robust. For instance, though they did not refer to them as such, in hindsight we can see that human flight became possible once would-be aviators came to understand and harness the order parameters that are part of the physics of flight: lift, drag, thrust and gravity. This is how reciprocal causality (i.e. both top-down and bottom-up simultaneously) becomes possible: The self-organization of the component parts causes the new pattern in the system to emerge, and this emergent pattern now affects the behavior of the parts (Juarrero, 1999). Emergent phenomena, as Larsen-Freeman and Cameron (2008: 60) propose, 'entrain the lower levels or scales of activity that have produced them in the first place'. Emergence thus allows systems to retain stability and functionality by responding to continuing disturbances based on their past experience of self-organization (Kelso, 1995).

Segue

We began this fairly lengthy, and possibly dense, chapter by seeking to understand the essence of the thing we refer to as 'complexity'. One way we did this was by defining and drawing a distinction between the complicated and the complex, terms that are often confused. As our examples show, taking a 'complex' view of language and related issues can be transformative, but it also necessitates a conceptual recalibration when thinking about many otherwise familiar issues. To stake out this novel ontological territory, we then briefly explored the origins of complexity thinking in the social sciences. In line with other social complexivists, we argued that complexity is best understood as a meta-theory that accompanies a set of powerful intellectual tools and concepts capable of informing diverse theories (e.g. theories of language and theories of learning). One of the main conceptual tools that is part of the complexity mindset for research, as we show, is adopting a relational rather than an object-based understanding of the field of applied linguistics. This deliberately entails thinking of complex systems as the fundamental unit of analysis. From this point of departure, we then reviewed a handful of CDST characteristics and principles crucial for understanding the behavior of complex systems. These not only inform the ways in which researchers can think about the social world and its phenomena, but they also provide new parameters for how to conduct research within social science – points we subsequently turn to in Chapter 3.

Finally, in our last section of this chapter, we shifted to the ways in which an understanding of complex dynamic behaviors becomes possible. Here, we made the case that self-organization and emergence are pivotal concepts in understanding and accounting for the dynamics of system change. Using these CDST insights allows researchers to value variation and processes as strongly as states and outcomes (Larsen-Freeman, 2012, 2013). Determining how such dynamics come about, where they unfold and the patterns that result are some of the primary goals of CDST (Larsen-Freeman, 1997). Many of the methods we introduce in Parts 2 and 3 of this book are also designed to assist researchers in describing and modeling the processes of self-organization in systems (Holland, 2006). As such a complex mechanism suggests, conceptualizing phenomena of interest using insight from self-organization requires applied linguists to think in a connected way about both outcomes and their processes (Larsen-Freeman & Cameron, 2008). This core conceptual tool illustrates well how CDST research entails an expansionist perspective of the field and requires appropriate methods compatible with this mode of scientific inquiry.

We would encourage our readers to explore other excellent sources of detailed exposition that are available in the field (e.g. Larsen-Freeman, 2017; Larsen-Freeman & Cameron, 2008). Some sources also address specific topics in our field (e.g. Dörnyei et al., 2015; de Bot et al., 2005), while others address broader issues in the social sciences (Byrne & Callaghan, 2014; Morin, 2008; Thelen & Smith, 1994).

References

Abraham, R. (2011) The genesis of complexity. *World Futures* 67, 380–394.

Abraham, R. and Shaw, D. (1992) *Dynamics: The Geometry of Behavior* (2nd edn). Redwood City, CA: Addison-Wesley.

Al-Hoorie, A.H. (2015) Human agency: Does the beach ball have free will? In Z. Dörnyei, P.D. MacIntyre and A. Henry (eds) *Motivational Dynamics in Language Learning* (pp. 55–72). Bristol: Multilingual Matters.

Alhadeff-Jones, M. (2008) Three generations of complexity theories: Nuances and ambiguities. *Educational Philosophy and Theory* 40 (1), 66–82.

Baba, K. and Nitta, R. (2014) Phase transitions in development of writing fluency from a complex dynamic systems perspective. *Language Learning* 64, 1–35.

Bak, P. (1996) *How Nature Works: The Science of Self-Organized Criticality*. New York: Springer.

Banzhaf, W. (2009) Self-organizing systems. In R. Meyers (ed.) *Encyclopedia of Complexity and Systems Science* (pp. 8040–8050). New York: Springer.

Beckner, C., Blythe, R., Bybee, J., Christiansen, M.H., Croft, W., Ellis, N.C., Holland, J., Ke, J., Larsen-Freeman, D. and Schonemann, T. (2009) Language is a complex adaptive system: Position paper. *Language Learning* 59 (s1), 1–27.

Boschetti, F., Hardy, P.Y., Grigg, N. and Horowitz, P. (2011) Can we learn how complex systems work? *Emergence: Complexity & Organization* 13 (4), 47–62.

Byrne, D. (1998) *Complexity Theory and the Social Sciences: An Introduction*. New York: Routledge.

Byrne, D. (2002) *Interpreting Quantitative Data*. Thousand Oaks, CA: SAGE.

Byrne, D. (2005) Complexity, configurations and cases. *Theory, Culture and Society* 22 (5), 95–111.

Byrne, D. (2009) Case-based methods: Why we need them; What they are; how to do them. In D. Byrne and C.C. Ragin (eds) *The SAGE Handbook of Case-Based Methods* (pp. 1–13). Thousand Oaks, CA: SAGE.

Byrne, D. (2011) *Applying Social Science*. Bristol: Policy Press.

Byrne, D. and Ragin, C. (eds) (2009) *The SAGE Handbook of Case-Based Methods*. Thousand Oaks, CA: SAGE.

Byrne, D. and Callaghan, G. (2014) *Complexity Theory and the Social Sciences: The State of the Art*. New York: Routledge.

Capra, F. and Luisi, P.L. (2014) *The Systems View of Life*. Cambridge: Cambridge University Press.

Castellani, B. and Hafferty, F. (2009) *Sociology and Complexity Science: A New Field of Inquiry*. Berlin: Springer.

Cilliers, P. (2000) Knowledge, complexity, and understanding. *Emergence* 2 (4), 7–13.

Cilliers, P. (2005) Complexity, deconstruction and relativism. *Theory, Culture and Society* 22, 255–267.

Cuban, L. (2010) The difference between 'complicated' and 'complex' matters. See https://larrycuban.wordpress.com/2010/06/08/the-difference-between-complicated-and-complex-matters/ (accessed 30 June 2019).

Davis, B. and Sumara, D. (2006) *Complexity and Education: Inquiries into Learning, Teaching and Research*. Mahwah, NJ: Lawrence Erlbaum.

de Bot, K. (2015) Rates of change: Timescales in second language development. In Z. Dörnyei, P.D. MacIntyre and A. Henry (eds) *Motivational Dynamics in Language Learning* (pp. 29–37). Bristol: Multilingual Matters.

de Bot, K., Lowie, W. and Verspoor, M. (2005) *Second Language Acquisition: An Advanced Resource Book*. London: Routledge.

Deacon, T. (2012) *Incomplete Nature: How Mind Emerged from Matter*. New York: W.W. Norton & Company.

De Villiers-Botha, T. and Cilliers, P. (2010) The complex 'I': The formation of identity in complex systems. In P. Cilliers and R. Preiser (eds) *Complexity, Difference, and Identity* (pp. 19–38). Dordrecht: Springer.

De Wolf, T. and Holvoet, T. (2005) Emergence versus self-organisation: Different concepts but promising when combined. In S. Brueckner, G. Di Marzo Serugendo, A. Karageorgos and R. Nagpal (eds) *Engineering Self-Organising Systems: Methodologies and Applications* (pp. 1–15). Berlin: Springer.

Dekker, S., Cilliers, P. and Hofmeyr, J.H. (2011) The complexity of failure: Implications of complexity theory for safety investigations. *Safety Science* 49, 939–945.

Dooley, K. (1997) A complex adaptive systems model of organization change. *Nonlinear Dynamics, Psychology, and Life Sciences* 1, 69–97.

Dörnyei, Z. (2014) Researching complex dynamic systems: 'Retrodictive qualitative modelling' in the language classroom. *Language Teaching* 47, 80–91.

Dörnyei, Z., MacIntyre, P.D. and Henry, A. (eds) (2015) *Motivational Dynamics in Language Learning*. Bristol: Multilingual Matters.

Douglas Fir Group (2016) A transdisciplinary framework for SLA in a multilingual world. *The Modern Language Journal* 100 (s), 19–47.

Ellis, N.C. and Larsen-Freeman, D. (eds) (2009) Language as a complex adaptive system [Special issue]. *Language Learning* 59 (s1).

Elman, J. (2003) It's about time. *Developmental Science* 6, 430–433.

Eoyang, G. (2003) Conditions for self-organizing in human systems. Unpublished doctoral dissertation, The Union Institute and University, Ohio.

Eoyang, G. (2004) The practitioner's landscape. *Emergence: Complexity & Organization* 6 (1/2), 55–60.

Eve, R., Horsfall, S. and Lee, M. (eds) (1997) *Chaos, Complexity, and Sociology: Myths, Models, and Theories*. Thousand Oaks, CA: SAGE.

Fogal, G.G. (2019a) Tracking microgenetic changes in authorial voice development from a complexity theory perspective. *Applied Linguistics* 40, 432–455. doi:10.1093/applin/amx031

Fogal, G.G. (2019b) Investigating variability in L2 development: Extending a complexity theory perspective on L2 writing studies and authorial voice. *Applied Linguistics*, Advance Online Access. doi:10.1093/applin/amz005

Gell-Mann, M. (1994) Complex adaptive systems. In G. Cowan, D. Pines and D. Meltzer (eds) *Complexity: Metaphors, Models and Reality* (pp. 17–45). Reading, MA: Addison-Wesley.

Gershenson, C. (2007) *Design and Control of Self-Organizing Systems*. Publisher: Author.

Gleick, J. (2008) *Chaos: Making a New Science*. New York: Penguin Books.

Goldstein, J. (1999) Emergence as a construct: History and issues. *Emergence: A Journal of Complexity Issues in Organizations and Management* 1 (1), 49–72.

Goldstein, J. (2000) Conceptual snares emergence: A construct amid a thicket of conceptual snares. *Emergence: A Journal of Complexity Issues in Organizations and Management* 2 (1), 5–22.

Goldstein, J. (2011a) Emergence in complex systems. In P. Allen, S. Maguire and B. McKelvey (eds) *The SAGE Handbook of Complexity and Management* (pp. 65–78). New York: SAGE.

Goldstein, J. (2011b) Probing the nature of complex systems: Parameters, modeling, interventions. *Emergence: Complexity & Organization* 13, 94–121.

Gorochowski, T., di Bernardo, M. and Grierson, C. (2011) Evolving dynamical networks: A formalism for describing complex systems. *Complexity* 17 (4), 18–25.

Haken, H. (2006) *Information and Self-Organization: A Macroscopic Approach to Complex Systems* (3rd edn). Berlin: Springer.

Haken, H. (2009) Synergetics: Basic concepts. In R. Meyers (ed.) *Encyclopedia of Complexity and Systems Science* (pp. 8926–8946). New York: Springer.

Harvey, D. (2009) Complexity and case. In D. Byrne and C.C. Ragin (eds) *The SAGE Handbook of Case-Based Methods* (pp. 15–38). Thousand Oaks, CA: SAGE.

Hilpert, J. and Marchand, G. (2018) Complex systems research in educational psychology: Aligning theory and method. *Educational Psychologist* 53, 185–202.

Hiver, P. (2015) Attractor states. In Z. Dörnyei, P.D. MacIntyre and A. Henry (eds) *Motivational Dynamics in Language Learning* (pp. 20–28). Bristol: Multilingual Matters.

Hiver, P. and Al-Hoorie, A.H. (2016) A 'dynamic ensemble' for second language research: Putting complexity theory into practice. *The Modern Language Journal* 100, 741–756.

Hiver, P. and Larsen-Freeman, D. (2020) Motivation: It *is* a relational system. In A.H. Al-Hoorie and P.D. MacIntyre (eds) *Contemporary Language Motivation Theory: 60 Years Since Gardner and Lambert (1959)*. Bristol: Multilingual Matters.

Holland, J.H. (1992) Complex adaptive systems. *Daedalus* 121, 17–30.

Holland, J.H. (1995) *Hidden Order: How Adaptation Builds Complexity*. Cambridge, MA: MIT Press.

Holland, J.H. (2006) Studying complex adaptive systems. *Journal of Systems Science and Complexity* 19, 1–8.

Holland, J.H. (2012) *Signals and Boundaries: Building Blocks for Complex Adaptive Systems*. Cambridge, MA: MIT Press.

Horn, J. (2008) Human research and complexity theory. *Educational Philosophy and Theory* 40, 130–143.

Howe, M.L. and Lewis, M.D. (2005) The importance of dynamic systems approaches for understanding development. *Developmental Review* 25, 247–251.

Human, O. (2015) Complexity: E-special introduction. *Theory, Culture & Society* 3, 1–20.

Johnson, N. (2009) *Simply Complexity: A Clear Guide to Complexity Theory*. Oxford: Oneworld Publications.

Jost, J., Bertschinger, N. and Olbrich, E. (2010) Emergence. *New Ideas in Psychology* 28, 265–273.

Juarrero, A. (1999) *Dynamics in Action: Intentional Behavior as a Complex System*. Cambridge, MA: MIT Press.

Kauffman, S. (1995) *At Home in the Universe: The Search for the Laws of Self-Organization and Complexity*. New York: Oxford University Press.

Kelso, J.A.S. (1995) *Dynamic Patterns: The Self-Organization of Brain and Behavior*. Cambridge, MA: MIT Press.

Kelso, J.A.S. (2002) Self-organizing dynamical systems. In N. Smelser and P. Baltes (eds) *International Encyclopedia of the Social and Behavioral Sciences* (pp. 13844–13850). Oxford: Elsevier.

Kelso, J.A.S. (2016) On the self-organizing origins of agency. *Trends in Cognitive Science* 20, 490–499.

Kiel, L. and Elliot, E. (eds) (1996) *Chaos Theory in the Social Sciences: Foundations and Applications*. Ann Arbor, MI: University of Michigan Press.

Klein, J. (2004) Interdisciplinarity and complexity: An evolving relationship. *Emergence: Complexity & Organization* 6 (1/2), 2–10.

Kloos, H. and Van Orden, G. (2009) Soft-assembled mechanisms for the grand theory. In J.P. Spencer, M. Thomas and J. McClelland (eds) *Toward a New Grand Theory of Development? Connectionism and Dynamics Systems Theory Reconsidered* (pp. 253–267). Oxford: Oxford University Press.

Koopmans, M. (2019) Education is a complex dynamical system: Challenges for research. *The Journal of Experimental Education*. Advance Online Access. doi:10.1080/00220 973.2019.1566199

Kra, B. (2009) Introduction to ergodic theory. In R. Meyers (ed.) *Encyclopedia of Complexity and Systems Science* (pp. 3053–3055). New York: Springer.

Kretzschmar, W. (2015) *Language and Complex Systems*. Cambridge: Cambridge University Press.

Kuhn, L. (2008) Complexity and educational research: A critical reflection. In M. Mason (ed.) *Complexity Theory and the Philosophy of Education* (pp. 169–180). Chichester: Wiley-Blackwell.

Lantolf, J. (2016, March) On the (in)commensurability of sociocultural theory and dynamic systems theory. Distinguished scholarship and service plenary given at the meeting of the American Association for Applied Linguistics, Orlando, FL.

Larsen-Freeman, D. (1997) Chaos/complexity science and second language acquisition. *Applied Linguistics* 18, 141–165.

Larsen-Freeman, D. (2010) The dynamic co-adaption of cognitive and social views: A chaos/complexity theory perspective. In R. Batstone (ed.) *Sociocognitive Perspectives on Second Language Use/Learning* (pp. 40–53). Oxford: Oxford University Press.

Larsen-Freeman, D. (2012) Complex, dynamic systems: A new transdisciplinary theme for applied linguistics? *Language Teaching* 45, 202–214.

Larsen-Freeman, D. (2013) Complexity theory: A new way to think. *Revista Brasileira de Linguistica Aplicada* 13, 369–373.

Larsen-Freeman, D. (2015) Ten 'lessons' from complex dynamic systems theory: What is on offer. In Z. Dörnyei, P.D. MacIntyre and A. Henry (eds) *Motivational Dynamics in Language Learning* (pp. 11–19). Bristol: Multilingual Matters.

Larsen-Freeman, D. (2016a) Classroom-oriented research from a complex systems perspective. *Studies in Second Language Learning and Teaching* 6, 377–393.

Larsen-Freeman, D. (2016b) The psychology of language learning and 'the science of the individual'. Paper presented at the Individuals in Contexts. Psychology of Language Learning 2 Conference, University of Jyväskylä, Finland.

Larsen-Freeman, D. (2017) Complexity theory: The lessons continue. In L. Ortega and Z. Han (eds) *Complexity Theory and Language Development: In Celebration of Diane Larsen-Freeman* (pp. 11–50). Amsterdam/Philadelphia, PA: John Benjamins.

Larsen-Freeman, D. (2019) On language learner agency: A complex dynamic systems theory perspective. *The Modern Language Journal* 103 (s), 61–79.

Larsen-Freeman, D. and Cameron, L. (2008) *Complex Systems and Applied Linguistics*. Oxford: Oxford University Press.

Larsen-Freeman, D. and Tedick, D.J. (2016) Teaching world languages: Thinking differently. In D. Gitomer and C. Bell (eds) *Handbook of Research on Teaching* (5th edn; pp. 1335–1388). Washington, DC: American Educational Research Association.

Lemke, J. (2000) Across the scales of time: Artifacts, activities, and meanings in ecosocial systems. *Mind, Culture, and Activity* 7, 273–290.

Lenzing, A. (2015) Relating regularities and dynamical systems in L2 development. *Language Learning* 65 (1), 89–112.

Lerner, R.M. and Overton, W.F. (2008) Exemplifying the integrations of the relational developmental system: Synthesizing theory, research, and application to promote positive development and social justice. *Journal of Adolescent Research* 23, 245–255.

Lewis, M. (2005) Bridging emotion theory and neurobiology through dynamic systems modeling. *Behavioral and Brain Sciences* 28, 169–245.

Lewontin, R. (1998) The evolution of cognition: Questions we will never answer. In D. Scarborough and S. Sternberg (eds) *An Invitation to Cognitive Science*, Volume 4: Methods, models and conceptual issues (pp. 107–132). Cambridge, MA: The MIT Press.

Lowie, W. and Verspoor, M. (2011) The dynamics of multilingualism: Levelt's speaking model revisited. In M.S. Schmid and W. Lowie (eds) *Modeling Bilingualism: From Structure to Chaos* (pp. 267–288). Philadelphia, PA: Benjamins.

Lowie, W. and Verspoor, M. (2015) Variability and variation in second language acquisition orders: A dynamic reevaluation. *Language Learning* 65, 63–88.

Lowie, W. and Verspoor, M. (2019) Individual differences and the ergodicity problem. *Language Learning* 69 (s1), 184–206. doi:10.1111/lang.12324.

Lowie, W., Plat, R. and de Bot, K. (2014) Pink noise in language production: A nonlinear approach to the multilingual lexicon. *Ecological Psychology* 26 (3), 216–228.

Mackenzie, A. (2005) The problem of the attractor: A singular generality between sciences and social theory. *Theory, Culture & Society* 22, 45–65.

Manson, S. (2001) Simplifying complexity: A review of complexity theory. *Geoforum* 32, 405–414.

Marchand, G. and Hilpert, J. (2018) Design considerations for education scholars interested in complex systems research. *Complicity: An International Journal of Complexity and Education* 15, 31–44.

Mason, M. (ed.) (2008) *Complexity Theory and the Philosophy of Education*. Chichester: Wiley-Blackwell.

Mercer, S. (2013) Towards a complexity-informed pedagogy for language learning. *Revista Brasileira de Linguistica Aplicada* 13 (2), 375–398.

Mercer, S. (2016) Complexity, language learning and the language classroom. In G. Hall (ed.) *The Routledge Handbook of English Language Teaching* (pp. 473–485). New York: Routledge.

Montuori, A. (2013) Complexity and transdisciplinarity: Reflections on theory and practice. *World Futures: The Journal of Global Education* 69, 200–230.

Morin, E. (1992) From the concept of system to the paradigm of complexity. *Journal of Social and Evolutionary Systems* 15, 371–385.

Morin, E. (2008) *On Complexity.* Cresskill, NJ: Hampton Press.

Morowitz, H. (1996) What's in a name? *Complexity* 1 (4), 7–8.

Newman, L. (2009) Human–environment interactions: Complex systems approaches for dynamic sustainable development. In R. Meyers (ed.) *Encyclopedia of Complexity and Systems Science* (pp. 4631–4643). New York: Springer.

Nowak, A., Vallacher, R. and Zochowski, M. (2005) The emergence of personality: Dynamic foundations of individual variation. *Developmental Review* 25, 351–385.

Nowak, A., Bui-Wrzosinska, L., Coleman, P., Vallacher, R., Jochemczyk, L. and Bartkowski, W. (2010) Seeking sustainable solutions: Using an attractor simulation platform for teaching multi-stakeholder negotiation in complex cases. *Negotiation Journal* 26, 49–68.

Nowotny, H. (2005) The increase of complexity and its reduction: Emergent interfaces between the natural sciences, humanities and social sciences. *Theory, Culture and Society* 22 (5), 15–31.

O'Sullivan, D. (2009) Complexity theory, nonlinear dynamic spatial systems, In R. Kitchin and N. Thrift (eds) *International Encyclopedia of Human Geography* (pp. 239–244). Oxford: Elsevier.

Osberg, D. and Biesta, G. (2010) The end/s of education: Complexity and the conundrum of the inclusive educational curriculum. *International Journal of Inclusive Education* 14, 593–607.

Overton, W.F. (2007) A coherent metatheory for dynamic systems: Relational organicism-contextualism. *Human Development* 50, 154–159.

Overton, W.F. (2013) A new paradigm for developmental science: Relationism and relational-developmental systems. *Applied Developmental Science* 17, 94–107.

Overton, W.F. (2015) Taking conceptual analyses seriously. *Research in Human Development* 12 (3/4), 163–171.

Overton, W.F. and Lerner, R.M. (2014) Fundamental concepts and methods in developmental science: A relational perspective. *Research in Human Development* 11, 63–73.

Peck, M.S. (1993) *Further Along the Road Less Travelled: The Unending Journey toward Spiritual Growth.* New York: Simon & Schuster.

Polat, B. and Kim, Y. (2014) Dynamics of complexity and accuracy: A longitudinal case study of advanced untutored development. *Applied Linguistics* 35 (2), 184–207.

Prigogine, I. and Stengers, I. (1984) *Order Out of Chaos.* New York: Bantam New Age.

Ragin, C.C. (2009) Reflections on casing and case-oriented research. In D. Byrne and C.C. Ragin (eds) *The SAGE Handbook of Case-Based Methods* (pp. 523–534). London: SAGE.

Reitsma, F. (2003) A response to simplifying complexity. *Geoforum* 34, 13–16.

Ridley, M. (2015) *The Evolution of Everything: How New Ideas Emerge.* New York: Harper Collins.

Rose, L., Rouhani, P. and Fischer, K. (2013) The science of the individual. *Mind, Brain, and Education* 7, 152–158.

Sawyer, K. (2005) *Social Emergence: Societies as Complex Systems.* New York: Cambridge University Press.

Schmid, M.S., Köpke, B. and de Bot, K. (2013) Language attrition as complex, non-linear development. *International Journal of Bilingualism* 17 (6), 675–683.

Seedhouse, P. (2010) Locusts, snowflakes, and recasts: Complexity theory and spoken interaction. *Classroom Discourse* 1, 4–24.

Strogatz, S. (2003) *Sync.* New York: Hyperion Books.

Straussfogel, D. and Von Schilling, C. (2009) Systems theory. In R. Kitchin and N. Thrift (eds) *International Encyclopedia of Human Geography* (pp. 151–158). Oxford: Elsevier.

Thelen, E. (2005) Dynamic systems theory and the complexity of change. *Psychoanalytic Dialogues* 15, 255–283.

Thelen, E. and Smith, L. (1994) *A Dynamic Systems Approach to Development of Cognition and Action.* Cambridge, MA: MIT Press.

Thelen, E. and Bates, E. (2003) Connectionism and dynamic systems: Are they really different? *Developmental Science* 6, 378–391.

Uprichard, E. (2013) Sampling: Bridging probability and nonprobability designs. *International Journal of Social Research Methodology* 16, 1–11.

Urry, J. (2003) *Global Complexity.* Cambridge: Polity Press.

Urry, J. (2005) The complexity turn. *Theory, Culture and Society* 22 (5), 1–14.

Ushioda, E. (2015) Context and complex dynamic systems theory. In Z. Dörnyei, P.D. MacIntyre and A. Henry (eds) *Motivational Dynamics in Language Learning* (pp. 47–54). Bristol: Multilingual Matters.

van Geert, P. (1998) We almost had a great future behind us: The contribution of nonlinear dynamics to developmental-science-in-the-making. *Developmental Science* 1, 143–159.

van Geert, P. (2008) The dynamic systems approach in the study of L1 and L2 acquisition: An introduction. *The Modern Language Journal* 92, 179–199.

van Geert, P. (2009) Complex dynamic systems of development. In R. Meyers (ed.) *Encyclopedia of Complexity and Systems Science* (pp. 1872–1916). New York: Springer.

Verspoor, M., Lowie, W. and van Dijk, M. (2008) Variability in L2 development from a dynamic systems perspective. *The Modern Language Journal* 92, 214–231.

Verspoor, M., Schmid, M.S. and Xu, X. (2012) A dynamic usage based perspective on L2 writing. *Journal of Second Language Writing* 21 (3), 239–263.

Walby, S. (2007) Complexity theory, systems theory, and multiple intersecting social inequalities. *Philosophy of the Social Sciences* 37, 449–470.

Weber, A. and Varela, F. (2002) Life after Kant: Natural purposes and the autopoietic foundations of biological individuality. *Phenomenology and the Cognitive Sciences* 1, 97–125.

3 Applying Complexity Theory to Research

The starting point of research is, as emphasized by Einstein and others, astonishment. As long as a problem remains unsolved we imagine many solutions. ... [But] the future is not given and therefore we have only a probabilistic description and there is no certainty.... Uncertainty and surprise are part of human destiny.

Prigogine (2005: 16)

CDST and the Philosophy of Science

Throughout numerous areas of investigation in social science, complexity theory is becoming *de rigueur* (Castellani & Hafferty, 2009). However, this is not merely because many scholars see it as a set of useful metaphors for thinking and theorizing about social phenomena. Complexity is an empirical reality (Morin, 2007, 2008) and – as with applied linguistics – has yielded significant insights into complex phenomena across many of the human and social disciplines. Consequently, applying complexity and dynamic systems theory (CDST) to research starts with the notion that complexity is real and progresses from there to investigate that reality. CDST research, then, is all about the inherent complexity of reality.

If that were all, then doing CDST research would be rather straight-forward (Byrne & Uprichard, 2012). Applied linguists would need fairly little bandwidth to accommodate CDST in their various areas of research. However, the fact is that different perspectives exist as to what the core scientific ideas within CDST are, what their significance is for doing research and what sort of meaningful results they will lead to in the enterprise of research (Verspoor *et al.*, 2011). In this chapter, we will survey a range of ideas through which we attempt to pin down some of the parameters for how to conduct CDST research within a social science such as applied linguistics. We examine philosophical and methodological issues that arise when researching the complex and dynamic social world, and discuss considerations that are part of planning and conducting studies informed by a CDST frame of reference. We start by revisiting the earlier question 'what is complexity?' (see Chapter 2) and, in a sense, widening the playing field by looking at multiple complexities – that is, drawing a distinction between dealing with complexity empirically and doing so in a way that is more paradigmatic in nature.

Earlier in this book, we pointed out that despite its fairly straightforward definition, there are many things complexity refers to in a technical sense. The work of some complexivists (Manson, 2001; Mitchell, 2009; Reitsma, 2003) highlights the many ideas that complexity uses as a referent, for example complexity as dimensionality or hierarchy, complexity as computational capacity, or complexity as degree of informational resources for creation. It is clear that these domains see complexity research as much more than merely applying metaphors from complexity, a conviction we share. Scholars from these different fields focus on one or more of these referents depending on the phenomena of interest (i.e. information, organization, computation, development) in their fields. However, since this chapter is concerned with the CDST philosophy of science, we will imagine a continuum of intellectual thought to help us explore a more important distinction made by complexivists in the social sciences – the distinction between a restricted and generalized complexity (Morin, 2007).

Restricted complexity

On one end, this continuum is populated by a non-CDST perspective of scientific inquiry. This non-CDST paradigm does not allow disorder, change and variability to be compatible with order, coherence and stability (Cilliers, 1998). Accompanying this perspective is an important scientific tool: the analytical method. In this intellectual tradition, things that are too complex to be grasped as a whole are divided into manageable units that can be analyzed separately and then put together again. This *modus operandi* rests on the idea that knowledge of basic constituting elements is required for knowing any larger whole, and that these must be broken down for study in an orderly and additive way. However, as should have been clear from the discussion and examples in Chapter 2, complexity is not constituted simply by the sum of components, and neither is it located at a specific, identifiable site in a system. Complexity is manifested at the level of the system itself, and results from the interaction between the components of a system.

Moving down the continuum of intellectual thought, into the realm of CDST perspectives, we find Edgar Morin's (2007) interesting and useful distinction between two forms of complexity thinking – restricted and generalized (aka general) complexity. Elsewhere, Byrne (2005) refers to this same distinction using the terms 'simple' and 'complex' complexity, terms slightly less catchy but that still correspond fundamentally with what Morin had in mind in comparing these two different ways of designing and doing CDST research.

The first of these, *restricted complexity*, deals with complexity empirically rather than epistemologically. That is, it embraces complexity by employing modes of thinking and explanation with which more conventional scientific perspectives are comfortable (Byrne & Callaghan, 2014). To extend this discussion back to our previous discussion of definitions of complexity, a restricted complexity viewpoint may rely on properties or metrics of existence exhibited in the world such as the number of connections or interactions, temporal and spatial variability or patterned structure present in a complex system. An example of dealing with complexity empirically would be explaining group or system properties first 'by modelling the participating individuals, then modelling their interactions, and then simulating the processes whereby collective properties emerge from the microsimulation' (Sawyer, 2005: 148).

Restricted complexity, as a mode of research, forms a hybrid between the principles of the conventional scientific method and developing an account of a complex reality. In this sense, it recognizes complexity as inherent to the human and social world but aims to 'decomplexify' it by availing itself of traditional issues such as the purposes (e.g. falsifying hypotheses) and tools (e.g. measurement validity and reliability) of more mainstream science. While CDST does not suggest abandoning these concepts wholesale, instead recalibrating these tasks with a complex and dynamic reality, some complexivists have observed that restricted complexity avoids fundamental epistemological and ontological questions with which generalized complexity actively grapples (Morin, 2007). These include questions regarding the nature of social reality, what constitutes knowing about that reality, whether and how that reality can be represented, etc.

Complexivists who practice a form of restricted complexity, such as Holland (2006), Johnson (2009) and Mitchell (2009), are interested in providing a sophisticated account of complexity that moves from multiplicity to simplicity and parsimony. Applied examples of restricted complexity can be seen in the way the social sciences study and model the behavior of financial markets, traffic systems, organizational structures, as well as health and epidemiology. Researchers in these areas apply restricted complexity in relation to rule-based models composed of many simple components interacting at a micro level in simple ways that give rise to complex adaptive behavior such as patterns of self-organization and emergent phenomena at a macro level. Holland (1998: 188, emphasis added) captures this mode of complexity by explaining that 'much complexity can be generated in systems defined by a few well-chosen rules. When we observe emergent phenomena we ought therefore try to discern the rules that generate the phenomenon.... In so doing we will *reduce* our complex observation of emergence to the interactions of simple mechanisms'.

There are several potential issues with this mode of complexity research that treats complexity primarily as a property of systems. One is the fact that not all complex systems are made up of simple elements, simple rules and simple interactions through time (Juarrero, 1999). This is especially the case with systems whose components can be thought of as sub-systems. Individuals are themselves complex systems, nested in other superordinate systems, and any of these systems is likely to be substantially more complex than anticipated. Another dilemma is the inability of this approach to complexity research to account for human agency and volition in the way that individuals or collectives act as causal agents in a system (see e.g. Al-Hoorie [2015] and Larsen-Freeman [2019] for an extended commentary on this point). Other complexivists, too, are wary of complexity-as-property research particularly when its methods are applied with little understanding or interest in the processes that give rise to them or their implications for any broader endeavors of human and social research (e.g. Byrne & Callaghan, 2014).

For these and other reasons, restricted complexity leads down a different pathway than generalized complexity. In the first case, CDST informs the way a scholar might craft an approach to doing science, and it results in designs that are more dynamic and contextually sensitive, but it would not necessarily result in any modifications to their practice in the sense that they would still be engaged in a conventional programme of research. Byrne and Callaghan (2014) offer their take on how restricted complexity is applied in research designs:

> The core idea behind the mechanism approach [of restricted complexity] is that we explain the state of a social system at a point in time and explain the trajectory of that system through past times by referring to a constellation both of internal control parameters and of the state(s) of systems with which the system of interest intersects. We generalize within a scoped range by considering that similar constellations might engender the same system state/trajectory for systems sufficiently similar to our system of interest. (Byrne & Callaghan, 2014: 48)

This is a precise description of what is meant by restricted complexity dealing with complexity empirically rather than epistemologically.

General complexity

As we look now to the other half of the distinction, let us return to Morin's (2007: 23) voice on the matter: 'restricted complexity rejects generalized complexity... because restricted complexity [does] not make the epistemological and paradigmatic' commitment required. And, because some forms of restricted complexity fail 'to take into account "emergence", history and context', they 'tend to be either wrong or trivial'

(Mouzelis, 1995: 5–6). Let us look more closely at the target of these criticisms.

While restricted complexity is focused on complex systems and on providing an accurate empirical representation of complex phenomena, *generalized complexity* goes much further: it entails a much broader reorientation to one's philosophy of science (Capra & Luisi, 2014) that highlights the generalized interdependence of everything and everyone. Complexity, if we see it as a meta-theory, is far more than mere method (Morin, 2008), and this reorientation impacts how we think about the world and how we engage in scientific inquiry across all fields (Cilliers, 2005). Morin (2007: 24) is clear on where his allegiance lies, stating that 'it is an error to think that one will find in complexity a method that can be applied automatically to the world'.

If complexity is more than mere method, as Morin suggests, we must look to this fundamental reorientation that accompanies generalized complexity and ask what it achieves in the enterprise of research. How can applied linguistics writ large benefit from taking up this approach? What we find here is that, similar to those Kuhn (1962/2012) outlined, generalized complexity has the ability to offer the applied linguistics research community a set of deliberate, consensus-forming and paradigm-shifting considerations regarding:

- what subjects or phenomena our scientific community values and chooses to study;
- the type of questions that are appropriate for inquiry in relation to these topics;
- how systematic investigation (i.e. scholarly research) should be structured and conducted (e.g. with regard to collection of evidence);
- how the results of such scientific investigation should be analyzed and interpreted (Harvey, 2009).

Morin and Cilliers go even further than these more conceptual implications for knowing and learning about the social world to highlight several unresolved conundrums with which generalized complexity commits itself to grappling. The first problem is the problem of time. As we have said earlier, all complex systems have a history and no system can be conceived of without taking that history into account. *Nonfinality* is an important aspect of this history; what this means is because final states do not exist for system development, complex systems are not defined by progressing toward an endpoint (Rose *et al.*, 2013). The practical significance of nonfinality is that what might seem to be an endpoint in a temporal window is likely just one of many stable points in an ongoing and iterative work in process. In other words, dynamic change is non-telic in the sense that complex dynamic processes progress through time without a predetermined, fixed goal (Howe & Lewis, 2005). The most salient purpose is an *autopoietic* one of self-regeneration (Maturana & Varela, 1980).

Yet another dilemma is the problem of representation which can be exemplified through Cilliers' (2000) question about how scholars should best perceive a subject – take for instance language, language use or language development – when in reality it is not something that is self-contained, existing inert and offline in an absolute sense, but instead has existence through dynamic interaction. Morin (2007: 6) sounds off on this notion by proposing that generalized complexity requires researchers 'to comprehend the relations between the whole and the parts. The knowledge of the parts is not enough, the knowledge of the whole as a whole is not enough, if one ignores its parts; one is thus brought to make a come and go in loop to gather the knowledge of the whole and its parts'. For instance, Kretzschmar (2015) makes a compelling case for linguistic phenomena such as speech, dialects and language change as being constituted in new ways each time they are examined, which by necessity calls for a richer, multidimensional and multi-temporal way of describing and representing these patterns and their associated processes. The view that phenomenologically tangible systems are units of analysis with concrete validity and coherence in time and space is one we have advanced previously (see Chapter 2). Representation, then, must begin from the premise that complex systems are constituted by rich interactions that are constantly changing. Generalized complexity is, in Cilliers' (2000: 9) words, 'incompressible' and the fact remains that any reduction of complexity will lead to distortions. However, because no perfect representation of a system can be achieved by researchers that is simpler than the system itself, things must inevitably be left out. This has real consequences for generalized complexity, and as a result these unavoidable limitations of the representations researchers use should be acknowledged.

Having discussed what these philosophical ideas might entail for a programme of research, we need to be clear where all this gets us as applied linguistics researchers. In one sense, we have come to think of restricted complexity as a sort of 'gateway drug' to generalized complexity, and we have witnessed firsthand that by studying complexity empirically (i.e. restricted complexity) individuals can adopt such a reorientation. For some, however, such a shift in paradigm may be a bridge too far. First, as Byrne and Callaghan (2014: 56) admit, 'any general complexity social science has to get beyond micro-determined emergence. It has to allow for structures with causal powers and it has to address human agency as capable of transcending narrow rules for behavior'. However, coming to grips with how to conceive of and represent causal forces in a non-reductionist framework poses significant intellectual challenges, and only some complexivists (e.g. Kelso, 2016; Larsen-Freeman, 2019) seem willing to entertain explicit agentic thought and action within human and social systems. We turn now to how such considerations for research would be possible within different intellectual traditions and explore the utility of such ontological frameworks for doing complexity research.

Complex realism: An ontology for CDST research

In his critique of the methodological wars of position between logical empiricists and radical hermeneuticists in the social sciences – both of whom adopt an equally naïve approach to the enterprise of research – Roy Bhaskar (2007: 192) argues that it is ironically 'when things are going well [that]…you just have knowledge and you take it that that knowledge is of the world. Ontology really only becomes relevant when you are not satisfied with knowledge, when what passes for knowledge is patently wrong or absurd'. In place of these factional philosophies of science, Bhaskar proposes that useful accounts of the human and social world must take as their starting point the fact that an inherent complexity – in the sense of exhibiting emergent behavior that cannot be anticipated from the behavior of its components – underlies that human and social reality. This is echoed by complexivists who also insist that methodology must reflect the distinctive (i.e. complex and dynamic) character of human and social phenomena (Byrne & Callaghan, 2014).

Ontology, in essence, represents an understanding of the world, of its categories and properties, and of the events both possible and impossible given the character of that world (Harvey, 2002). In response to concerns that the scientific community had disengaged with the necessary ontological thinking behind scientific inquiry, Bhaskar's work (1975/1997, 1989, 2007) attempted to fashion a new worldview that would correspond more closely with the growing understanding of the complex and situated nature of all social and human phenomena. This new worldview, named critical realism, is compared with its alternatives by Byrne and Callaghan (2014: 33): 'In contrast with positivism this recognizes that our scientific (in the widest sense of the meaning of that term) descriptions of reality are social constructions. [But] in contrast with relativism it recognizes that they are constructs made from reality and therefore shaped by reality'.

Connections between realism as an ontology and fields closer to home do exist (see e.g. Bastardas-Boada, 2014; Bouchard, 2018; Cochran-Smith *et al.*, 2014). As Danermark *et al.* (2002: 10) suggest, the hallmarks of this critical realism are (1) that there exists a human and social reality which is stratified, differentiated, structured and changing; (2) that our knowledge about this reality is always fallible; but (3) that there are some theoretical and methodological tools we can use in order to inform us about that reality. This stands in stark contrast to the 'explanatory myths' embodied by the relativist and reductionist positions (Archer, 1998: 193). As the first ontology informed by complexity thinking, critical realism stakes a claim on the ways in which we can and should proceed as researchers of that complex social reality. Primarily, its position is that 'if the [social] sciences are to remain coherent enterprises, their explanatory protocols must embrace... the existence of an objective moment of experience, some part of which stands over and against our attempts to understand and manipulate our world' (Harvey, 2009: 24).

Importantly for our efforts as researchers, critical realism does not imply that this reality is either fixed or empirically inaccessible (Danermark *et al.*, 2002). This notion, one we explore later in this chapter under the rubrics of complex causality and explanation beyond the unique instance, is fully compatible with the principles of CDST, which do not reject empirical investigations (Diane Larsen-Freeman, personal communication, 16 December 2018). As Byrne and Callaghan (2014: 74–75) propose, adopting such a critical realist ontology leads researchers to design and conduct research by 'try[ing] to explore what things – complex systems – are, and how they became what they are' which, because it subsequently 'allows for effective human action and has the potential to provide a basis for human action', can be seen as 'one of the most valuable of all investigative techniques in the repertoire of complexity science as an empirical project'. This is particularly important given renewed calls in our field to capitalize on applied linguistics research as both the site and the vehicle for social action (e.g. Ortega, 2012, 2019).

This ontology, through the work of David L. Harvey (2001, 2002) and Michael Reed (Reed & Harvey, 1992, 1997), has come to be known as complex realism. Complex realism, these and other scholars propose, offers the most compatible philosophy of science to doing CDST research. Complex realism holds that there is a 'real' reality. However, given that reality is dynamic, shaped by inside and outside forces, and emerges over time, it is not meaningful to try to isolate and grasp all aspects of it. Because of the nature of reality, it can only be apprehended imperfectly and probabilistically. This reality must also be properly qualified to allow an active role for agency. Complex realism treads a middle way between realism and relativism, and adopts a problem-driven approach to research by relying on a pragmatic balance of methods determined by the object of inquiry. But, what of other non-positivistic perspectives, and might postmodernism be a viable alternative as some have suggested?

CDST and postmodernist, poststructuralist thinking

In her thorough overview of the many ways CDST has impacted the field of applied linguistics in recent years, Larsen-Freeman (2017) makes a convincing argument that CDST is rooted in principles that aim to reform science, not reject it. We could not agree more and find Larsen-Freeman's perspective refreshing and welcome. Inspired, for example, by the work of Paul Cilliers (1998), Larsen-Freeman (2017) demonstrates the shared resonances between a CDST perspective of the world, rejecting the goal of reducibility as a path to scientific understanding, and insights from poststructuralist and postmodernist thinking – both recognizing that empirical accounts and understandings can only be partial and provisional. The poststructural, postmodern, constructivist paradigms highlight the concepts of distributedness and multiplicity, and question the search for simple truths, objectivity and absolute certainty. As Larsen-Freeman (2017) makes clear, however, because of their radically different ontologies these perspectives sharply diverge from CDST in their view of how to proceed in a world marked by contingency, emergence and complexity.

The poststructuralist/postmodernist penchant for seeing both the means and ends of the scientific enterprise as fundamentally flawed and worthy of deconstruction, is not shared by complexivists who instead seek to reconstruct science (Price, 1997). CDST does not view knowledge as arbitrary, neither does it see the world essentially as verbally/discursively constructed, nor does it seek to 'dispense with *things*' entirely (Foucault, 1972: 48, our emphasis). In observing these perspectives' easy adoption of notions such as nonlinearity, interconnectedness, context dependence and nonfinality, complexivists have cautioned that the project of CDST remains firmly grounded in the scientific tradition (Byrne & Callaghan, 2014) with some characterizing postmodernism as a 'strategic misinterpretation of legitimate scientific ideas' (Turner, 1997). Even social complexivists who some might describe as drawing on postmodern thought (e.g. Paul Cilliers) are really much closer in thinking to a critical realist perspective: 'If relativism is maintained consistently, it becomes an absolute position. From this one can see that a relativist is nothing but a disappointed fundamentalist' (Cilliers, 2000: 12).

Postmodernists decline to consider a realm beyond the objects of discourse, given their view that all beliefs and actions are constructions and that there are no neutral, factual or definitive accounts of any human or social phenomena (Byrne, 2011). According to Archer (2000: 22), this is an 'anti-humanist stance' that ironically reifies 'process-without-a-maker, discourse-without-a-speaker, and texts-without-an-author' (Archer, 2000: 20). In his blistering takedown of such perspectives in social science research, Westergaard (2003) writes:

> I think the strand of postmodernism which I found most unfortunate was, again, an epistemological relativism which, if taken to its logical conclusion, makes you think 'well, what the hell are we doing?' If we can only look at perceptions, and at other people's perceptions only as they are coloured by our own perceptions, what are we in this business for at all? (Westergaard, 2003: 2)

A similarly vibrant critique exists in our own field (e.g. Block, 2014: 17; Gregg, 2000; Kubota, 2016: 487), given the recent prominence of the *post*-positions (i.e. postmodernism, poststructuralism and postcolonialism). Without discounting the very legitimate critical perspectives that are now widely recognized by applied linguists of all stripes (e.g. Douglas Fir Group, 2016; Ortega, 2019), such critiques rightly problematize these approaches to applied linguistics as positions that by default reject most assumptions of scientific inquiry, and argue instead for '*trans*- ideas' (e.g. *trans*lingual, *trans*humanist, *trans*cultural) as an antidote to such 'empty pluralism' (Pennycook, 2018: 34).

Postmodernism 'has been succeeded by a new sensibility and configuration' (Peters *et al.*, 2018: 1299), and while postmodern and poststructural characterizations may resonate with CDST's rejection of universal and reductionist accounts and its emphasis on local understandings, most complexity theorists do accept that there is a reality 'out there', albeit one characterized by complex human and social interactions occurring in spatiotemporal contexts that a classical science cannot help explain (Price, 1997). We must admit that this is also our viewpoint, and we suspect it is shared by many other applied linguists working in the CDST paradigm (see e.g. Larsen-Freeman [2017] for just one example).

At the risk of over-caricaturizing the *post*-positions, an anti-rationalist and absolute-relativist approach to scientific inquiry strikes us, though not only us (see e.g. Archer, 2000; Bhaskar, 1975/1997; Byrne, 1998, 2011), as devaluing the function of research – particularly in an applied social science such as the field of applied linguistics – and as entirely unuseful both for informing our understanding of a complex dynamic world and for actual CDST research practice. We would therefore disagree with calls for a return to postmodern thinking as a way to advance transdisciplinary applied linguistics (e.g. Atkinson, 2019: 114; McNamara, 2015: 474–475). Instead, we adopt a view, similar to Byrne and Callaghan (2014), that CDST's contribution to research is in how it moves beyond arguments between the two extremes of positivism and relativism, of thought and of action, of what is internal and what is external and of what exists and what comes to be constructed. Rather, CDST enables a notion of knowledge which is real but bounded by the complex and dynamic contingencies of the social world.

Key Tasks of CDST Research

Henry Louis Mencken, a renowned 20th-century American essayist and social commentator, once observed that 'there is always an easy solution to every problem – neat, plausible and wrong' (cited in Norman, 2011: 41). In this section, we reflect on the lessons we have learned firsthand from the challenge of doing complexity research, and from searching for easy solutions and often finding they were, just as Mencken describes them, neat, plausible but wrong. The goal of presenting such lessons is to systematically raise awareness of some of the things that 'good' applications of CDST research might do and some of the key tasks that will ensure the quality of CDST research overall. Again, we would like to assure our readers that we have no bully pulpit here, and are simply interested in helping others share the hard-won lessons we have learned.

The first lesson we have learned is about transparency in adopting a CDST framework for research. Good applications of CDST research will be transparent about the reasons for choosing to adopt a complexity framework and specifying why situating a study within this perspective is a sound theoretical and empirical choice (see also Hiver & Papi, 2020; Larsen-Freeman & Cameron, 2008b). The reason we advocate for this is that within applied linguistics, as in other disciplines, no thematic or topical area inherently functions within the CDST paradigm, but instead it is the choice of adopting a given perspective that illuminates or obscures certain aspects of the phenomenon under investigation. Articulating how CDST informs their perspective or approach to research explicitly can help researchers situate the design of their study, their research questions, data analyses and the results and discussion more broadly within this perspective (Lowie, 2017). This can also guard against using CDST too loosely (in the sense that anything with multiple interacting parts can be construed as CDST research) and in an opportunistic, *post hoc* manner.

Related to transparency is the methodological reform movement recently witnessed in the social sciences more generally, and in applied linguistics more specifically. This movement was originally motivated by a perceived replication crisis blighting various fields including biology, genetics, medicine and psychology (Schooler, 2014). In response, more interest has been directed toward replication, a practice which used to be an afterthought and certainly not entertained by major journals (Porte, 2012). This movement has also emphasized the value of open science practices, such as open materials, open data and preregistration (Marsden et al., 2018a). Preregistration refers to specifying the details of one's research plan in advance (e.g. what hypotheses to test, the sample size, instruments to be used, statistical tests to apply and criteria to exclude data and to handle missing data) that the researcher commits to adhering to regardless of whether the results are favorable to the theory under investigation. The standard approach is to articulate all these decisions and log them at a website dedicated to preregistration (e.g. https://osf.io/), which then generates a time-stamped preregistration protocol. Some journals also offer researchers the chance to pre-register their studies on the journal's own website along with the study rationale (e.g. *Language Learning*; Marsden et al., 2018b). The journal editors then send out the research plan for peer review. Plans that receive favorable reviews are conferred *in-principle acceptance*, in that they are guaranteed publication regardless of the results the researcher will eventually obtain. Another promising open science initiative is multi-site registered replication (Morgan-Short *et al.*, 2018), where teams of researchers independently attempt to replicate a finding while following the same preregistered protocols. All these initiatives aim to attain more rigor and precision in the published literature. Although CDST certainly endorses these initiatives, few actual CDST studies have followed these open science principles to-date.

Another best practice we have learned from good applications of CDST research is to examine a system's complex (i.e. interconnected) structure *as well as* its dynamic behavior. After all, as we are reminded by Stroup (1997), structure is, in fact, the system's long-term behavior. Applied linguistics research to-date has had a more conventional product or outcome focus, and a particular added value of research from a CDST perspective comes from investigating how processes evolve over time (Verspoor *et al.*, 2011). Framed this way, we are no longer left to choose between designs that examine processes of becoming and those that shed light on outcomes and patterns of being. Instead, applied linguistics research using the CDST perspective requires researchers to talk in a connected way about both the outcomes and the processes through which those outcomes are reached, and to acknowledge how entwined these are. In order to accomplish this task, CDST research must 'describe the system, its constituents, their contingencies, and also their interactions' (de Bot & Larsen-Freeman, 2011: 23).

Borrowing from previous work (Hiver & Al-Hoorie, 2016; Koopmans, 2019; Larsen-Freeman & Cameron, 2008a; Moss & Haertel, 2016), here we present a practical catalog of considerations which can inform good applications of CDST research flexibly. This *dynamic ensemble* is a user guide for planning and designing CDST research. It is compatible with the methods we introduce in Parts 2 and 3 of the book, and presents questions that can be consulted at multiple junctures in the research process to inform the choice of research problems, development of hypotheses, sampling of participants, types of data collected, and analysis and interpretation. These begin with the operational and contextual considerations, and progress to macro-system and micro-structure considerations.

Operational decisions

In designing a study, deliberately deciding what to case as a complex system, the unit of analysis and level(s) (e.g. a whole-system level, a micro-components level) at which to investigate and analyze that system and the timescale(s), temporal window or duration at which a phenomenon is to be studied is a useful point of entry. These decisions will impact the type of questions appropriate for exploration, the types of evidence that can be collected and, ultimately, the theoretical and empirical advances made (Uprichard, 2013). With regard to operationalizing the system, we are concerned with questions such as:

- What is the complex system under investigation?
- What gives this case phenomenological validity?
- Who are the agents in the system?

The goal in CDST research will rarely be to represent the entire complex system in question. In pragmatically deciding the level of granularity to adopt in a study, researchers may not be able to claim comprehensiveness of all the dimensions that bear on a phenomenon (Cilliers, 2001). However, settling on precise levels of detail in data collection and analysis can telescope the analytical focus or perspective breadth of a study to simultaneously explore only the most conspicuous segments, aspects or interactions of a system. Regarding the level of granularity of choice, researchers are concerned with the following questions:

- On what timescale(s) will the system outcome(s), system behavior(s) or complex phenomena of interest be examined?
- What type(s) and what level(s) of data are required to study the system or the phenomena of interest?
- What do the chosen levels of granularity enable the researcher to investigate that other levels would not?

Greater clarity and precision in choosing an appropriate level of granularity may narrow the focus of attention, producing relatively arbitrary boundaries in data collection and analysis. However, specifying upfront the level of granularity for a study can produce structural definition in data and still capture the complex causal dynamics of a system without reducing and overly simplifying its essential aspects.

Contextual decisions

As we have tried to convey in Chapter 2, context functions as a way of bracketing a system within an environment and giving ecological coherence to that system, its actions and its states (Byrne & Ragin, 2009). This is key for research designs. Context encompasses the initial situational conditions that can either limit or facilitate certain processes and outcomes. These conditions will include features that are directly observable (i.e. that can be recorded or measured) or that are otherwise empirically relevant (i.e. salient in the dataset) to the makeup and location of the system, and which co-adapt with it. Relevant guiding considerations relating to context include:

- What are the contextual factors that are part of the environmental frame of reference for the system, its dynamic actions and its patterned outcomes?

- How do these contextual factors permeate the system that is part of the context and influence system behavior?
- How does the system adapt to the context it is embedded in, and vice versa?

In Chapter 2, we laid out a rationale for seeing systems as the basic structural building blocks of the complex social world. To this we could add that context is pragmatically constrained to include the cognitive, psychological and social aspects that form the immediate environment of a system's ecology. Extending this one step further, then, a network is the architectural superstructure in which these systems are embedded (Kadushin, 2012). A multi-node hub is composed of interconnected systems, their relationships and processes which together form the foundational web of the complex social world. This consideration leads to a range of possibilities in conducting and designing research with linked and nested systems. The questions researchers might consider related to systemic networks include:

- To which other systems (i.e. nodes) does the system of interest link?
- What is the nature of these networked relationships (e.g. co-adaptive, competitive)?
- For the system under investigation, what processes ensue in coordination with other systems?

Because any single system is just one of many nodes embedded within this dynamic network of interwoven systems, progressively unraveling which systems are networked and the precise dimensions in which they reciprocate forms a sophisticated agenda for a given strand of CDST research. On the other hand, none of this suggests that systems be treated as contiguous or networked simply because they are sampled together. Systems can only be thought of as adjacent or networked if they are bounded together in some phenomenologically meaningful way (see Chapter 2 for more on this).

Macro-system decisions

One might ask, 'what is it that systems do?'. In response, many complexivists see the pivotal characteristic of complex systems as that of dynamic change and adaptation (Verspoor et al., 2011). Whereas emergent outcomes account for the dynamic state in which a system has stabilized, adaptive change provides a temporal narrative for the process of how and why the system got there and where it may be going. These are points we elaborate on at some length in Chapter 2. Because this change is constant, researchers interested in fingerprinting this moving target through their research designs (see also Lowie, 2017) might consider the following questions related to dynamic processes:

- What general principles of change (e.g. coordinative structures) and specific mechanisms of change (e.g. bifurcations) exist for this system?
- What trajectory has the system followed through state space, and how did it get to where it is?
- What signature dynamics (e.g. self-organization) have produced the system outcomes, and why?

Patterns or trajectories of change over time are essential for understanding the complexities of system development. And as we have explained earlier, just as the emergent outcomes for a system are not unlimited, the trajectories to those outcomes are also finite, although the system's dynamic behavior may include rich variations that are diachronically asymmetrical (Elman, 2003; Koopmans, 2014).

As we mentioned at the start of this section, CDST research treats emergent outcomes and the processes through which those outcomes are reached in a connected way, acknowledging how entangled these are. For researchers, it may seem counterintuitive that emergent outcomes at the system level have no direct counterpart at the lower component level (Holland, 2012). However, the fact that higher-order patterns of dynamic equilibrium for a system are emergent allows for a more accurate and parsimonious explanation than is possible by aggregating the individual components and their interactions (Jörg, 2011). Questions that researchers might attend to concerning emergent outcomes as they design and conduct CDST research include:

- What dynamic outcome configurations emerge for this system, and how/why?
- What pockets of stability (i.e. attractor states) does the system tend toward over time, and why?
- What are the characteristics of these patterns of stability for the system in the state landscape?
- What variability exists around these patterns of stability?

To reiterate an earlier point, the number of novel emergent outcomes observable in the social world is finite (see Chapter 2) (De Wolf & Holvoet, 2005). Consequently, identifying these may reduce much of the unpredictability of complex systems' functioning and allow researchers to make informed choices about how to interact with respective outcomes (Vallacher *et al.*, 2015).

Micro-structure questions

As other CDST scholars also emphasize, the task of describing and explaining system behavior is key to CDST research and must take into account the makeup of that complex system (see e.g. de Bot & Larsen-Freeman, 2011: 23). Questions the CDST researcher might consider in describing the system and its constituents include:

- What are the constituent parts that make up the system under investigation?
- Which are the most prominent components of the system in a given process of change, or for an emergent outcome, and why?

The dilemma this presents is that isolating individual system components for examination – regardless of the level of sophistication applied to their analysis – cannot give a true measure of their influence. Social complexivists have raised concerns regarding this type of research design (Byrne & Callaghan, 2014; Ragin, 2004). Ultimately, CDST rules out the possibility of adequately understanding a complex system and its behavior by examining only one level or manifestation of it. Thus, rather than seeing the whole system and its parts as being in tension, frequent 'level jumping' (Davis & Sumara, 2006: 26) in data collection and analysis may be necessary in CDST research.

System outcomes are not the result of sums of components, but of dynamic interactions. This means that interactions between components of a system and with the environment are a system's lifeblood. If there is no potential for components to interact, there is no complexity (Vallacher et al., 2015). Exploring these internal dynamics when designing and conducting CDST research can be guided by the following considerations:

- What types of relationships and interactions exist between system components, and what are their characteristics?
- How do these exchanges manifest and affect system behavior?
- How do these relationships change over time?

We have found it helpful to explore these internal dynamics from the perspective of their manifestations and their latent characteristics. The manifestation of interaction is the specific observable behavior between the components themselves, between multiple systems and with the environment. The latent characteristics give interactions their causal and functional coherence, and include the aim, purpose or intention of the interaction; its directionality, intensity, frequency and duration; its utility and the rewards or costs that accrue from it.

These interactions are themselves dynamic, and because system change is contingent in large part on these interactions, they are essential to understanding a system's self-organized processes and emergent outcomes (Overton, 2013).

Parameters reveal yet another layer of understanding for designing and conducting CDST research. Some parameters (i.e. order parameters/ constraint parameters) reduce the degrees of freedom within which components are able to interact (Gaustello & Liebovitch, 2009) and specify the changes and interactions possible within a system (Haken, 2009). These guidelines for interaction among a system's elements function as operating rules for interpreting system behavior. Here the question guiding research designs might be:

• What are the guidelines and constraints that specify the changes and interactions possible within a system, and how do they influence the system's behavior?

Part of the reason why our complex world does not exhibit infinite permutations is because of order parameters. Once these rules are known, it becomes possible to make more robust observations and potentially influence movement toward a desired outcome (Morrison, 2012).

Other parameters (i.e. control parameters/driving parameters) are critical dimensions or values of a system (e.g. temperature, interest rates, stress, taxes) which fluctuate and as a result may effect a change in system behavior and outcome (Haken, 2009). Control parameters are particularly useful for intentionally inducing change in a system. Determining which control parameters a system is particularly sensitive to is a key task of CDST research and is one productive way of finding the 'motors of change' (Larsen-Freeman & Cameron, 2008a: 70) for intervention. Here, the consideration for research designs would be:

• What are the critical dimensions or values of a system (e.g. the motors of change) which, when they fluctuate, may result in a change in outcome?

System intervention in CDST research, then, may entail setting the conditions and shaping the path of emergent outcomes from a good enough design of the relevant control parameters (Byrne & Uprichard, 2012).

We have outlined some of the lessons we have learned firsthand from the challenge of doing complexity research, framing these within what we see as key tasks of CDST research. Here, we have been inspired by de Bot and Larsen-Freeman (2011: 23) who write that 'teasing out the relationships and describing their dynamics for systems at different levels of scale are key tasks of the researcher working from a [C]DST perspective'. Using this as guidance, the core objectives of 'good' CDST research in applied linguistics are to (a) represent and understand specific complex systems at various scales of description; (b) identify and understand the dynamic patterns of change, emergent system outcomes and behavior in the environment; (c) trace, understand and where possible model the complex mechanisms and processes by which these patterns arise; and (d) capture, understand and apply the relevant parameters for influencing the behavior of the systems (Hiver & Al-Hoorie, 2016).

Once we have accomplished these already challenging tasks, as researchers, we begin to wonder how much farther we can and should go. After all, de Bot and Larsen-Freeman (2011: 23) also affirm that CDST 'undoes the conventional expectation that a good theory is one that describes, explains, and predicts. Description and explanation are possible, and these may be good enough'. CDST research, most complexivists would agree, should be useful in the way that all good research should be (Byrne, 1998; Byrne & Uprichard, 2012; Gershenson, 2008). As Byrne and Callaghan (2014: 12) write regarding scholars in the applied social sciences – of which we also count applied linguists – 'We are not just describers, we are makers and the most important mode through which we make is in application'. But, does the enterprise of conventional research contravene the assumptions necessary for investigating a complex and dynamic reality? Is CDST research compatible with hypothesis testing, causal explanation and generalization? Is CDST research appropriate for intervention and practical application? We turn now to exploring these important questions.

Methodological Questions in CDST Research

On 8 April 1986, in a lecture to the Royal Society of London on the 300th anniversary of Newton's *Principia*, Sir James Lighthill (1986) made the following statement:

> I speak...once again on behalf of the broad global fraternity of practitioners of mechanics. We are all deeply conscious today that the enthusiasm of our forebears for the marvelous achievements of Newtonian mechanics led them to make generalizations in this area of predictability which... we tended to believe before 1960, but which we now recognize as false. We collectively wish to apologize for having misled the general educated public by spreading ideas about determinism of systems satisfying Newton's laws of motion that, after 1960, were proven to be incorrect. I am trying to make belated amends by explaining both the very different picture that we now discern, and the reasons for it having been uncovered so late. (Lighthill, 1986: 38)

What Lighthill went on to explain in his lecture is that with the discovery of the principles of complexity and of complex systems, the limits to generalizability and predictability became apparent and scientists had to make good-faith efforts to come to grips with these limits and address them in research methodology.

In this section, we turn to examining what these issues might look like when they are part of a programme of CDST research.

Generalizability

Variability is at the heart of CDST (Lowie, 2017). Systems in context feature multiple components, each interacting in unique ways with the others. The strength provided by CDST is its approach to investigating this inherent variation and how qualitatively new patterns and functions are formed (Larsen-Freeman, 2012, 2013). But what this also means is that we may need to reconsider conventional notions of generalizability. One inherent quality of researching related phenomena from a CDST perspective is the deliberate focus on the complex mechanisms or processes through which the outcome is reached (Thelen, 2005; Verspoor *et al.*, 2011). Researchers investigating such emergent phenomena would perhaps want to be able to make claims beyond the unique instance. Fortunately, the number of novel emergent outcomes observable in the social world seems finite (De Wolf & Holvoet, 2005), and the complex social world presents a set of phenomenological outcomes and self-organized processes, which are found in recurring instances and guises (Jost *et al.*, 2010). Because these attractor states (see Chapter 2) are so marked for similar systems, investigating them can offer insights that still have general relevance.

Due to the complexities involved in generalizing within a paradigm that values openness to context, the importance of initial conditions, interconnectedness, soft-assembly and nonlinear change and self-organization, it is worth considering whether the project of generalization is a valid one, and how researchers might approach it. Some scholars, for instance, see varying logics of generalizability (see e.g. Moss & Haertel [2016] for further discussion). We must admit that not all complexivists agree that the enterprise of generalizing across contexts, time and systems is necessary or indeed realizable. For instance, some have cautioned that assuming an understanding of human and social phenomena only when there is a high degree of predictability and generalizability is questionable and relies on simplistic and deterministic principles of 'fixity' (Allen & Boulton, 2011: 164). This is particularly the case for those operating within a strong general complexity frame of reference (Morin, 2001, 2008).

Complexity, we must also affirm, is not simply the result of lack of information or unrefined measurement. In a complex and dynamic world, researchers are faced with real limitations to our ability to understand phenomena of interest. This is the case because complexity assumes a degree of uncertainty in interpreting the behavior of individual elements inside a system and the collective behavior of the system; this extends also to the way the system interacts with other systems in its environment and

how those systems respond to changes in the environment (McDaniel &
Driebe, 2005). These scholars posit that in place of grand impressions
of certainty, embracing uncertainty is the fundamental underpinning of
complexity science as it allows researchers to examine variability as a
default function of existence – rather than as noise (Allen & Boulton,
2011). As de Bot and Larsen-Freeman (2011: 23) remind us, 'instead of
generalizable predictions, then, we are content to point to tendencies,
patterns, and contingencies. Instead of single causal variables, we have
interconnecting parts and subsystems that co-adapt and that may display
sudden emergence of new modes of behavior'.

There is no disputing these points, and CDST researchers must accept
the complex dynamic nature of reality and operate within it. Juarrero
(1999: 258), for instance, similarly reminds us that 'the price we pay for
the potential of true novelty and creativity is uncertainty'. While we take
up these notions in a more concrete way by exemplifying what is and is
not possible in each method introduced in Parts 2 and 3, here we are also
guided by the thinking of complexity methodologists David Byrne and
Charles Ragin (2009: 1) who propose that 'the central project of any science is the elucidation of causes that extend beyond the unique specific
instance' (see also Byrne & Callaghan, 2014).

CDST research holds a core set of operational assumptions, namely
that complex outcomes and their dynamics of change 'depend on all of
the whole, the parts, the interactions among parts and whole, and the
interactions of any system with other complex systems among which it is
nested and with which it intersects' (Byrne & Ragin, 2009: 2). For these
complexivists, scientific inquiry should have generalizing claims, but they
are equally categorical that 'generalizing is not the same as universalizing' (Byrne & Ragin, 2009: 1). Generalizing in CDST research, then,
should be best understood as the act of developing an understanding of
a phenomenon that goes beyond the unique instance and involves paying
'careful attention to the limitations of our knowledge claims in time and
space' (Byrne & Ragin, 2009: 9).

Other methodologists have explored how such alternate approaches
to a nomothetic, and variable-based, mode of generating explanations
that are invariant across time and settings would work in practice
(Velicer et al., 2014). These are motivated by the perceived shortcomings
of the postmodernist approach to this enterprise – i.e. that everything is
relative and essentially unknowable (Lee, 1997; Price, 1997) – and are
instead informed, broadly, by a complex realist perspective that what
we observe in the world is real and that it is the product of complex and
contingent causal mechanisms which may not be directly accessible to us
(Byrne, 1998). Writing on this issue, Mouzelis (1995: 152) makes a convincing argument that 'the only interesting substantive generalizations…
are those that take into full account context in terms of time and space'.
As we have proposed in Chapter 2, discovering 'what works' within a

CDST research paradigm may only be possible by articulating for whom, in what settings, under what conditions and when. Others call for greater caution regarding generalizing claims (e.g. Biesta, 2007) and propose that 'research can tell us what *worked*, but not necessarily what *works*' (Diane Larsen-Freeman, personal communication, 16 December 2018).

One potential CDST approach is generalizing within a system, across contexts. The question here is whether a particular account of phenomena of interest that is established as valid and reliable for the system in one context would be generalizable to other contexts where other conditions are at play. For instance, if certain system behavior or self-organized development is understood to lead to a particular emergent outcome, this approach to generalizing would entail finding out, in a fairly systematic way, the extent to which such an explanation holds when the system is in another environment entirely. To take an example closer to home, if patterns of language use and language learning can be accounted for successfully in one setting or one classroom, it would be necessary to ask whether these patterns are also maintained in another setting or classroom. Generalizing within a system and across contexts is sometimes referred to as the 'generalization gradient' (Velicer *et al.*, 2014: 429), which refers to the relative strength or the degree to which an understanding that extends beyond the unique instance varies on a continuum of applicability. An added caveat, however, is that 'from all the failures to replicate experiments, one wonders if this is even possible in the human world using positivism' (Diane Larsen-Freeman, personal communication, 16 December 2018).

Another alternative is to generalize within a system, across time, instances or occasions. As the focus of CDST research is often related to a system's variability across time (Lowie, 2017), generalization should also be thought of in terms of the strength of an explanation for such variability across time (Velicer *et al.*, 2014). For example, to evaluate the effect of policy initiatives on changes in language use trends within a multilingual community, the focus would be on the 'replicability' of these patterns of change in the language community over time, not on attempting to generalize from one community to another or a focus on how such policies impact other communities (cf. van Geert & Steenbeek [2014] for alternative ideas in policy research). Some of the time-series designs introduced in Parts 2 and 3 which are low-N but high-T recommend such replication across multiple occasions – sometimes called a box-score approach. That is, in order for an account of a system's variability to be accepted as valid and reliable – even if that change is nonlinear and discontinuous, the understanding is that it should be coherent across time.

Yet another approach, when generalizing to a heterogeneous population is not warranted, would be to generalize to homogeneous systems, cases or subgroups. This is similar to the notion of ergodic systems in which wholes exhibit the same behavior and properties as their parts over time, and vice versa. Systems and processes exhibit such ergodicity when sequences in time or samples in space are representative of the whole entity or developmental trajectory. The ergodic principle is often violated when using large-N group-based designs that examine only variation between individuals (Hamaker, 2012; Koopmans, 2014, 2019), but it is in fact the default option for many of the case-based methods we introduce in Parts 2 and 3 of this book. Developing an in-depth familiarity with the systems being examined allows researchers to capture aspects of their complexity. Casing systems as the units of analysis in this way also enables researchers to study more than just a handful of systems at a time, which opens up the possibility of generalizing across cases and datasets. Some case-based methods, such as qualitative comparative analysis (see Chapter 4), even feature the possibility of including an entire population of systems or sub-systems in a sample.

A final approach would be to capitalize on the inherent variability of complex systems and, as Larsen-Freeman and Cameron (2008a) propose, draw generalized conclusions about the dynamics of systems. This is similar to several lines of research that van Geert and Steenbeek (2014) advocate for:

> [O]ne line of research that is now becoming increasingly important focuses on the statistical structure of patterns of intraindividual variability, and to use such patterns to discover general properties of the underlying complex dynamic systems from which [this] variability originates... Yet another line of research is to apply predictions based on very general system descriptions... to observations made in educational systems, for instance. (van Geert & Steenbeek, 2014: 35)

There may, in fact, be research topics or issues 'especially on high levels of effect aggregation [where] it is primarily inter-individual variability that matters' (van Geert & Steenbeek, 2014: 34), but this will not always be the case. One point of clarification is that, as van Geert and Steenbeek (2014: 33, our emphasis) propose, 'this reasoning is based on the tacit assumption that the nature of the causes governing (co-)variation as it occurs *between* individuals is the same as the nature of the causes governing (co-)variation occurring *within* individuals'. For research that focuses on within-system dynamics, van Geert (2011: 276) emphasizes that CDST helps scholars to go beyond the unique specific instance by 'generat[ing] theory-based descriptions of individual trajectories in a non-trivial sense'.

Causality

Causality, Byrne and Callaghan (2014: 11) propose, is 'a fundamental task of any science which seeks both to explain and to be useful'. It is a way of conceptualizing the real world and observations about life.

The way that scholars in the social sciences think about causality has been heavily influenced by ideas which originate from a neo-positivist paradigm prevalent in the natural sciences – ideas which are frequently transposed onto the social sciences (Byrne, 1998). At its core, this manner of looking at causality concerns expectations that life is ordered deterministically, that it is governed by absolute laws and that this order and regularity allows inference from the particular instance to the general conditions of existence (Groff, 2008). It relies on decomposing a system into discrete elements or variables, varying them through randomized controlled experiments to understand a system's outcome or behavior and what has caused it, and to predict its future behavior (Gershenson, 2008).

Like others who work within a CDST paradigm, we would characterize this ideology of simple mono-causality – i.e. outcomes being driven by a single, linear causal agent – as flawed and misleading (Mainzer, 2007). Even within medicine, a hard science built on randomized controlled experiments, notions of etiology and causality have for some time now developed in ways that prioritize multifactorial, related and intersequenced causal explanations (e.g. Kleinberg & Hripcsak, 2011; Koopman, 1977; Rizzi & Pedersen, 1992; Ward, 2009). Adopting a simplistic view of causes and their effects in the face of the complexity of the social and human world, according to Turner (1997), is analogous to trying to push a string. The Newtonian assumption that effects cannot occur without specific causes relies on condensed, single-factor explanations of causality rather than diffuse and system-level ones (Radford, 2008). This is clearly inadequate for the CDST paradigm with its concern for open systems and their nestedness, networked links and feedback sensitivity (Hedström & Ylikoski, 2010; Morrison, 2012). This is also why developing a different logic of explanation is critical to advancing what Byrne and Ragin (2009: 1) have called 'the central project' of research: going beyond the purely idiographic without resorting to being radically nomothetic, while still elucidating causation.

How, then, might the notion of causality be reconciled with what we have said previously about complex dynamic systems? To start to make any progress in resolving this issue, some complexivists propose that 'we have to think first not about causes in complex systems but about the nature of effects. We should start with the question: what is an effect?' (Byrne & Callaghan, 2014: 174). We have spent much of Chapter 2 exploring just such questions by elaborating key insights about systems and their operation within a CDST perspective. A fuller answer to this question, other experts suggest, lies in developing more nuanced notions of a complex and dynamic causality (Larsen-Freeman & Cameron, 2008a). This is what Alicia Juarrero (2011: 162), for example, calls a 'billiard-ball understanding of causality'.

The position CDST takes on causality in the complex social and human world is that, most often, (a) effects and outcomes are produced through a combination of complex conditions, (b) that several different combinations of conditions can produce the same phenomena and (c) that certain conditions can have a different impact on an outcome at different times depending on the context (Jörg, 2011). This complex, networked type of causality is at the heart of a transdisciplinary approach to scientific inquiry (see also Kleinberg, 2013), on which we have much more to say below.

No single rule or principle governs or determines the makeup, development or behavior of complex systems (Holland, 1995). As Bouchard (2018: 270) writes regarding the critical realist stance on causality, 'because social and cultural changes are also multilayered, realist researchers are... more interested in multiple determinations – that is, the causal potential of multiple factors interacting in complex ways, with each factor having a particular effect on other factors'. This revised notion of causality is *complex* because it is likely to be multivariate, multilevel and path dependent; it is *dynamic* because it may involve contingent, co-adaptive processes that are nonlinear and non-proportional. The most uphill task, then, may be in acknowledging that 'everything counts' (Thelen, 2005: 261) when it comes to how effects are caused.

A further intriguing aspect of the human social world is the distinctive character of complex social causality since any account of causes and outcomes must contend with and account for conscious human agency (Byrne & Callaghan, 2014). On this point, Hedström (2005: 72) concurs: 'Most of us agree that individuals exist and that they have causal powers that enable them to bring about change and to transcend social expectations'. Human agency then is itself a complex casual force as humans hunt causes (i.e. establish what might cause changes in the future state of the system) and use causes (i.e. implement choice actions which will result in a particular future rather than another future) (Hedström & Ylikoski, 2010). Byrne and Callaghan (2014: 176) write convincingly on how human agency contributes to further causal complexity: 'in a world of social conflict, at whatever level, there are multiple actors with competing interests and objectives. So it is not a matter just of establishing causal parameters and acting on that establishment to achieve a desired future state'.

While a complex and dynamic treatment of causality and causal mechanisms remains more of a conceptual exercise at this stage, and will become more concrete as we revisit these notions through the various research methods we introduce in Parts 2 and 3, for the time being we can propose several guiding principles that are broadly applicable to the field of applied linguistics and might allow a more nuanced view of causality:

(1) *Multiplicity*: Patterns flow from conditions, and identifying the causal conditions at play for a given outcome is a crucial first step

(Kleinberg, 2013). Note our deliberate use of the plural. Thinking in terms of multiplicity should be the CDST default as more often than not there are likely to be a handful of central causative factors along with various peripheral – and in some instances even hidden – ones (Stroup, 1997). Here, researchers would reference aspects of the system and its context that are most likely to have an impact on, and in turn to be impacted by, the outcome. Establishing these is a necessary step, but one that is not sufficient on its own (Thelen, 2005). Adding further intrigue to the mix, here we can also borrow a maxim from the realm of computer programming where coders acknowledge TMTOWTDI (there is more than one way to do it). Systems have more than one way of reaching outcomes, and this is precisely what the CDST principle of *equifinality* suggests: the same outcome may be achieved with different initial conditions and via different trajectories.

(2) *Interdependence*: Our readers will recall the technical meaning of complexity: what is woven together and leads to emergent outcomes. Given the prominence of interconnectedness in a system, examining the interdependent links between the conditions and factors that appear to have causal significance will offer as much insight into the workings of the system's outcome as determining what these factors are (Larsen-Freeman & Cameron, 2008b). The element-to-element and element-to-context relationships that involve loops of reinforcing (i.e. positive) and damping (i.e. negative) feedback will allow these causal factors to trigger, interact with and even counteract each other. Knowing something about these multilevel interdependencies is vital in unraveling the causal threads of a system's outcome (Lewis, 2005).

(3) *Hysteresis*: Time is central to understanding complex causality (Koopmans, 2014, 2019). However, the default understanding of time should be that the point of departure for a cause may not always be what it appears to be (de Bot, 2015). Hysteresis concerns the system's previous history and those initial conditions' influence on subsequent outcomes. Time 1 predicts Time 2, and the interaction of both Time 1 and Time 2 predicts Time 3. In this way, history both provides the initial time frame which is necessary to begin thinking about causality, and contributes to the expanding picture of how effects come about (Jörg, 2011). Previous points in time will contribute causally to present points in time, and these in combination will continue to contribute causally to future points in time. On the hysteretic aspects of causal influence in complex dynamic systems, we have written elsewhere about an *incubation effect* (Joe et al., 2017), which is the delay between instigating initial conditions of implementation for an intervention and the emergence of effects. CDST principles show that outcomes may not immediately reveal their underlying cause if the

source of that cause is a process whose sustained effect has a much earlier inception (Larsen-Freeman, 2017).

(4) *Directionality*: Causality is not a static determinant of a system's outcome. Causes and effects can reciprocate in progressive bidirectional cycles where each modifies the other functionally (Byrne & Callaghan, 2014). Thus, these reciprocal and recursive flows of causes and effects add another important dimension to how systems come to be what they are, or how they come to behave as they do (Larsen-Freeman & Cameron, 2008a). Causes shape effects, which then return the favor and reshape the causes, where each is at once an antecedent and a consequence of the other (van Geert, 1998). The capacity to decipher these cycles is likely to result in completely new ways of thinking about outcomes.

(5) *Stochasticity*: To compound the foregoing factors, there is also an unpredictable, diffuse quality to outcomes. This introduces an element of nonlinearity and non-proportionateness to how effects come about, often reflected in human behavior which appears to have no immediate effect because the antecedents require time and persistence before the effect unfolds (Morrison, 2012). Yet another angle to this is the fact that, contingent on context, different mechanisms operate to produce different outcomes. Similarly, different mechanisms may produce the same outcome (Byrne & Ragin, 2009). In the place of equal and opposite reactions, then, applied linguistics researchers must think instead of contingent, threshold effects which build up over time until they cascade into one or another outcome (Gershenson, 2008).

Methodological Experimentation and Transdisciplinarity

Until fairly recently, applied linguistics research favored analytical methods for partitioning and isolating objects of inquiry into discrete variables or mechanisms to determine current behavior, track the past or predict a future. This 'preference for the [methodological] artifice of simplicity' (Larsen-Freeman & Cameron, 2008a: 1) stands in contrast to the way in which CDST informs an approach to scientific inquiry (Ellis & Larsen-Freeman, 2006). A conventional, componential way of researching applied linguistics may be compelling in its simplicity and apparent coherence, but it does not lend itself to dealing with complex effects or situations where results and outcomes are multi-determined – a hallmark of how the human, social world functions.

Despite our general enthusiasm toward CDST for applied linguistics research throughout these first few chapters, we are perfectly aware that CDST research is not without its own set of challenges. Most of these we have experienced firsthand in our own research. With regard to methodological choices, some questions for consideration include: (1) What does doing impactful applied linguistics research from a CDST perspective actually entail? (2) Does CDST research require applied linguistics researchers to discard existing methodological toolkits? and (3) How should a genuinely meaningful programme of CDST research be designed and conducted?

First, it is worth being explicit about the methodological contribution CDST makes to the study of applied linguistics: the logic of CDST can be used as an aid to designing a programme of research that prioritizes adaptive and developmental processes (Larsen-Freeman & Cameron, 2008a) – focusing on the how and why of a phenomenon – and is equally suited to questions of emergent outcomes and holistic pattern finding. In addition, while many degrees of freedom exist with regard to the methods of data elicitation and analysis (ideas we elaborate on in Parts 2 and 3), as a meta-theory CDST does not offer ready-made research templates – nor should it be expected to.

Recent work has proposed ways in which complexity constrains methodological choices while at the same time encouraging innovation and diversification (Hiver & Al-Hoorie, 2016). Other researchers have begun to expand the toolbox of methods available to conduct research in a dynamic vein (Verspoor et al., 2011; Dörnyei et al., 2015). Collectively, this work features individual and group-based methods with emergent, recursive and iterative designs that are suited to studying dynamic change in context and interconnectedness. Our field is therefore following other social and human disciplines that also seek to understand complexity by routinely drawing on and innovating with existing methods.

Secondly, we must also admit what we feel does not go nearly far enough to qualify as CDST-informed research: approaching complex dynamic phenomena in applied linguistics from a purely semantic or metaphorical point of view, and formulating descriptions of those with a language borrowed from CDST. Instead, as we see it, using ideas from CDST requires researchers to identify pressing issues that need addressing or questions that demand answers, and then determine how to shed light on possible solutions (Larsen-Freeman, 2016), a CDST research task that Castellani (2018: 248) calls 'addressing the adjacent possible'. At one level this might mean using ideas from CDST to analyze empirical data and provide more complex descriptions, analyses and interpretations of applied linguistics phenomena.

Flexibility and pragmatism are necessary to advance the study of such complex dynamic phenomena, and experimentation with data collection and analysis techniques that are amenable to CDST research in applied linguistics is to be encouraged. Blending research methods, which we discuss toward the end of this book, is a genuinely productive way to produce a more multidimensional understanding of an issue than adhering to tightly prescriptive methods, and this underscores the value of methodological diversity for CDST research. However, as we propose throughout the chapters in Parts 2 and 3 in this book, researchers should also endeavor to be meticulous and well-informed so that every step within a research design resonates with the principles of CDST (Larsen-Freeman, 2012).

Because CDST is a meta-theory, it does not dictate the use of unique research methods, nor does it exclude existing research methods as long as those methods are fundamentally congruent with the principles of complexity (Byrne, 2011; Mason, 2008). Instead, complexity is grounded in the phenomenological reality of the social world and calls for an inquiry-driven approach to research that emerges from the needs of inquiry, not one determined by disciplinary boundaries (Morin, 2008). So, while CDST provides a truer perspective for looking at existing problems and opens the door to reconfiguring the field's programme of knowledge, in a sense there are no such things as methods of complexity because CDST encourages innovation and diversification in understanding complex social phenomena (Wolf-Branigin, 2013). This reality is demonstrated well by the fact that many of the methods we introduce in Parts 3 and 4 are not used exclusively by complexivists in the social sciences and are not described as 'CDST methods' *per se*.

As a further example, we find it to be a rather persistent misunderstanding among newcomers to CDST that quantitative data elicitation and analyses are poorly suited to CDST-informed empirical research or that qualitative designs are inherently more compatible with dynamic change and interconnectedness (e.g. Molenaar *et al.*, 2014; Valsiner *et al.*, 2009). Qualitative research designs do not by themselves guarantee a more complex and dynamic perspective for research, particularly if the research design is not inherently connected to or informed by the conceptual framework of CDST (see e.g. Dörnyei *et al.* [2015] on this topic). CDST might gain greater traction in applied linguistics research if scholars recognized that CDST encourages repurposing existing methods and techniques – both qualitative and quantitative, individual and group based – to ensure they are congruent with its philosophy of science (van Geert, 2008).

As others have noted, the selection of methods for complexity-based inquiry in applied linguistics does not suggest an either/or choice, and from CDST's philosophy of science, advocating a qualitative-only approach is neither defensible nor pragmatic for the range of phenomena that necessitate investigation (Molenaar *et al.*, 2014; Valsiner *et al.*, 2009). CDST adopts a problem-driven, inclusive approach to social inquiry that encourages expansion of existing methodological repertoires. By its transdisciplinary nature, CDST also opens the door to constructing a programme of research that cuts across topical, thematic, methodological or discipline-specific lines, and offers a broad solution to how CDST research can position its contribution to doing applied linguistics research.[1]

Multidisciplinary approaches to research, Larsen-Freeman (2012) reminds us, feature multiple disciplines contributing distinct perspectives on a shared problem space. Unfortunately, these are additive and rarely characterized by interaction across disciplinary lines (see Moss & Haertel [2016] for an extended discussion). Perhaps, *cross-disciplinary* approaches to research offer greater promise in this regard. Yet, here too we find a state of affairs in which 'one discipline assum[es] a dominant role and draw[s] upon the other whatever can be accommodated within its scheme of things' (Widdowson, 2005: 18), leaving these efforts open to potential distortions and lopsided intellectual progeny. This has been problematized well by recent reviews of trends in scientific inquiry which report the numerous attempts at cross-pollination between up to four or five subdisciplines (Mutz *et al.*, 2015) – 'nutrigenomics', 'recombinant-memetics' and 'neurolaw' are real examples.

Yet another attempt to engineer a creative collision of sorts are *inter-disciplinary* approaches to research. These position research and practice as being informed by several different perspectives at once. However, as some scholars caution, 'it is simply not possible to see things from two different perspectives at the same time' (Widdowson, 2005: 19), and what may look like integrated perspectives are often in fact 'different views of the same topic or problem in serial order but without any explicit integration' (Klein, 2010: 17). A further issue concerns the question of how methodological rigor and conceptual clarity are possible when competing 'integrated' fields inform the circumscribed area of study (Mutz *et al.*, 2015).

Transdisciplinarity offers one solution to these dilemmas (Hirsch Hadorn *et al.*, 2008). The goal of transdisciplinary research is to build 'a comprehensive general view, a theoretical synthesis or an integrative framework' (Klein, 2007: 39) that works at a 'supra-disciplinary, more abstract level offering a general set of patterns, outcomes, and descriptions that can be applied to many different sorts of systems' (Larsen-Freeman & Cameron, 2008a: 15–16). A transdisciplinary approach to scientific inquiry creates unity beyond disciplinary boundaries and turns toward a problem-oriented approach (Halliday & Burns, 2006). This is precisely what CDST research does: it transcends knowledge boundaries and renders the dominant disciplinary frames of reference and methodological silos redundant (Byrne & Callaghan, 2014: 3). What transdisciplinary research leaves in place of disciplinary boundaries is a problem-oriented approach to scientific inquiry that creates unity beyond the disciplinary perspectives (Klein, 2004), and the implications of these efforts are far reaching as they allow researchers to achieve common scientific goals (Hirsch Hadorn *et al.*, 2010). The idea in transdisciplinary research is to identify pressing issues that need addressing or questions that demand answers, and then determine the most appropriate object theories, methods (typically multi-method), models, etc., to shed light on possible solutions (Al-Hoorie & Hiver, 2019; Larsen-Freeman, 2017). This is why CDST has such potential to add value to the empirical study of phenomena of interest in applied linguistics.

An excellent example of how CDST is the natural precursor for transdisciplinary approaches to research can be found in how the initiative underlying such ideas led to the genesis of the Santa Fe Institute,[2] an intellectual hub whose 'existence seems to be predicated on the porousness of... boundaries between disciplines, or even their nonexistence' (Harris & Krakauer, 2016). Mitchell (2009) recounts how the Santa Fe Institute came about:

> By the mid-twentieth century, many scientists realized that such phenomena cannot be pigeonholed into any single discipline but require [a new] understanding based on scientific foundations that have not yet been invented. Several attempts at building those foundations include (among others) the fields of cybernetics, synergetics, systems science, and, more recently, the science of complex systems. In 1984, a diverse interdisciplinary group of twenty-four prominent scientists and mathematicians met in the high desert of Santa Fe, New Mexico, to discuss these 'emerging syntheses in science'. Their goal was to plot out the founding of a new research institute that would 'pursue research on a large number of highly complex and interactive systems which can be properly studied only in an interdisciplinary environment' and 'promote a unity of knowledge and a recognition of shared responsibility that will stand in sharp contrast to the present growing polarization of intellectual cultures'. Thus the Santa Fe Institute was created as a center for the study of complex systems. (Mitchell, 2009: x)

The methodological openness and experimentation that we advocate above, and which the chapters in Parts 2 and 3 of this book showcase, is a hallmark of moving beyond discipline-specific approaches to address common problems – the very definition of transdisciplinarity (Hirsch Hadorn et al., 2010; Nicolescu, 2008). As a final illustration of transdisciplinary research, David Krakauer – current director of the Santa Fe Institute – explains in an interview (Harris & Krakauer, 2016) on this topic:

> I don't like to call the way we do it interdisciplinary, because that's in some sense genuflecting in the direction of a superstition that I know people take seriously. So what happens when you ignore all of that and say, 'Let's certainly use the skills that we've acquired in the disciplines, but let's leave them at the door and just be intelligent about complex problems'?

This, we feel, is precisely what transdisciplinary research in applied linguistics is about: using all available research tools at our disposal to be intelligent about complex problems (see also King & Mackey, 2016).

Segue

The purpose of the current chapter, which we hope was less dry than the previous one, was to chart out what the CDST perspective might entail for a programme of social science research, more specifically in applied linguistics, that strives for compatibility with a complex and dynamic philosophy of science. We provided an overview of some of the philosophical and methodological issues that arise when researching the complex and dynamic social world. We did this by drawing a distinction between dealing with complexity empirically and doing so in a way that is more paradigmatic in nature. We then expanded on a novel ontology – complex realism – that underpins CDST research.

Following from our previous work in this area (Hiver & Al-Hoorie, 2016), we attempted to draw some coherence around the key tasks of CDST research. In the final portion of this chapter, we then thought about big questions and offered some preliminary thoughts to stimulate thinking on these issues in CDST research. Much more than just a fashion statement or a bandwagon, we see CDST as a rigorous aid to thinking and theorizing about social phenomena that represents a challenge to conventional methods of scientific thought. Clearly, when doing such research in a transdisciplinary way, an expansion of available methods is called for. This is the goal we turn to now in Parts 2 and 3 of this book.

Notes

(1)   Interested readers are encouraged to explore the Map of the Complexity Sciences, a visual diagram of the transdisciplinary nature of complexity theory created and curated by Brian Castellani (http://www.art-sciencefactory.com/complexity-map_feb09.html). We introduce this resource further in Chapter 19.

(2)   Interested readers will find much to explore at www.santafe.edu/ and can also embark on a fascinating journey of learning more about CDST at the Santa Fe Institute's center for educating the public on complexity science (www.complexityexplorer.com/). We introduce these sources further in Chapter 19.

References

Al-Hoorie, A.H. (2015) Human agency: Does the beach ball have free will? In Z. Dörnyei, P.D. MacIntyre and A. Henry (eds) *Motivational Dynamics in Language Learning* (pp. 55–72). Bristol: Multilingual Matters.

Al-Hoorie, A.H. and Hiver, P. (2019, March) Beyond the Quantitative–Qualitative Divide: Toward a Transdisciplinary Integration of Research Purposes and Methods for CDST. Paper presented at the meeting of the American Association for Applied Linguistics, Atlanta, GA.

Allen, P. and Boulton, J. (2011) Complexity and limits to knowledge: The importance of uncertainty. In P. Allen, S. Maguire and B. McKelvey (eds) *The SAGE Handbook of Complexity and Management* (pp. 164–181). London: SAGE.

Archer, M.S. (1998) Realism in the social sciences. In R. Bhaskar, M.S. Archer, A. Collier, T. Lawson and A. Norrie (eds) *Critical Realism: Essential Readings* (pp. 189–205). New York: Routledge.

Archer, M.S. (2000) *Being Human: The Problem of Agency.* Cambridge: Cambridge University Press.

Atkinson, D. (2019) Second language acquisition beyond borders? The Douglas Fir Group searches for transdisciplinary identity. *The Modern Language Journal* 103 (s), 113–121.

Bastardas-Boada, A. (2014) Towards a complex-figurational socio-linguistics: Some contributions from physics, ecology and the sciences of complexity. *History of the Human Sciences* 27 (3), 55–75.

Biesta, G. (2007) Why 'what works' won't work: Evidence-based practice and the democratic deficit in educational research. *Educational Theory* 57 (1), 1–22.

Bhaskar, R. (1975/1997) *A Realist Theory of Science.* New York: Verso.

Bhaskar, R. (1989) *Reclaiming Reality: A Critical Introduction to Contemporary Philosophy.* London: Verso.

Bhaskar, R. (2007) Theorizing ontology. In C. Lawson, J. Latsis and N. Martins (eds) *Contributions to Social Ontology* (pp. 192–204). London: Routledge.

Block, D. (2014) *Social Class in Applied Linguistics.* New York: Routledge.

Bouchard, J. (2018) On language, culture, and controversies. *Asian Englishes* 20 (3), 268–278.

Byrne, D. (1998) *Complexity Theory and the Social Sciences: An Introduction.* New York: Routledge.

Byrne, D. (2005) Complexity, configurations and cases. *Theory, Culture and Society* 22 (5), 95–111.

Byrne, D. (2011) *Applying Social Science.* Bristol: Policy Press.

Byrne, D. and Ragin, C. (eds) (2009) *The SAGE Handbook of Case-Based Methods.* Thousand Oaks, CA: SAGE.

Byrne, D. and Uprichard, E. (2012) Useful complex causality. In E. Kincaid (ed.) *The Oxford Handbook of Philosophy of Social Science* (pp. 109–129). Oxford: Oxford University Press.

Byrne, D. and Callaghan, G. (2014) *Complexity Theory and the Social Sciences: The State of the Art.* New York: Routledge.

Capra, F. and Luisi, P.L. (2014) *The Systems View of Life.* Cambridge: Cambridge University Press.

Castellani, B. (2018) *The Defiance of Global Commitment: A Complex Social Psychology.* New York: Routledge.

Castellani, B. and Hafferty, F. (2009) *Sociology and Complexity Science: A New Field of Inquiry.* Berlin: Springer.

Cilliers, P. (1998) *Complexity and Postmodernism: Understanding Complex Systems.* London: Routledge.

Cilliers, P. (2000) Knowledge, complexity, and understanding. *Emergence* 2 (4), 7–13.

Cilliers, P. (2001) Boundaries, hierarchies and networks in complex systems. *International Journal of Innovation Management* 5 (2), 135–47.

Cilliers, P. (2005) Complexity, deconstruction and relativism. *Theory, Culture and Society* 22, 255–267.

Cochran-Smith, M., Ell, F., Ludlow, L., Grudnoff, L., Haigh, M. and Hill, M. (2014) When complexity theory meets critical realism: A platform for research on initial teacher education. *Teacher Education Quarterly* 41 (1), 105–122.

Danermark, B., Ekstrom, M., Jacobsen, L. and Karlsson, J.C. (2002) *Explaining Society.* London: Routledge.

Davis, B. and Sumara, D. (2006) *Complexity and Education: Inquiries into Learning, Teaching, Teaching and Research.* New York: Routledge.

de Bot, K. (2015) Rates of change: Timescales in second language development. In Z. Dörnyei, P.D. MacIntyre and A. Henry (eds) *Motivational Dynamics in Language Learning* (pp. 29–37). Bristol: Multilingual Matters.

de Bot, K. and Larsen-Freeman, D. (2011) Researching second language development from a dynamic systems theory perspective. In M. Verspoor, K. de Bot and W. Lowie (eds) *A Dynamic Approach to Second Language Development* (pp. 5–23). Amsterdam/ Philadelphia, PA: John Benjamins.

De Wolf, T. and Holvoet, T. (2005) Emergence versus self-organisation: Different concepts but promising when combined. In S. Brueckner, G. Di Marzo Serugendo, A. Karageorgos and R. Nagpal (eds) *Engineering Self-Organising Systems: Methodologies and Applications* (pp. 1–15). Berlin: Springer.

Dörnyei, Z., MacIntyre, P.D. and Henry, A. (eds) (2015) *Motivational Dynamics in Language Learning*. Bristol: Multilingual Matters.

Douglas Fir Group (2016) A transdisciplinary framework for SLA in a multilingual world. *The Modern Language Journal* 100 (s), 19–47.

Ellis, N.C. and Larsen-Freeman, D. (2006) Language emergence: Implications for applied linguistics: Introduction to the special issue. *Applied Linguistics* 27, 558–589.

Elman, J. (2003) It's about time. *Developmental Science* 6, 430–433.

Foucault, M. (1972) *The Archaeology of Knowledge and the Discourse on Language*. New York: Pantheon.

Gaustello, S. and Liebovitch, L. (2009) Introduction to nonlinear dynamics and complexity. In S. Gaustello, M. Koopmans and D. Pincus (eds) *Chaos and Complexity in Psychology* (pp. 1–40). Cambridge: Cambridge University Press.

Gershenson, C. (ed.) (2008) *Complexity: 5 Questions*. Copenhagen: Automatic Press.

Gregg, K.R. (2000) A theory for every occasion: Postmodernism and SLA. *Second Language Research* 16, 383–399.

Groff, R. (ed.) (2008) *Revitalizing Causality: Realism about Causality in Philosophy and Social Science*. New York: Routledge.

Haken, H. (2009) Synergetics: Basic concepts. In R. Meyers (ed.) *Encyclopedia of Complexity and Systems Science* (pp. 8926–8946). New York: Springer.

Halliday, M. and Burns, A. (2006) Applied linguistics: Thematic pursuits or disciplinary moorings? *Journal of Applied Linguistics* 3, 113–128.

Hamaker, E.L. (2012) Why researchers should think 'within-person': A paradigmatic rationale. In M.R. Mehl and T.S. Conner (eds) *Handbook of Methods for Studying Daily Life* (pp. 43–61). New York: Guilford.

Harris, S. and Krakauer, D. (2016) *Complexity and Stupidity*. The Waking Up Podcast. See https://samharris.org/complexity-stupidity/ (accessed 1 July 2019).

Harvey, D.L. (2001) Chaos and complexity: Their bearing on social policy research. *Social Issues* 1 (2). See http://www.whb.co.uk/socialissues/harvey.htm (accessed 30 June 2019).

Harvey, D.L. (2002) Agency and community: A critical realist paradigm. *Journal for the Theory of Social Behaviour* 32 (2), 163–194.

Harvey, D.L. (2009) Complexity and case. In D. Byrne and C.C. Ragin (eds) *The SAGE Handbook of Case-Based Methods* (pp. 15–38). Thousand Oaks, CA: SAGE.

Hedström, P. (2005) *Dissecting the Social*. Cambridge: Cambridge University Press.

Hedström, P. and Ylikoski, P. (2010) Casual mechanisms in the social sciences. *Annual Review of Sociology* 32 (1), 46–67.

Hirsch Hadorn, G., Hoffmann-Riem, H., Biber-Klemm, S., Grossenbacher-Mansuy, W., Joye, D., Pohl, C., Wiesmann, U. and Zemp, E. (eds) (2008) *Handbook of Transdisciplinary Research*. Dordrecht: Springer.

Hirsch Hadorn, G., Pohl, C. and Bammer, G. (2010) Solving problems through transdisciplinary research. In R. Frodeman, J.T. Klein and C. Mitcham (eds) *Oxford Handbook of Interdisciplinarity* (pp. 231–252). Oxford: Oxford University Press.

Hiver, P. and Al-Hoorie, A.H. (2016) A 'dynamic ensemble' for second language research: Putting complexity theory into practice. *The Modern Language Journal* 100, 741–756.

Hiver, P. and Papi, M. (2020) Complexity theory and L2 motivation. In M. Lamb, K. Csizér, A. Henry and S. Ryan (eds) *Palgrave Handbook of Motivation for Language Learning*. Basingstoke: Palgrave Macmillan.

Holland, J.H. (1995) *Hidden Order: How Adaptation Builds Complexity*. Cambridge, MA: MIT Press.

Holland, J.H. (1998) *Emergence: From Chaos to Order*. Oxford: Oxford University Press.

Holland, J.H. (2006) Studying complex adaptive systems. *Journal of Systems Science and Complexity* 19, 1–8.

Holland, J.H. (2012) *Signals and Boundaries: Building Blocks for Complex Adaptive Systems*. Cambridge, MA: MIT Press.

Howe, M.L. and Lewis, M.D. (2005) The importance of dynamic systems approaches for understanding development. *Developmental Review* 25, 247–251

Joe, H.-K., Hiver, P. and Al-Hoorie, A.H. (2017) Classroom social climate, self-determined motivation, willingness to communicate, and achievement: A study of structural relationships in instructed second language settings. *Learning and Individual Differences* 53, 133–144.

Johnson, N.F. (2009) *Simply Complexity: A Clear Guide to Complexity Theory*. Oxford: Oneworld Publications.

Jörg, T. (2011) *New Thinking in Complexity for the Social Sciences and Humanities: A Generative, Transdisciplinary Approach*. Dordrecht: Springer.

Jost, J., Bertschinger, N. and Olbrich, E. (2010) Emergence. *New Ideas in Psychology* 28, 265–273.

Juarrero, A. (1999) *Dynamics in Action: Intentional Behavior as a Complex System*. Cambridge, MA: MIT Press.

Juarrero, A. (2011) Causality and explanation. In P. Allen, S. Maguire and B. McKelvey (eds) *The SAGE Handbook of Complexity and Management* (pp. 155–163). London: SAGE.

Kadushin, C. (2012) *Understanding Social Networks: Theories, Concepts, and Findings*. Oxford: Oxford University Press.

Kelso, J.A.S. (2016) On the self-organizing origins of agency. *Trends in Cognitive Science* 20, 490–499.

King, K. and Mackey, A. (2016) Research methodology in second language studies: Trends, concerns, and new directions. *The Modern Language Journal* 100 (s), 209–227.

Klein, J.T. (2004) Interdisciplinarity and complexity: An evolving relationship. *Emergence: Complexity & Organization* 6 (1/2), 2–10.

Klein, J.T. (2007) Interdisciplinary approaches in social science research. In W. Outhwaite and S.P. Turner (eds) *The SAGE Handbook of Social Science Methodology* (pp. 32–49). London: SAGE.

Klein, J.T. (2010) A taxonomy of interdisciplinarity. In R. Frodeman, J.T. Klein and C. Mitcham (eds) *Oxford Handbook of Interdisciplinarity* (pp. 15–30). Oxford: Oxford University Press.

Kleinberg, S. (2013) *Causality, Probability, and Time*. Cambridge: Cambridge University Press.

Kleinberg, S. and Hripcsak, G. (2011) A review of causal inference for biomedical informatics. *Journal of Biomedical Informatics* 44, 1102–1112.

Koopman, J.S. (1977) Causal models and sources of interaction. *American Journal of Epidemiology* 106, 439–444.

Koopmans, M. (2014) Change, self-organization and the search for causality in educational research and practice. *Complicity: An International Journal of Complexity and Education* 11 (1), 20–39.

Koopmans, M. (2019) Education is a complex dynamical system: Challenges for research. *The Journal of Experimental Education*. Advance Online Access. doi:10.1080/00220 973.2019.1566199

Kretzschmar, W. (2015) *Language and Complex Systems.* Cambridge: Cambridge University Press.

Kubota, R. (2016) The multi/plural turn, postcolonial theory, and neoliberal multiculturalism: Complicities and implications for applied linguistics. *Applied Linguistics* 37 (4), 474–494.

Kuhn, T.S. (1962/2012) *The Structure of Scientific Revolutions* (4th edn). Chicago, IL: University of Chicago Press.

Larsen-Freeman, D. (2012) Complex, dynamic systems: A new transdisciplinary theme for applied linguistics? *Language Teaching* 45, 202–214.

Larsen-Freeman, D. (2013) Complexity theory: A new way to think. *Revista Brasileira de Linguística Aplicada* 13, 369–373.

Larsen-Freeman, D. (2016) Classroom-oriented research from a complex systems perspective. *Studies in Second Language Learning and Teaching* 6, 377–393.

Larsen-Freeman, D. (2017) Complexity theory: The lessons continue. In L. Ortega and Z. Han (eds) *Complexity Theory and Language Development: In Celebration of Diane Larsen-Freeman* (pp. 11–50). Amsterdam/Philadelphia, PA: John Benjamins.

Larsen-Freeman, D. (2019) On language learner agency: A complex dynamic systems theory perspective. *The Modern Language Journal* 103 (s), xx–xx.

Larsen-Freeman, D. and Cameron, L. (2008a) *Complex Systems and Applied Linguistics.* Oxford: Oxford University Press.

Larsen-Freeman, D. and Cameron, L. (2008b) Research methodology on language development from a complex systems perspective. *The Modern Language Journal* 92, 200–213.

Lee, M.E. (1997) From enlightenment to chaos: Toward nonmodern social theory. In R.A. Eve, S. Horsfall and M.E. Lee (eds) *Chaos, Complexity, and Sociology: Myths, Model, and Theories* (pp. 15–29). Thousand Oaks, CA: SAGE.

Lewis, M. (2005) Bridging emotion theory and neurobiology through dynamic systems modeling. *Behavioral and Brain Sciences* 28, 169–245.

Lighthill, J. (1986) The recently recognized failure of predictability in Newtonian dynamics. *Proceedings of the Royal Society of London A* 407, 35–48.

Lowie, W. (2017) Lost in state space?: Methodological considerations in Complex Dynamic Theory approaches to second language development research. In L. Ortega and Z. Han (eds) *Complexity Theory and Language Development: In Celebration of Diane Larsen-Freeman* (pp. 123–141). Amsterdam/Philadelphia, PA: John Benjamins.

Mainzer, K. (2007) *Thinking in Complexity: The Computational Dynamics of Matter, Mind, and Mankind* (5th edn). Berlin: Springer.

Manson, S. (2001) Simplifying complexity: A review of complexity theory. *Geoforum* 32, 405–414.

Marsden, E., Morgan-Short, K., Thompson, S. and Abugaber, D. (2018a) Replication in second language research: Narrative and systematic reviews and recommendations for the field. *Language Learning* 68, 321–391.

Marsden, E., Morgan-Short, K., Trofimovich, P. and Ellis, N.C. (2018b) Introducing registered reports at Language Learning: Promoting transparency, replication, and a synthetic ethic in the language sciences. *Language Learning* 68, 309–320.

Mason, M. (ed.) (2008) *Complexity Theory and the Philosophy of Education.* Chichester: Wiley-Blackwell.

Maturana, H.R. and Varela, F.J. (eds) (1980) *Autopoiesis and Cognition: The Realization of the Living.* Dordrecht: Reidel.

McDaniel, R.R. and Driebe, D.J. (2005) Uncertainty and surprise: An introduction. In R.R. McDaniel and D.J. Driebe (eds) *Uncertainty and Surprise in Complex Systems: Questions on Working with the Unexpected* (pp. 3–11). Berlin: Springer.

McNamara, T. (2015) Applied linguistics: The challenge of theory. *Applied Linguistics* 36 (4), 466–477.

Mitchell, M. (2009) *Complexity: A Guided Tour*. Oxford: Oxford University Press.

Molenaar, P., Lerner, R. and Newell, K. (2014) Developmental systems theory and methodology: A view of the issues. In P.C.M. Molenaar, R.M. Lerner and K.M. Newell (eds) *Handbook of Developmental Systems Theory and Methodology* (pp. 3–15). New York: Guilford.

Morgan-Short, K., Marsden, E., Heil, J., Issa II, B.I., Leow, R.P., Mikhaylova, A., Mikołajczak, S., Moreno, N., Slabakova, R. and Szudarski, P. (2018) Multisite replication in second language acquisition research: Attention to form during listening and reading comprehension. *Language Learning* 68, 392–437.

Morin, E. (2001) *Seven Complex Lessons in Education for the Future*. Paris: United Nations Educational, Scientific, and Cultural Organization.

Morin, E. (2007) Restricted complexity, general complexity. In C. Gershenson, D. Aerts and B. Edmonds (eds) *Worldviews, Science and Us: Philosophy and Complexity* (pp. 5–29). Singapore: World Scientific.

Morin, E. (2008) *On Complexity*. Cresskill, NJ: Hampton Press.

Morrison, K. (2012) Searching for causality in the wrong places. *International Journal of Social Research Methodology* 15, 15–30.

Moss, P.A. and Haertel, E.H. (2016) Engaging methodological pluralism. In D. Gitomer and C. Bell (eds) *Handbook of Research on Teaching* (5th edn; pp. 127–248). Washington, DC: American Educational Research Association.

Mouzelis, N. (1995) *Sociological Theory: What Went Wrong?* London: Routledge.

Mutz, R., Bornmann, L. and Daniel, H.-D. (2014) Cross-disciplinary research: What configurations of fields of science are found in grant proposals today? *Research Evaluation* 24 (1), 30–36.

Nicolescu, B. (ed.) (2008) *Transdisciplinarity: Theory and Practice*. Cresskill, NJ: Hampton Press.

Norman, D. (2011) *Living with Complexity*. Cambridge, MA: MIT Press.

Ortega, L. (2012) Epistemological diversity and moral ends of research in instructed SLA. *Language Teaching Research* 16, 206–226.

Ortega, L. (2019) SLA and the study of equitable multilingualism. *The Modern Language Journal* 103 (s), 23–38.

Overton, W.F. (2013) A new paradigm for developmental science: Relationism and relational-developmental systems. *Applied Developmental Science* 17, 94–107.

Pennycook, A. (2018) *Posthumanist Applied Linguistics*. New York: Routledge.

Peters, M.A., Tesar, M. and Jackson, L. (2018) After postmodernism in educational theory? A collective writing experiment and thought survey. Introduction to the Special Issue. *Educational Philosophy and Theory* 50, 1299–1307.

Price, B. (1997) The myth of postmodern science. In R.A. Eve, S. Horsfall and M.E. Lee (eds) *Chaos, Complexity, and Sociology: Myths, Model, and Theories* (pp. 3–14). Thousand Oaks, CA: SAGE.

Prigogine, I. (2005) Surprises in a half century. In R.R. McDaniel and D.J. Driebe (eds) *Uncertainty and Surprise in Complex Systems: Questions on Working with the Unexpected* (pp. 13–16). Berlin: Springer.

Radford, M. (2008) Prediction, control and the challenge to complexity. *Oxford Review of Education* 34, 505–520.

Ragin, C.C. (2004) Turning the tables: How case-oriented research challenges variable-oriented research. In H.E. Brady and D. Collier (eds) *Rethinking Social Inquiry: Diverse Tools, Shared Standards* (pp. 123–138). Lanham, MD: Rowman and Littlefield.

Reed, M. and Harvey, D.L. (1992) The new science and the old: Complexity and realism in the social sciences. *Journal for the Theory of Social Behaviour* 22, 356–379.

Reed, M. and Harvey, D.L. (1997) Social science as the study of complex systems. In L.D. Kiel and E. Elliott (eds) *Chaos Theory in the Social Sciences: Foundations and Applications* (pp. 295–324). Ann Arbor, MI: University of Michigan Press.

Reitsma, F. (2003) A response to simplifying complexity. *Geoforum* 34, 13–16.

Rizzi, D.A. and Pedersen, S.A. (1992) Causality in medicine: Towards a theory and terminology. *Theoretical Medicine* 13, 233–254.

Porte, G.K. (2012) *Replication Research in Applied Linguistics.* Cambridge: Cambridge University Press.

Rose, L., Rouhani, P. and Fischer, K. (2013) The science of the individual. *Mind, Brain, and Education* 7, 152–158.

Sawyer, K. (2005) *Social Emergence: Societies as Complex Systems.* New York: Cambridge University Press.

Schooler, J.W. (2014) Metascience could rescue the 'replication crisis'. *Nature* 515 (7525), 9. doi:10.1038/515009a

Stroup, W. (1997) Webs of chaos: Implications for research designs. In R.A. Eve, S. Horsfall and M.E. Lee (eds) *Chaos, Complexity, and Sociology: Myths, Model, and Theories* (pp. 125–140). Thousand Oaks, CA: SAGE.

Thelen, E. (2005) Dynamic systems theory and the complexity of change. *Psychoanalytic Dialogues* 15, 255–283.

Turner, F. (1997) Forward: Chaos and social science. In R.A. Eve, S. Horsfall and M.E. Lee (eds) *Chaos, Complexity, and Sociology: Myths, Model, and Theories* (pp. xi–xxvii). Thousand Oaks, CA: SAGE.

Uprichard, E. (2013) Sampling: Bridging probability and nonprobability designs. *International Journal of Social Research Methodology* 16, 1–11.

Vallacher, R.R., van Geert, P. and Nowak, A. (2015) The intrinsic dynamics of psychological process. *Current Directions in Psychological Science* 24, 58–64.

Valsiner, J., Molenaar, P., Lyra, M. and Chaudhary, N. (eds) (2009) *Dynamic Process Methodology in the Social and Developmental Sciences.* New York: Springer.

van Geert, P. (1998) We almost had a great future behind us: The contribution of nonlinear dynamics to developmental-science-in-the-making. *Developmental Science* 1 (1), 143–159.

van Geert, P. (2008) The dynamic systems approach in the study of L1 and L2 acquisition: An introduction. *The Modern Language Journal* 92, 179–199.

van Geert, P. (2011) The contribution of complex dynamic systems to development. *Child Development Perspectives* 5, 273–278.

van Geert, P. and Steenbeek, H. (2014) The good, the bad and the ugly? The dynamic interplay between educational practice, policy and research. *Complicity: An International Journal of Complexity and Education* 11 (2), 22–39.

Velicer, W., Babbin, S. and Palumbo, R. (2014) Idiographic applications: Issues of ergodicity and generalizability. In P. Molenaar, R. Lerner and K. Newell (eds) *Handbook of Developmental Systems Theory and Methodology* (pp. 425–441). New York: Guilford Press.

Verspoor, M., de Bot, K. and Lowie, W. (eds) (2011) *A Dynamic Approach to Second Language Development: Methods and Techniques.* Amsterdam/Philadelphia, PA: John Benjamins.

Ward, A.C. (2009) Causal criteria and the problem of complex causation. *Medical Health Care and Philosophy* 12, 333–343.

Westergaard, J. (2003) Interview with John Westergaard. *Network* 85, 1–2.

Widdowson, H.G. (2005) Applied linguistics, interdisciplinarity, and disparate realities. In P. Bruthiaux, D. Atkinson, W. Eggington, W. Grabe and V. Ramanathan (eds) *Directions in Applied Linguistics* (pp. 12–25). Clevedon: Multilingual Matters.

Wolf-Branigin, M. (2013) *Using Complexity Theory for Research and Program Evaluation.* Oxford: Oxford University Press.

Part 2
Qualitative Methods

4 Qualitative Comparative Analysis

Overview

Qualitative comparative analysis (QCA) is a case-based approach to researching complexity that originated in Charles Ragin's (2009) work in sociology. While developing QCA, Ragin's intention was to come up with an original and 'synthetic' comparison strategy. The idea behind this method of analysis was to focus entirely on the complexity inherent in the social world through comparison and synthesis, and to strike a balance between the case-oriented, qualitative approaches to research that featured rich descriptive data and the variable-oriented, quantitative approaches that give researchers a robust explanatory framework for advancing causal claims. The goal of this strategy was to integrate the best features of a case-oriented approach with the best features of a variable-oriented approach (Ragin, 2014).

Like several other research designs (e.g. think here of grounded theory), QCA can be seen both as a broader approach to research and as a focused technique depending on how it is applied. As an approach – which is how we treat it in this chapter – it encompasses everything from case sampling to various phases of data analysis and extends to interpretation (Rihoux & Lobe, 2009). Its purpose is to enable researchers to make deliberate comparisons of multiple cases and by doing so provide data-driven 'how' and 'why' explanations for complex phenomena. This means QCA tends to be an intermediate to large-N research design. From this perspective, QCA embodies some key strengths of the holistic qualitative approaches, in the sense that each individual case is considered as a complex whole that needs to be understood for analysis.

QCA assumes two important but seemingly contradictory objectives: the first objective is to develop in-depth descriptions of the cases being examined and capture their complexity by gathering comprehensive information about those cases; the second is to provide generalizable findings (see our discussion of these issues in Chapter 3) about the complex causal processes at play in the functioning of these cases and systematically investigate these by analyzing a suitable type and number of cases (i.e. usually in the double digits) (Rihoux & Lobe, 2009). The notion of multiple (i.e. many causes) and contingent (i.e. context-specific) causality in QCA is also a novel one, when compared to how causality is thought of in more variable-oriented experimental designs, but this perspective goes hand in hand with complexity. The position QCA takes on causality in the complex social and human world is that, most often, (a) effects and outcomes are produced through a combination of complex conditions, (b) several different combinations of conditions can produce the same phenomena and (c) certain conditions can have a different impact on an outcome at different times depending on context. Translated to the kind of development that cases experience over time, this means that different causal pathways can lead to the same complex outcome for different cases, which illustrates the principle of equifinality.

QCA also incorporates some of the key strengths of quantitative, analytic approaches into its design. First, it enables researchers to study more than just a handful of cases at a time, which opens up the possibility of generalizing across cases and datasets. There is even the possibility to include an entire population in a sample, provided all cases satisfy the outcome criterion for inclusion (Ragin, 2014) – think, for example, of studying an outcome of plurilingualism or language attrition in a community and including all relevant participants from that setting in the sample. This potential for comprehensive comparative analytical insights is a benefit that most other designs cannot claim.

The comparative analysis of QCA relies on Boolean 1s and 0s to code cases and their causal conditions into categorical 'independent' variables that are thought to influence a complex outcome. The Boolean 1s show that a causal condition has a present or positive value for the case, whereas 0s indicate that the causal condition has an absent or null value. Although they operate at a much more global level, affecting a whole system or sets of systems, complex outcomes or phenomena of interest are equivalent to what we might think of as a 'dependent' variable. Examples of such complex outcomes within a language sphere might include new forms of multimodal literacy, patterns of language discourse across institutions, language development outcomes, emergent configurations of intercultural communication and even the adoption of novel language policies. Using Boolean 1s and 0s as variable codes enables a researcher to identify regularities and patterns for causal conditions within a dataset, which in turn leads to a parsimonious expression of the fewest possible conditions, from among the greater set of conditions in the analysis which, in combination, can explain a complex outcome in the cases being examined.

This brings us to QCA and its use as a collection of data analysis techniques: like QCA as a larger approach, it draws on the logic of set-theory (i.e. a domain of mathematics that deals with the formal properties of sets as units) and its assumptions of complex causality. QCA is after all a set-theoretic research template (Ragin, 1999a, 1999b). Developing a causal explanation of a complex outcome using QCA techniques first requires a researcher to articulate the complex outcome of interest and then select the causal conditions. Conditions are equivalent to the term 'variables' in more widespread use, and, as previously noted, QCA uses the 1s and 0s of Boolean algebra to code conditions that are thought to influence a specified outcome in the cases being compared. *Crisp set* QCA (csQCA), the original Boolean analytical technique, is used for discrete variables. In csQCA, all the cases are assigned one of two possible 'crisp' categorical membership values for each condition or 'set' included in a study: 1, membership in the set; and 0, non-membership in the set. The second analytic technique, termed *fuzzy set* QCA (fsQCA), refers to a situation in which membership values are not as clear-cut but instead may range from partial membership to full membership. In fsQCA, each case being compared is assigned membership values ranging from 0 (i.e. non-membership) for each causal condition to 1 (i.e. full membership) (Ragin, 2009). Scores between these two values indicate partial membership, and relative scores indicate degrees of membership, thus reflecting the 'fuzzy' set (i.e. non-dichotomous) logic (see e.g. Hiver *et al.* [2019] for one application of this). The third and most advanced analytical technique is *multi-value* QCA (mvQCA), which is mid-way between csQCA and fsQCA.

Research Questions

QCA is designed to uncover patterns of invariance (i.e. beyond the unique instance) in explaining complex outcomes and constant associations between causal conditions and phenomena of interest. However, because probabilistic relationships alone do not satisfy the stringent requirements for demonstrating causality in QCA, researchers must get very close to their data and become extremely familiar with the cases they have chosen to study (Byrne, 2005, 2009a). This sort of understanding is more consistent with how we often think of, understand and characterize qualitatively distinct outcomes. When does a walk become a run, when does infant babbling become intelligible and when does new information become familiar? We know they are different and can point to how, but also think about them in terms of tendencies rather than hard and fast rules. Some questions that QCA allows researchers to explore include:

- What combination of conditions leads to a certain state or outcome?
- Are there any deviant cases that do not demonstrate the outcome of interest?
- How do conditions intersect or interact to produce a certain state or outcome?
- Which conditions are essential or inessential, desirable or undesirable, and sufficient or insufficient for producing an outcome of interest?

- Are there any cases that function as evidence for illustrating a theoretical understanding of the outcome of interest?
- Are there any cases that function as counterfactuals for a theoretical understanding of the outcome of interest?
- When looking at causal conditions for a complex outcome, can cross-sample conclusions or outcome-specific generalizations be established?
- What collective-level insights can help explain variation at the individual level of data?
- What empirical regularities can be used to evaluate and interpret cases against theoretical and substantive criteria?

When asking such questions as these, it can be a challenge to unravel causal complexity. After all, many aspects of the social world confound attempts to understand their inherent complexity. It can be an uphill challenge to explain what and how something worked, even after the fact. Outcomes of interest in applied linguistics, as in most human and social domains, rarely have a single cause, and QCA – like complexity theory demands – soundly rejects the notion that there is a single causal condition capable of generating a complex outcome (Byrne, 2005). In addition, conditions and causes rarely operate in isolation. It is most often the combined effect of various conditions and how they intersect through time and in context that produces outcomes. Merely acknowledging this is not enough, and QCA formalizes this into its design logic.

Technical Features

QCA begins with defining the outcome of interest (i.e. sufficiently narrowing down a phenomenon to research it) and casing the outcome (i.e. recruiting a typical sample that will guarantee relevant data about that phenomenon) to establish which conditions, in which combination, can be said to contribute to this complex outcome. QCA can be both exploratory and confirmatory. Although the results of exploratory QCA might need to be taken with caution and corroborated through further research, this method is also helpful as a confirmatory tool when researchers already have a theory or a set of expectations.

*BYRNE AND RAGIN (2009: 1–2, ORIGINAL EMPHASIS),
BOTH SOCIAL COMPLEXIVISTS, TAKE A FIRM STANCE
ON THE FUNDAMENTAL TASK OF RESEARCH:*

The central project of any science is the elucidation of causes that extend beyond the unique specific instance. ... However, we want to qualify and elaborate somewhat on these fundamental premises. First, we want to make it clear that for us generalizing is not the same as universalizing. It is important to be able to develop an understanding of causation that goes beyond the unique instance – the object of ideographic inquiry. However, it is just as important to be able to specify the limits of that generalization. We cannot establish universal laws in the social sciences. There is no valid nomothetic project. ... Case-based methods help us both to elucidate causation *and* to specify the range of applicability of our account of causal mechanisms. The emphasis on the plural form of mechanism in the preceding sentence is very important. It is not just that different mechanisms operate to produce, contingently in context, different outcomes. It is rather that different mechanisms may produce the same outcome.

As we mentioned previously, QCA relies on the use of Boolean algebra. In a Boolean analysis of some case-based data, all the variables included, both independent and dependent variables, must be nominal scale measures. Variables that are interval-scale measures are transformed into multicategory nominal scales. Boolean algebra allows two conditions or states for all variables (the reason why they must be nominal): true (i.e. present) and false (i.e. absent). In QCA, these are represented by the binary values 1, indicating true, positive or present, and 0, indicating false, null or absent. Using the aggregated data, QCA analyses address the issue of whether the conditions thought to exist in an outcome of interest are present or absent.

In order to use these Boolean values of 1 and 0 for qualitative comparisons, scholars reconstruct a raw data matrix with all the cases sampled in one column and all the conditions that contribute to the associated outcome of interest in subsequent columns. This is called a 'truth table' (see the following example study) and the idea behind it is rather simple but elegant: once the data are recoded into nominal variables and populated with their binary values, each row of the various combinations of independent variables and their values result in an output or outcome variable (i.e. do these conditions result in the outcome of interest?) that can be taken into account for subsequent inferential and causal analyses. For instance, in the following example study, the outcome column shows whether or not each row of conditions results in institutional success. By analyzing the combinations of conditions across participants in the truth table, the researcher is able to settle on a parsimonious minimal formula that offers an empirically robust explanation of the phenomena under investigation. In these analyses, the number of instances each condition occurs does not feature directly in any computations, and this is because frequency criteria are less important in QCA than in conventional statistical analyses. Note also that the outcome variable must be either 1 or 0 for each case, not a probability or a mean value.

Boolean notation uses uppercase to indicate the presence of a condition, and lowercase to indicate its absence. For a final outcome Y (i.e. the outcome of interest) that has three causal conditions A, B and C, there are various potential solutions for determining how the outcome emerges in the cases sampled for examination: $Y = Abc + aBc + abC + ABc + AbC + aBC + ABC + abc$. The plus sign operator shows that each additional formula listed also fully produces the complex outcome. This operator is equivalent to OR, meaning that when using the preceding three conditions, Abc OR aBc OR any of the other combinations, all lead to the same outcome Y. The best way to think about this is in logical terms (OR, AND, NOT are in fact termed 'logical operators' in QCA), not mathematical ones – for example, there are a variety of ways to lose weight and if a person does any one of them they will lose weight. Note that the last formula indicating the absence of all causal conditions identified in the dataset tends to be unlikely (Ragin, 2006).

BERG-SCHLOSSER ET AL. (2009: 9) LIST THE ASSUMPTIONS THAT ARE NOT TAKEN ON BOARD FOR CAUSAL RELATIONS IN QCA:

It is crucial to bear in mind that QCA does *not* take on board some basic assumptions that lie at the heart of the mainstream (variable-based) statistical approach (and thus underlie most statistical techniques). In QCA:

- Permanent causality is *not* assumed.
- Uniformity of causal effects is *not* assumed.
- Unit homogeneity is not assumed.
- Additivity is not assumed.
- Causal symmetry is not assumed.

Other core mainstream statistical assumptions, such as linearity and so on, are not taken on board either.

Causal conditions are considered in various configurations and against their degree of necessity and sufficiency for contributing to a complex outcome (Ragin, 2014). Causal conditions that by themselves produce a complex outcome are defined as *sufficient*. Conditions are defined as *necessary* if they must be present for a complex outcome to occur. A summary of the possibilities when these are combined is shown in Table 4.1. A causal condition is deemed neither necessary nor sufficient if it appears in only a subset of the combinations of conditions that produce a complex outcome: $Y = AC + Bc$. Here, none of the causal conditions are uniquely necessary or sufficient to produce the outcome Y; either of them would suffice. A condition is necessary but not sufficient if it is capable of producing an outcome in combination with other causes and

Table 4.1   A summary of possible configurations of causal conditions

	Sufficient	Insufficient
	$Y = C$	$Y = AB + BC$
Necessary	The causal condition C is the singular and only cause that produces the complex outcome Y.	The causal condition B is capable of producing the complex outcome Y in combination with other conditions and appears in all such combinations.
	$Y = A + bC$	$Y = AC + Bc$
Unnecessary	The causal condition A is capable of producing the complex outcome Y but is not the only condition with this capacity to produce the outcome.	The causal condition B appears in only a subset of the combinations of conditions that produce the complex outcome Y. The same is true of A.

appears in all such combinations: $Y = AB + BC$. Here, B is necessary but not sufficient. A condition is sufficient but not necessary if it is capable of producing the outcome but is not the only cause with this capacity to produce the outcome: $Y = A + bC$. Here, A is sufficient but not necessary. Finally, a causal condition is both necessary and sufficient if it is the singular and only cause that produces an outcome: $Y = C$.

The comparative and combinatorial logic of QCA might seem to add levels of complexity to the way outcomes can be understood, but quite the opposite is true (Byrne, 2005, 2009a). Necessity and sufficiency become important when attempting to simplify complexity in a dataset. One of the most fundamental and straightforward ways this is done is through minimization. Essentially, the minimization rule states that if two Boolean expressions (e.g. $Y = ABc + aBc$) differ in the presence and absence of only one causal condition but produce the same outcome, then for analysis purposes the causal dimensions that do not distinguish the two expressions can be considered irrelevant or redundant and removed to arrive at a simpler combined expression: $Y = Bc$. To minimize this expression, we would say that one condition may be either present (A) or absent (a), but outcome Y will still occur. The notion of *implicants* – causal conditions thought to be either necessary and/or sufficient for an outcome of interest – is also relevant here: if a set of conditions Abc reflect an identical condition A, then the first can be considered a subset and the more refined set (i.e. the latter) is a more parsimonious representation of this subset. Other subsets are also possible.

Example Study

In his study of high- and low-performing state schools in the North East region of England, Byrne (2009b) was curious to examine what combination of conditions set successful schools apart from unsuccessful schools. He defined the complex outcome in terms of 'institutional success', which in a performative setting such as the UK is associated with

the specific goal of maximizing student performance in public examina-
tions. He then cased the outcome by sampling all 126 secondary-level
public schools in the North East region of England. Rather than inferring
from a partial sample, using the entire population as his case-set allowed
Byrne to advance some strong causal claims about the underlying conditions that enhanced the schools' success or lack thereof.

As we have mentioned, adopting QCA as an analytical technique also
entails understanding cases in terms of the different combinations of their
attributes – that is, as diverse 'configurations of memberships' (Ragin,
1999a: 1225). Byrne's (2009b) analytical strategy illustrates this well.
Relying on formal descriptive inspection reports of public schools, Byrne
(2009b) undertook to establish the complex reasons underlying this outcome of relative institutional success. Developing a causal explanation of
an outcome requires a researcher to select the causal conditions, and Byrne
set out to identify underlying conditions that make a difference in schools
and about which something can be done to influence their levels of success.

Table 4.2 presents a small subset of this whole dataset (Byrne, 2009b:
264). Recall that truth tables combine the sampled respondents in rows
with the list of causal conditions thought to lead to the outcome of
interest represented in columns. The more causal conditions being investigated, the more columns the truth table will have, and the larger the
case-set being sampled, the more rows are included in the truth table.

Part of investigating complex causality using QCA is the assumption
that the case-set will be large enough to reveal interesting cross-case patterns, while still small enough to allow a researcher to gain a meaningful level of familiarity with each individual case (Yin, 2014). This was
Byrne's intention in limiting the scope of conditions to those most salient

Table 4.2   Truth table

School	X_1	X_2	X_3	X_4	X_5	X_6	X_7	X_8	Y
C	1	0	0	0	0	1	1	1	1
D	1	0	0	0	0	1	1	1	1
E	1	1	0	1	1	1	0	1	0
F	1	0	0	1	0	1	1	1	0
H	0	0	0	1	1	1	1	1	0
A	0	0	1	0	0	1	1	1	1
B	0	0	0	0	1	1	1	1	1
I	0	0	0	1	0	1	0	1	0
J	0	0	0	0	0	1	1	1	0
L	1	0	0	0	1	1	1	1	0

Note: X_1 = disruptive students; X_2 = high staff turnover; X_3 = existence of a mentoring scheme;
X_4 = deprived students; X_5 = special needs students; X_6 = co-educational student body; X_7 = student absenteeism; X_8 = free school meals; Y = institutional success.

in the comprehensive inspection documents from which his dataset drew. Having more cases always means more heterogeneity (Ragin, 2006), and as the number of cases in the case-set decreases, there is a corresponding increase – as an artifact of the methodology – in the likelihood that they will share causally relevant conditions. Too small a sample will most likely not reveal meaningful causal configurations.

As QCA progresses, contradictions are solved and the causal conditions are minimized (i.e. trimmed) in order to keep the fewest possible causal conditions that still result in the outcome. This analysis aims to obtain a parsimonious minimal formula that holds for all of the cases being compared. That is, when the QCA analysis is complete, the number of cases that share this combination of conditions and also display the outcome of interest should be as high as possible (Ragin, 2009). For Byrne (2009b), summarizing the case-specific details in truth table rows allowed him to determine which causal conditions, or combinations of conditions, were necessary or sufficient for the outcome of institutional success that was being investigated. Through this analysis, the data established that teacher-led intensive mentoring of students was the most important feature of successful schools serving high-need student populations in the set.

Annotated readings

Ragin, C.C. (2014) *The Comparative Method: Moving beyond Qualitative and Quantitative Strategies*. Oakland, CA: University of California Press.

This is a comprehensive overview of Ragin's synthetic comparison approach and how it improves on purely variable-centric and case-centric methods. It progresses from topics such as sampling and casing, to basic concepts in Boolean logic, and a more advanced extension of Boolean mathematics.

Rihoux, B. and Lobe, B. (2009) The case for qualitative comparative analysis (QCA): Adding leverage for thick cross-case comparison. In D. Byrne and C.C. Ragin (eds) *The SAGE Handbook of Case-Based Methods* (pp. 222–242). London: SAGE.

The authors of this extended chapter discuss the important question 'what is a "case"?' and provide a reader-friendly template for applying QCA in research designs through a sequence of 15 steps. They also review the main purposes for adopting QCA as a technique or as an approach. The 15 steps are illustrated through examples and the entire sequence is contextualized with reader-friendly visuals.

Rihoux, B. and Ragin, C.C. (eds) (2009) *Configurational Comparative Methods: QCA and Related Methods*. Thousand Oaks, CA: SAGE.

This is an in-depth treatment of QCA and its many variations (i.e. fsQCA, mvQCA, MSDO/MDSO) by the originator of QCA (Charles Ragin) and a foremost authority on its application (Benoît Rihoux). Chapters provide a comprehensive overview that ranges from definitions of a 'case' to the epistemological foundations of QCA.

Schneider, C. and Wagemann, C. (2012) *Set-Theoretic Methods for the Social Sciences: A Guide to Qualitative Comparative Analysis*. Cambridge: Cambridge University Press.

The authors spend most of this book demonstrating how QCA fits within the logic of set-theoretic designs and how it would work as a practical design for research. This book falls on the more applied side than some other books and complements these other, more theoretical works nicely.

COMPASSS (COMPArative Methods for Systematic cross-caSe analySis).

Compasss.org (www.compasss.org) is a worldwide network for QCA scholars and practitioners who share a common interest in theoretical and methodological advancements in a systematic comparative case approach to research. The network's website is designed to further disseminate case-based methods that are informed by configurational logic, premised on the existence of multiple causality, and value a careful qualitative understanding of research cases and populations. This website hosts working papers, a bibliography on associated methods and applications, as well as links to nearly 20 data analytic software packages for such comparative configurational methods.

References

Berg-Schlosser, D., De Meur, G., Rihoux, B. and Ragin, C.C. (2009) Qualitative comparative analysis (QCA) as an approach. In B. Rihoux and C.C. Ragin (eds) *Configurational Comparative Methods: QCA and Related Methods* (pp. 1–18). Thousand Oaks, CA: SAGE.

Byrne, D. (2005) Complexity, configurations and cases. *Theory, Culture and Society* 22, 95–111.

Byrne, D. (2009a) Case-based methods: Why we need them; What they are; How to do them. In D. Byrne and C.C. Ragin (eds) *The SAGE Handbook of Case-Based Methods* (pp. 1–13). Thousand Oaks, CA: SAGE.

Byrne, D. (2009b) Complex realists and configurational approaches to cases: A radical synthesis. In D. Byrne and C.C. Ragin (eds) *The SAGE Handbook of Case-Based Methods* (pp. 101–112). Thousand Oaks, CA: SAGE.

Byrne, D. and Ragin, C.C. (eds) (2009) *The SAGE Handbook of Case-Based Methods*. Thousand Oaks, CA: SAGE.

Hiver, P., Obando, G., Sang, Y., Tahmouresi, S., Zhou, A. and Zhou, Y. (2019) Reframing the L2 learning experience as narrative reconstructions of classroom learning. *Studies in Second Language Learning and Teaching* 9 (1), 85–118. doi:10.14746/ssllt.2019.9.1.5

Ragin, C.C. (1999a) The distinctiveness of case-oriented research. *Health Services Research* 34, 1137–1151.

Ragin, C.C. (1999b) Using qualitative comparative analysis to study causal complexity. *Health Services Research* 34, 1225–1239.

Ragin, C.C. (2006) Set relations in social research: Evaluating their consistency and coverage. *Political Analysis* 14, 291–310. doi:10.1093/pan/mpj019

Ragin, C.C. (2009) Qualitative comparative analysis (QCA) as an approach. In B. Rihoux and C.C. Ragin (eds) *Configurational Comparative Methods: Qualitative Comparative Analysis (QCA) and Related Techniques* (pp. 1–18). Thousand Oaks, CA: SAGE.

Ragin, C.C. (2014) *The Comparative Method: Moving beyond Qualitative and Quantitative Strategies*. Oakland, CA: University of California Press.

Rihoux, B. and Lobe, B. (2009) The case for qualitative comparative analysis (QCA): Adding leverage for thick cross-case comparison. In D. Byrne and C.C. Ragin (eds) *The SAGE Handbook of Case-Based Methods* (pp. 222–242). London: SAGE.

Rihoux, B. and Ragin, C.C. (eds) (2009) *Configurational Comparative Methods: QCA and Related Methods*. Thousand Oaks, CA: SAGE.

Schneider, C. and Wagemann, C. (2012) *Set-Theoretic Methods for the Social Sciences: A Guide to Qualitative Comparative Analysis*. Cambridge: Cambridge University Press.

Yin, R.K. (2014) *Case Study Research: Design and Methods* (5th edn). Thousand Oaks, CA: SAGE.

5 Process Tracing

Overview

Process tracing originated in the field of cognitive psychology early in the 1970s as a way of examining intermediate steps and better understanding the heuristics through which individuals make decisions. Nearly a decade later, it began to see application in the study of political science, political history and political psychology. For obvious reasons, these disciplines, with their focus on human events and timespans, are interested in complex causal explanation and in drilling down to the mechanisms that can explain how and why an intervening causal chain led to an emergent outcome. Causal mechanisms, within this tradition (see also Chapter 3), do not reside in a 'black box of unobservability' (Bennett & Checkel, 2015: 41), but are conceived of in the complexity and dynamic systems theory (CDST) sense of probabilistic and stochastic events 'which produce an outcome by the interaction of a number of parts' (Beach & Pedersen, 2013: 1).

Process tracing can be described as a within-case method (i.e. a special case of case-study) for explaining complex causal mechanisms at a micro level of granularity (Checkel, 2006). Proponents of process tracing use it to provide evidence-based historical explanations and to make causal inferences from historical cases. Process tracing, when it is applied, is the systematic use of evidence from within a case (i.e. often a system) to make inferences about causal explanations of that case, its dynamic behavior and its emergent outcomes (Mahoney, 2012, 2015). Drawing such inferences from prior events and historical data is a seemingly intuitive way of making sense of their importance. However, this way of doing research is also fraught with potential inferential errors (see e.g. Gerring, 2005, 2010), and scholars caution that process tracing must be principled as it is not merely 'detective work based on hunches and intuition' from temporal sequences of events (Bennett & Checkel, 2015: 22). More often than not, intervening events, influences or processes are not simple or linear and do not have independent effects on the nature, the timing or the magnitude of a complex outcome.

*BENNETT AND CHECKEL (2015: 6) INTRODUCE
A METAPHOR TO ILLUSTRATE THE PURPOSE OF
PROCESS TRACING:*

If one had a row of fifty dominoes lying on the table after they had pre-viously been standing, how could one make inferences about whether the first domino caused the last to fall through a domino process, or whether wind, a bump of the table, or some other force caused the dominoes to fall? The answer, George and Bennett argued, was to use evidence on the intervening processes posited by each of the alternative explanations. Did anyone hear a succession of dominoes? Do the posi-tions of the fallen dominoes shed light on how they fell? And so on.

Process tracing is a versatile method that draws on within-case data. These data may be quantitative, quasi-quantitative or entirely qualitative in design (Collier, 2011). Within-case evidence here refers to evidence from within the temporal, spatial or substantive unit defined as a case (i.e. a system). This evidence will often include many temporal and situ-ational factors, and process tracing has parallels in historiography as it relies on microscopic tracing of a dynamic trajectory and examines evi-dence for competing explanations through a sequence of inferential tests (Bennett, 2006, 2008). Process tracing can progress (a) backward into a system's context and history; (b) forward into the dynamic mechanisms of change; (c) upward into the network of systems that anchor and inter-act with the case being examined; and (d) downward into the system's components, interactions and parameters to explain complex causal pro-cesses for a given outcome (Beach & Pedersen, 2013).

*BEACH AND PEDERSEN (2013: 69) DISCUSS THE ISSUE
OF 'CAUSAL MECHANISMS' IN NON-MECHANISTIC
COMPLEX SYSTEMS:*

In process-case studies, we attempt to analyze whether a theorized causal mechanism exists in an individual case. Therefore, we are inter-ested in making what can be termed within-case inferences, meaning that we use empirical evidence collected from a particular case to infer that all of the parts of a hypothesized causal mechanism were actually present in that case.

Process-tracing methods cannot be used to make cross-case infer-ences that involve concluding based on evidence drawn from a sample of comparable cases that a causal relationship exists across a population of a given theoretical phenomenon. Other forms of inferential tools, such as comparative methods, are necessary to make cross-case inferences.

Process tracing differs from the kind of cross-sectional analysis that involves collecting and examining data across a range of units. Process tracing involves temporal within-case data that attempt to systematically examine processes within individual cases. Whatever the outcome of interest, process tracing can be seen as the analysis of 'evidence on [case-specific] processes, sequences, and events within a case or system for the purpose of either developing or testing hypotheses' about the complex causal representation of that case and whether and how it generated the outcome of interest (Bennett & Checkel, 2015: 7).

Research Questions

Many of the questions that process tracing allows applied linguists to propose and explore have to do with the temporal and causal nature of events in the social and human spheres we are concerned with. In large-N analyses, especially cross-sectional designs, researchers are often forced to deal with causal factors in a relatively crude way, along a single dimension or using a very small number of categories (Gerring, 2005, 2010). In contrast, the within-case analysis used by process tracing affords the opportunity to attend much more closely to multiple dimensions of causal mechanisms (Checkel, 2006). Some questions that process tracing usefully enables applied linguistics researchers to explore include:

- How and why does an intervening causal chain lead to an emergent outcome?
- Are the complex causal mechanisms at play for an outcome of interest observable in action?
- What can the study of processes and sequences of events within a case (i.e. a system) reveal about its emergent outcomes?
- How does the conjoint occurrence of certain events and factors feed into the dynamic trajectory of a case?
- What evidence can we expect to see if only part of a complex causal mechanism exists? What counts as evidence for alternative hypotheses about these? What can be concluded when the predicted evidence is not found?
- What is the temporal dimension (long or short term) of the mechanisms identified, and what is the time horizon of the emergent outcome?
- What parameters or regularities govern system behavior over its time span?
- What is the scope of a set of complex causal mechanisms in a system's outcome of interest?

The use of process tracing to test and refine hypotheses about causal mechanisms can clarify the scope of conditions under which a hypothesis is transferable to other cases. The goal in process tracing is only ever to obtain an approximation of the complex causal mechanisms, and not something approaching an isomorphic reality. This is because explanation via complex and dynamic mechanisms means the former are always incomplete and provisional, and every explanation can be modified and revised if it can be shown that its hypothesized processes are not evident at other levels of analysis (Checkel, 2006). In this way too, process tracing opens the possibility for researchers to examine nested processes and the fractal nature of a system's dynamics.

Technical Features

As a single-case method, the ordinary starting point for process tracing is the prior state of knowledge about the complex outcome of interest. This outcome of interest must be defined qualitatively in a set-theoretic manner by indicating its presence or absence, and the case selected for investigation – usually a typical case (Mahoney, 2012, 2015). This point of departure will determine the extent to which the case study follows (a) a deductive path dedicated to testing whether evidence exists for hypothesized causal mechanisms or (b) an inductive path dedicated to inferring more general causal explanations from the empirical evidence and facts of a particular case. Process tracing proceeds in the latter of these ways when there is little prior knowledge for cases being examined or in instances where phenomena or outcomes are not well explained by existing theories (Bennett & Checkel, 2015). Once promising potential explanations are uncovered inductively, they can then be tested more deductively against evidence at different levels of time and scale within that case or in other cases. It is also important, at least initially in a process tracing study, to cast a wide net and generate alternative explanations in order to avoid confirmation bias and to take equifinality seriously by considering alternative causal pathways through which the outcome of interest might have occurred (Gerring, 2005, 2010).

Empirical material is then gathered and evaluated for its content, accuracy and probability and used as the basis of observations of causal mechanisms (Collier, 2011). One key distinction that scholars who adopt this method often make is between mechanisms that are thought to exist at a micro level, a macro level or that link the two. A more pragmatic reality would be that mechanisms can exist at both a macro and a micro level and, additionally, can span these levels and everything that lies between. Indeed, the choice of which level to adopt in analyzing a complex causal mechanism depends very much on first determining the level at which empirical manifestations of those complex causal mechanisms are most meaningful (Checkel, 2006). For instance, the study of how a baseball pitcher soft-assembles their throwing mechanics with each pitch would require a different level than the fine-motor skills used by an artist to grasp their tools. In the realm of applied linguistics, studying language change at a societal scale would ride on particular explanatory mechanisms and demand a certain level of explanation, whereas other factors would come into play for language variation at the level of an individual language user.

Because time is the dimension that gives causes and outcomes their coherence, mechanisms can also vary based on the length of time they are thought to be acting and on the time horizon of the outcome of interest (Mahoney, 2012, 2015). One type concerns *incremental causal mechanisms*, whose impact only becomes significant once they have been in action over a sustained period of time. This mirrors the well-known principle in complexity that causes and their effects are, among other things, rarely linear and proportionate. Another type is *threshold mechanisms*, also referred to as 'punctuated equilibrium' (Beach & Pedersen, 2013: 56), where very little happens for long periods until a cusp is reached – parallel to Per Bak's notion of self-organized criticality – and then relatively rapid and profound change unfolds.

It is also helpful to think of the types of data that are useful for process tracing analysis. In fact, many types of evidence can be used in process tracing, ranging from interviews to archival data. However, a key premise of process tracing is the idea that some pieces of evidence provide higher inferential power than others (Bennett, 2006; Collier, 2011). This type of evidence is said to have a higher *probative value* – meaning that it has the quality or function of demonstrating something or affording stronger, more relevant evidence for a conclusion than other, less relevant evidence. For example, in legal cases that aim to assign responsibility for liability in accidents, it may satisfy jurors' curiosity to have a comprehensive life-history of the individuals involved, but this evidence is not guaranteed to have much probative value (i.e. it may or may not be relevant) for judging the events in question or the case at hand. The tricky part about developing complex causal explanations based on these data is that process tracing involves identifying and describing potentially infinite steps between chosen starting and ending points in a hypothesized process. In addition, these in-between steps may appear to be at somewhat arbitrary increments of time and levels of detail in the analysis (Checkel, 2006; Gerring, 2005). Fortunately, an explanation that a process tracing researcher derives inductively from a case does not necessarily need to be tested against a different case in order to build confidence in it. Instead, to ensure rigor during analysis it can be tested against different and independent evidence in the same case from which it was derived (Beach & Pedersen, 2013).

BEACH AND PEDERSEN (2013: 73) CONSIDER DATA OBSERVATIONS ONLY ONE STEP ON THE WAY TO BUILDING EVIDENCE FOR COMPLEX CAUSAL PROCESSES:

In process-tracing, another type of empirical material is gathered. Collier, Brady, and Seawright suggest that this type of material be termed 'causal process observations' (CPO), defined as 'an insight or piece of data that provides information about the context or mechanism and contributes a different kind of leverage in causal inference'. In process-tracing, this assessment is undertaken using case-specific contextual knowledge; therefore, we can depict the evaluation process symbolically as o + k → e, where o is an observation, k is case-specific knowledge, and e is the resulting evidence produced by the evaluation process. After evaluation, empirical material can be termed evidence, which can then be used to make inferences that update our confidence in the presence of a hypothesized causal mechanism.

Extending this notion of the quality of evidence used to trace a process, more evidence (in the form of more data points or observations) is not always more useful. This is simply because process tracing places a greater importance on the probative value of evidence. In this sense, process tracing mirrors Bayesian logic that relies on the use of evidence and evidentiary tests to affirm some explanations and disprove others (Bennett, 2006, 2008). To some extent, the heuristics of Bayesian logic inform the analytical techniques that process tracing relies on. Bayesian logic provides a way to use evidence to update one's beliefs or understanding of existing evidence – sometimes known as priors – in the likelihood that alternative explanations are true.

Rather than being presented in narrative form, process tracing case studies and the evidence accumulated (i.e. the dataset) in accounting for the complex outcome of interest is usually presented as a stepwise test of each part of a causal mechanism, with evidentiary tests for and against the theorized causal factors presented at each turn. As an overview of the analytical steps, Bennett and Checkel (2015: 21–31) propose a sequence of steps to ensure that, ultimately, applications of process tracing analysis are rigorous, systematic and transparent.

First, prior expectations for complex causal mechanisms and their potential explanatory scope should be specified. Then, Bennett and Checkel propose that researchers select a representative or crucial case and *make a justifiable decision on the starting point for gathering evidence*. This temporal juncture chosen should be an operationally meaningful, and not an arbitrary point, from which process tracing can begin.

This step is critical, and in the same way that a researcher's decision to gather evidence can be critiqued for being too detailed or not detailed enough, the point in time selected as the start of process tracing can be critiqued for being too distant or too proximate a point in time. For Bennett and Checkel, a critical juncture is one that can be identified in retrospect at which a process displayed greater degrees of freedom and was most open to alternative contingent paths and outcomes.

Next, because conclusions in process tracing hinge on the value of collected evidence, Bennett and Checkel (2015) suggest the need to *consider the potential biases of evidentiary sources that might render observations more or less empirically convincing.* To avoid this type of selection bias, researchers should consider the context and the origin of evidence in assessing the robustness of that evidence.

Following this, Bennett and Checkel (2015) recommend *casting a wide net for alternative explanations in the search for causal mechanisms* that lead to a complex outcome. Doing so requires additional effort to consider a wide range of alternative explanations and to track down evidence that would affirm or disprove these alternate processes. However, the consequences of not taking into account such potentially viable explanations might render the findings unconvincing, due to the potential for confirmation bias and failure to address equifinality (i.e. the possibility of multiple pathways leading to the same outcome). Accepting a single explanation for a complex process too early on, and without considering alternatives, could leave the research design open to criticisms of lack of rigor.

Subsequently, Bennett and Checkel (2015) propose that *the analytical steps should be equally tough on the alternative explanations*, and advise researchers to gradually eliminate these alternative explanations if their core expectations about the causal process are disconfirmed. From a Bayesian logic perspective, as the evidence accumulates, process tracing should generate more detailed evidence for the explanations that increasingly appear to be true for a posterior (Bennett, 2006, 2008). To counteract confirmation bias, researchers should outline in advance the predictions of a wide range of alternative explanations, and then consider supporting evidence and counter evidence for each explanation.

BENNETT AND CHECKEL (2015: 278) LIST WHAT IS NEEDED FOR EVIDENCE TO DRAW MEANINGFULLY ON THE HEURISTICS OF BAYESIAN LOGIC:

In Bayes's approach, we need three key pieces of information, in addition to the evidence itself, to calculate this posterior probability. First, we need to start with a 'prior' probability, or a probability that expresses our initial confidence that a theory is true even before looking at the new evidence. Second, we need information on the likelihood that, if a theory is true in a case, we will find a particular kind of evidence in that case. This is referred to as the evidence conditional on the theory. Third, we need to know the likelihood that we would find the same evidence even if the explanation of interest is false. This is often referred to as the false positive rate, or the likelihood that evidence or a diagnostic test will show up positive even when a theory is false.

Once sufficient evidence has been collected, there is a need to *decide when to stop gathering and analyzing evidence*. This is a determination that can only be made once the diverse and independent streams of evidence have been gathered and contrasted. Using Bayesian logic, the decision to stop pursuing a given stream of evidence becomes acceptable once evidence is so repetitive that gathering more of that same kind of evidence has a low probability of revising one's prior expectations through alternative explanations (Bennett, 2008). This form of conclusiveness in data collection has parallels with the notion of reaching 'saturation' in most case-based research designs.

Finally, Bennett and Checkel (2015) advise ways to compensate for the limitations of single-case or so-called 'no-variance' designs by combining process tracing, where feasible, with cross-case comparisons, being open to inductive and unanticipated insights and acknowledging that, because not all forms of evidence are available or consistent, not all good process tracing is perfectly infallible or comprehensive.

Example Study

In a study of impressive breadth and depth, although from a domain outside of applied linguistics, Elisabeth Wood (2000) set out to trace the process of democratic change in El Salvador and to explain this nation's transitions from dictatorship to democracy. Wood's aim was to explore the mechanisms at play in this causal chain and construct a model of the intervening processes by collecting evidence and submitting that evidence to the tests described above. Through this evidence, she demonstrated how economic and political calculations of the costs and benefits can lead to regime preferences and conflict, and at each step she was able to either affirm or disprove the hypotheses she constructed.

Wood's point of departure in this case was that the status quo in El Salvador was characterized by the reliance of elites on repressive labor systems and economic institutions. The need to control the political system to maintain such repressive labor practices led these elites to adopt authoritarian preferences. Through tests of evidence, she was able to show that the elites allied with hardline military officers to undermine the

reformists who sought to modernize and liberalize politics and economics in the country. The consequence of this, however, was political exclu-
sion of the majority of the working class which, unsurprisingly, led to
insurgent collective action to overthrow the oligarchic state institutions.
Wood (2000) summarizes the intermediate steps:

> Insurgency dampens the usual returns for the elite – assets are destroyed,
> costly strikes occur, security costs rise, investment is suspended, and
> taxes increase. If sustained long enough, expected returns under democ-
> racy look attractive in comparison – if the distributional terms of the
> transition do not greatly threaten the status quo distribution of property
> rights. (Wood, 2000: 15)

Broadly speaking, Wood's process tracing demonstrated that insurgency played a causal role in catalyzing economic change that saw the
elites relinquishing their control over economic institutions. This economic change subsequently pushed El Salvador along a democratic path.
Wood carefully considered a potential alternative model that situated the
rise of new economic conditions in the more liberal labor-market dynamics of the 1970s and 1980s. However, on examining the evidence for this
alternative, she sustained her claim that it was labor insurgency that
triggered new economic behavior by the business elite. By scrutinizing
the availability of counter evidence, Wood was able to reject alternative
explanations.

The final part of Wood's study traced the last steps in the causal
chain, from political negotiations to democracy. She demonstrated that
for this piece of the causal chain to hold up, the political elites in El
Salvador first had to feel secure that their economic interests would be
safeguarded under democracy, and second that the insurgents would
commit to renouncing their recourse to violence and compete electorally
at the ballot box. This second task could only be accomplished if the
insurgents, too, embraced democracy and built a political organization
and an economic base of their own to support their party. Thus, to the
extent that insurgency resulted in novel cost–benefit analyses that triggered economic change and the subsequent recalibration of the political
institutions, it can be seen as a key causal mechanism in the transition of
El Salvador to democracy.

Annotated readings

Bennett, A. and Checkel, J. (eds) (2015) *Process Tracing: From Metaphor to Analytic
Tool.* Cambridge: Cambridge University Press.

This anthology contains chapters by some of the leading process tracing scholars in the
social sciences. These chapters showcase both applied demonstrations and theoretical
principles of best practice in process tracing. Readers will also find a treatment of issues

relating to standards in process tracing, causal analysis and inferencing, the analysis of complex mechanisms and what process tracing offers, beyond methods, to a practitioner in the social sciences. This book is the best starting point for discovering process tracing methods.

Beach, D. and Pedersen, R.B. (2013) *Process Tracing Methods: Foundations and Guidelines*. Ann Arbor, MI: The University of Michigan Press.

The authors of this volume explore the philosophical underpinnings of using probabilistic and stochastic causal mechanisms to explain social phenomena with illustrative examples. They also provide a straightforward and reader-friendly introduction to the Bayesian logic of priors and posteriors that forms the basis for making conclusions based on this method. They round off the book with advice on selecting cases and collecting evidence, as well as practical checklists for process tracing analysis designed to (a) test hypotheses, (b) build theory and (c) explain outcomes.

References

Beach, D. and Pedersen, R.B. (2013) *Process Tracing Methods: Foundations and Guidelines*. Ann Arbor, MI: The University of Michigan Press.

Bennett, A. (2006) Stirring the frequentist pot with a dash of Bayes. *Political Analysis* 14, 339–344. doi:10.1093/pan/mpj011

Bennett, A. (2008) Process-tracing: A Bayesian perspective. In J.M. Box-Steffensmeier, H.E. Brady and D. Collier (eds) *The Oxford Handbook of Political Methodology* (pp. 702–721). Oxford: Oxford University Press.

Bennett, A. and Checkel, J. (eds) (2015) *Process Tracing: From Metaphor to Analytic Tool*. Cambridge: Cambridge University Press.

Checkel, J. (2006) Tracing causal mechanisms. *International Studies Review* 8, 362–370. doi:10.1111/j.1468-2486.2006.00598_2.x

Collier, D. (2011) Understanding process tracing. *PS: Political Science and Politics* 44, 823–830. doi:10.1017/S1049096511001429

Gerring, J. (2005) Causation: A unified framework for the social sciences. *Journal of Theoretical Politics* 17, 163–198. doi:10.1177/0951629805050859

Gerring, J. (2010) Causal mechanisms: Yes but… *Comparative Political Studies* 43, 1499–1526. doi:10.1177/0010414010376911

Mahoney, J. (2012) The logic of process tracing tests in the social sciences. *Sociological Research Methods* 41, 570–597. doi:10.1177/0049124112437709

Mahoney, J. (2015) Process tracing and historical explanation. *Security Studies* 24, 200–218. doi:10.1080/09636412.2015.1036610

Wood, E.J. (2000) *Forging Democracy from Below: Insurgent Transitions in South Africa and El Salvador*. Cambridge: Cambridge University Press.

6 Concept Mapping

Overview

An old adage says that 'a picture is worth a thousand words'. We feel this is apt for the topic of the current chapter – a method that relies on pictures that happen to be composed of words. Concept mapping is a theoretically grounded diagrammatic method first developed in the 1970s by Joseph Novak at Cornell University and built on by his colleagues at the Institute for Human & Machine Cognition (Novak, 2010). Concept mapping is a tool for representing aspects of knowledge (e.g. about a complex system) and specifying the links connecting them through the construction of concept maps (CMaps) that serve as the basis for action (Novak & Cañas, 2006, 2007, 2008). In this way, researchers might think of CMaps as incorporating elements of flowcharts, mind maps, visual organizers and diagrams all rolled into one. A close cousin of CMaps is System Mapping, a method with at least one recent application in our field (Fogal, forthcoming).

First, we need to disambiguate several similar terms. A *mind map* is a center-focused representation, often with branches of associated ideas radiating out from a central node (see Figure 6.1). These ideas do not need to be tightly related or categorized, but initially only need to be loosely associated. Concept mapping, however, looks and functions differently. It is designed to reflect the basis of a complex system's actual organization or its actual functioning. For this reason, CMaps are constructed to help researchers make better sense of real-world systems (Moon *et al.*, 2011). The primary objective of concept mapping is to serve as the basis for action within a complexity and dynamic systems theory (CDST) perspective. With this in mind, the point of departure in a CMap is the system-level structure of complex phenomena. CMaps are often considered a means of representing concepts and relationships that are hierarchical (see Figure 6.2); however, the more fundamental requirement is that the structure of a CMap should reflect the systems' nature and content, and for this reason CMaps can represent non-hierarchical systems or knowledge equally well (Derbentseva *et al.*, 2006).

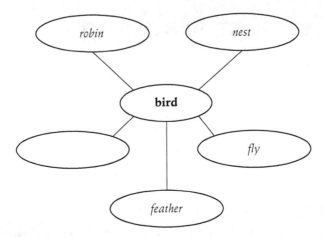

Figure 6.1 A simple mind map

The purpose of concept mapping is to build an aggregate visual diagram of a real-world system and its mechanisms. This diagram is designed to help pinpoint issues of concern in the organization or functioning of the system, and then to strategically intervene in ways that optimize system functioning and solve any such problems (Moon *et al.*, 2011). In the field of applied linguistics, there are numerous complex processes that researchers would potentially want to understand, including those at a broader level (e.g. how technology influences language and the creation of culture, how language ideology affects communities or how language encounters throughout individuals' life experiences impact their identity) and those at a much narrower level (e.g. how an individual's multilingualism impacts their cognitive resources, how an important topic is represented in a particular text or how a language test influences language pedagogy in a particular classroom). Because of its underlying objectives, concept mapping relies more on system-internal considerations than on formalizing aspects of broader systemic networks in its models. It is unique in this sense when compared with several other methods we present in this volume. Concept mapping integrates input from multiple sources and can accommodate differing interests or pockets of expertise, and for these reasons it is a participatory approach that has 'become increasingly valued and useful within a world of systems thinking and growing networks' (Kane & Trochim, 2007: viii).

A CMap is developed within a *context frame*. As the starting point for process tracing, projects can be defined by an explicit focus question, a well-articulated objective, an issue that requires a response or a problem that requires a solution of some sort (Moon *et al.*, 2011; Safayeni *et al.*, 2005). For instance, the context frame of a CMap for deciding what to include in a unit of language instruction would be very different from the context frame of a CMap for optimizing decision-making on national

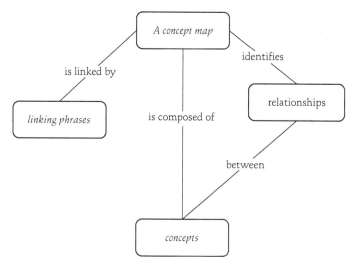

Figure 6.2 A simple concept map

language policy (e.g. the latter would include stakeholder details, information on costs and benefits and a time horizon for implementing the
policy, among other things). Even domain-specific context frames will
differ, as the context frame of a CMap for addressing nationwide declin-
ing enrollments in foreign language classes will be distinct from that of a
CMap for examining barriers to language learning engagement in non-
compulsory settings. We elaborate on concept frames later in this chapter.

A key component of a CMap is a *proposition* composed of at least
two nodes or *concepts* and their functional relationship (see Figure 6.2).
Propositions can be seen as units of meaning in the CMap. They are often
declarative in nature. Concepts may be system agents or components,
events, objects, information or processes, or just perceived patterns and
regularities (Novak & Cañas, 2006, 2007, 2008). Relationships express
precise meanings and may illustrate interactions or sequences. A collection of such linked concepts is structurally connected to other such
propositions through a *crosslink*, which shows the relationships between
ideas in different segments of the CMap. By using thematic clusters, concept mapping produces a spatiotemporal representation of a system and
the structural links between clusters.

KANE AND TROCHIM (2007: 2) OFFER THEIR VIEW OF HOW CONCEPT MAPPING IS USEFUL FOR SOCIAL SCIENCE RESEARCH:

Concept mapping seeks the open contribution of participant stakeholders' ideas on a specific issue, organizes the ideas, and portrays them in

pictures or maps that are readily understood. Using the resulting concept map as a foundation, researchers can measure any number of variables of interest—such as the importance or feasibility of participant ideas—and display them as patterns on the map. They can then compare two or more patterns—in the aggregate and in their details—using pattern matching to look at consensus and consistency over time, along with bivariate displays known as 'go zones', to identify the potential courses of action or types of measurement. The concept mapping process is useful as an integrating framework throughout the life cycle of a project, from the initial conceptualization of the project, to the development of actions, programs, and/or measures, to the initial implementation of them, and finally to evaluation and reformulation.

Since its inception, concept mapping has been used for knowledge elicitation and management, organizational learning and collaborative operations and for complex-systemic problem-solving. Concept mapping was famously used by Disney to represent its brand positioning and branding strategy, and a cursory web search turns up hundreds of images of CMaps ranging from the relatively mundane to the wildly elaborate. Its current applications extend from education to corporations and public policy, with the adoption of concept mapping even emerging at NASA and at the US Department of Defense (Moon *et al.*, 2011).

Research Questions

Moon *et al.* (2011) caution that it is easy to build CMaps, but much less easy to build good CMaps. Their concern here is that almost any domain of knowledge, any phenomena or any complex system can be represented diagrammatically using propositions and crosslinks. However, it only becomes an effective use of concept mapping when the CMap is employed as the basis for action or intervention in a problem space of some sort. CMaps, in other words, always serve to describe the current state of a system or an issue within the system, and should then be used to help the researchers form a consensus about the future desired state of the system or the resolution of that issue (Novak & Cañas, 2006, 2007, 2008).

MOON ET AL. (2011: 24) SHARE THEIR EXPERIENCE ON THE TRADECRAFT OF CONCEPT MAPPING:

Were it not for ease of creation and use, we suspect the global use of Concept Mapping would not have grown over the past three decades, spreading from classrooms to boardrooms, migrating from butcher paper to the Internet. The ease of Concept Mapping is its greatest strength. The most powerful ideas are often the simplest. And, yet, as practitioners with thousands of hours of Concept Mapping experience between us, our eyebrows are drawn upward when we hear the truism uttered. What we really hear is: '(Good, Novakian) Concept Maps are (not so) easy to (efficiently and effectively) make and use'. Moreover, facilitating others in making good Concept Maps is even more difficult. Concept Mapping is not just a procedure, it is a skill set.

This also raises the issue that there may be times when a CMap constructed for a particular purpose or course of action appears to be incomplete or lacking in comprehensiveness (Derbentseva *et al.*, 2006). This is to be expected, and the reality is that no CMap is ever definitively finished because complex systemic knowledge, problems and solutions are not fixed but often exist in dynamic flux. Fortunately, CMaps can be seen as constant works in progress that can be updated and revised. The challenge is simply knowing when the level of detail present in the represented concepts and in their links is adequate for the researchers' purpose (Kane & Trochim, 2007).

Concept mapping allows researchers to explore questions that vary in scope, such as:

- Is a system functioning as it is intended, achieving what it was intended to achieve or serving the purpose it was intended for?
- On which concepts and relationships does a system's continued functioning ride?
- How does a system reach its optimal level of functioning (for a given purpose) or stay on track throughout its developmental life cycle?
- If a system is not functioning as intended, what are the issues that need to be resolved?
- What course of action would most effectively improve a specific area of less-than-optimal system functioning?
- Which system issues are relatively more important or should have higher priority for optimizing system functioning?
- How do different objectives and system-level outcomes change the priority of factors for optimal system functioning?
- What is the feasibility of two competing ideas or processes in the life cycle of a system's development?
- What stake do the system's agents have in the desired system outcome and do their incentive structures match up with the intended purpose or architecture of the system?
- Do a system's emergent states and dynamic processes of change correspond with original expectations or intentions for the system?

- What are the best uses of limited available resources to solve specific system issues or for reaching long-term system goals?

Technical Features

The initial steps for creating a CMap are similar to most techniques of visual brainstorming (Novak, 2010). These include steps such as defining a focus question, objective or issue; identifying the key concepts for inclusion and articulating these; arranging the concepts spatially using some notion of priority; creating links; revising spatial arrangement accordingly; and creating crosslinks among the propositions.

KANE AND TROCHIM (2007: 27) LIST SOME IMPORTANT ISSUES THAT ARISE WHILE PREPARING FOR THE CONCEPT MAPPING PROCESS:

Preparation is the most important step in the concept mapping process because thoughtful decisions at this stage will help ensure a smooth and meaningful process, and errors made here may be amplified as the process unfolds.... The preparation stage involves several tasks:

- Define the Issue. Identify the core need, interest, or issue to be examined.
- Initiate the Process. Define the need for a concept mapping project and move it forward as appropriate, driven by the goals and desired outcomes, through initiator(s) who may be either an individual or a team put together to ensure both political and practical coverage for the project.
- Select the Facilitator. Choose a person from outside or inside the organization who will facilitate and enable the process.
- Determine Goals and Purposes. Identify the goals and desired outcomes of the concept mapping project.
- Define the Focus. Discuss the goal and the focus of the concept mapping.
- Select the Participants. Choose the people who will participate in the concept mapping, informed by goals and purposes, as well as the resulting focus statements.
- Determine Participation Methods. Identify whether goals of the process are best served using on-site versus remote brainstorming, sorting, and rating, as well as appropriate stakeholder group sizes for each step.

Once these preliminary steps have been used iteratively to build the skeleton CMap, the core purpose of concept mapping kicks in: using the CMap as the basis for action or intervention in a problem space of some sort (Novak & Cañas, 2006, 2007, 2008). Here, we use the term *problem space* in a non-generic way and refer to its CDST meaning: a state space that includes potential tasks or information that the system is processing, or developmental goals or solutions toward which the system may be working. Examples of these might be optimizing learning in classroom settings, streamlining the flow of information in social networks, increasing individual interactions, mitigating breakdowns in communication or facilitating uptake of new strategies and behaviors (Figure 6.3).

A focus question (e.g. how can schools encourage greater voluntary enrolment in second language [L2] learning?), objective (e.g. to maximize L2 learning from limited instructional resources) or issue (e.g. low parental involvement in L2 learners' development) guides the purpose for which a CMap is constructed and the scope of ideas included in it. As we mentioned above, a CMap is developed within the boundaries of a context frame. A context frame refers to the conceptual and developmental outer bounds that a CMap can be expected to take within its purview and represent diagrammatically. They can also be seen as the spatio-temporal dimensions of a CMap. Context frames help to maintain a big

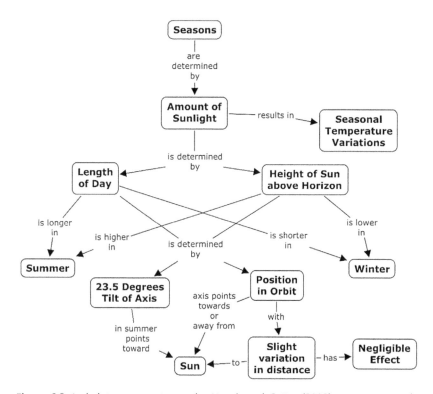

Figure 6.3 A skeleton concept map by Novak and Cañas (2008) to represent why seasons change (Reproduced with permission)

picture view of the research project as the purpose for which the CMap is being constructed plays back into the decisions made regarding how comprehensive, detailed and refined the CMap should be (Safayeni *et al.*, 2005). Figure 6.4 shows one example of what this might look like. It is important to note that the scope of a CMap is not always predetermined and researchers should keep an open mind if the issues or objectives that originally present themselves to the concept mappers point to deeper ones with time and further mapping (Kane & Trochim, 2007).

Articulating the key concepts for inclusion in the CMap is also a task that requires careful thought. Randomly listed concepts may not satisfy the needs of the CMap, and will often benefit from further unpacking of latent concepts (Kane & Trochim, 2007). This process can create opportunities for differentiating between sub-concepts and their relations and seeing how previously unrelated concepts might fall under a higher-order

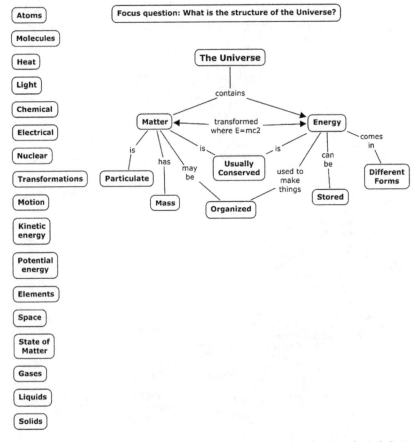

Figure 6.4 Focus question, context frame and concept map by Novak and Cañas (2008) to represent the structure of the universe (Reproduced with permission)

concept. Crafting the linking words presents another challenge as the resulting propositions (i.e. concepts combined with their link) must be simple and meaningful, and must express declarative propositional value. Looking at Figure 6.4, we can see that 'matter → has → mass' or 'energy → can be → stored' stand independently, as they should, in their propositional coherence (Moon *et al.*, 2011). The example in Figure 6.5, however, illustrates a lack of propositional coherence. Pulling apart the 'string' or 'run-on' proposition shows that the final piece (Figure 6.6) does not express any declarative propositional value. Making the string propositionally coherent would require us to use new connecting words or links (Figure 6.7). While there are no restrictions on the kinds of phrases that can serve as links or that can be used to label relationships, these should obviously be clear, concise and diverse. Often, a decent thesaurus can augment the concept mapper's capacity to describe these links.

| This book → is about → research methods → and concept mapping. |

Figure 6.5 An example of a concept map that lacks propositional coherence

| ...research methods → and concept mapping. |

Figure 6.6 An example of a proposition that does not express a declarative value

| Concept mapping → is a → research method. |

Figure 6.7 An example of a concept map that expresses a declarative value

The user-friendliness that comes with concept mapping is often related to the spatial features of a CMap, which aid in finding a balanced overall structure for the CMap's strategic intended purpose. This is why arranging the concepts spatially and revising this organization is so crucial to the success of a CMap (Moon *et al.*, 2011). Diagrammatic methods such as concept mapping rely heavily on shape-meaning coherence in listing and arranging the concepts by some notion of inclusiveness, categorization, importance or priority, and in using the available space for propositions and deliberately placing crosslinks in the CMap (Derbentseva *et al.*, 2006; Safayeni *et al.*, 2005). For example, a procedural CMap that is only able to represent time as a linear progression of events may be too rigid and inflexible to be of any use because in real developmental situations, temporality is often cyclical or iterative, and may be extended or disrupted according to the nature of a system and its dynamics (Kane & Trochim, 2007). It is this spatial organization that provides data for action and, executed well, allows CMaps to be used efficiently from the initial conceptualization of the action needed, to their implementation and evaluation.

To reiterate, concept mapping depicts a system's interconnected workings, its states and dynamic processes of change. It represents these diagrammatically, and in turn sets out to do something about them – what Kane and Trochim (2007: xiii) refer to as a 'concept systems approach'. It thus draws on Kurt Lewin's often-cited maxim that 'there is nothing so practical as a good theory' and is particularly suited for building large-scale, concrete models of systems. Finally, the principled use of CMaps also requires researchers, somewhat ironically, to know when to refrain from concept mapping, and when to adopt other methods that are better suited to the problems or questions at hand (Moon *et al.*, 2011).

MOON ET AL. (2011: 41–42) DESCRIBE SOME OF THE PITFALLS OF TAKING SHORTCUTS WHILE CONCEPT MAPPING:

We have already mentioned many of the novice errors we have seen new Concept Mappers make, most of which we made ourselves. Experiencing these errors a few times is a valuable learning experience, making it really possible to avoid them and introduce a level of true professionalism into Concept Mapping. The errors include:

- Rushing or skipping altogether the introduction to Concept Mapping for the knower.
- Writing sentences or verbose phrases into concepts.
- Complacency in capturing the concepts as the knower expresses them.
- Incessantly moving elements in front of the knower.
- Jumping too quickly into creating links between concepts.
- Banally repeating linking words.
- Restructuring the Concept Map outside of the view of the knower.
- Incautiously setting up links to temporary resources or resource locations.

With the wider adoption of concept mapping for both data curation and dissemination, software such as CmapTools (https://cmap.ihmc.us/cmaptools) has been developed to address the analytical needs of stakeholders in governance, industry and the public sphere who rely on these methods. There are also CMap libraries online. For instance, Concept Systems, Inc. is a research, evaluation and consulting agency founded by Mary Kane, which has compiled a topical list of recent peer-reviewed publications that either employ or review concept mapping methods (https://www.conceptsystems.com/gw/bibliography).

Example Study

Dare *et al*. (2017), who research educational inclusion, were intrigued by existing findings suggesting that students with special learning needs benefit from individualized programmes to realize their full potential. They surmised that students who have higher than typical academic ability are no exception, and that when such students' educational needs are overlooked, this may result in talent loss. They designed a mixed-method concept mapping study to investigate high-ability learners and their motivations for educational acceleration through dual enrolment – a programme in which students are enrolled in two levels of school simultaneously (e.g. high school students take their own classes and junior college classes).

The design included secondary students ($n = 12$) who attended university while completing high school. They found that students expressed predominantly self-determined (i.e. intrinsic) motivations to accelerate through this concurrent enrollment. The participants proceeded to structure a set of 85 reasons for concurrent enrollment by sorting the data into meaningful groups through a group concept mapping process. Students' CMap revealed seven connected themes that focused on preparing for university, demonstrating initiative, getting ahead, love of learning, finding self-fulfillment, seeking challenge and socializing.

In order to include a comparative element, Dare *et al*. (2017) also examined how educators ($n = 12$) categorized students' motivations to choose concurrent enrollment. They felt that educators' categorizations are important because these educators act as gatekeepers in students' choice to accelerate: they inform students about acceleration, identify suitable candidates, guide students in educational planning and support students who accelerate.

As a quantitative follow-up, Dare *et al*. (2017) then applied multidimensional scaling and hierarchical cluster analysis (both of which are visual partitioning methods) to the CMap data in order to create a cluster solution of students' categorizations and contrast it with those of the educators. First, using multidimensional scaling, the researchers created an x–y plot of the 85 categorized statements for each group. In their data point map, distances between 85 statements correspond to how frequently the statements were sorted together. After creating the data point map, average grouping patterns were analyzed by applying the statistical technique hierarchical cluster analysis. Hierarchical cluster analysis examines similarities between the data points and produces a range of cluster solutions showing meaningful groupings of these data points which reflect distinct concepts with conceptual clarity.

For the educators' data, Dare *et al*. (2017) determined that a five-cluster solution of the CMap data resulted in the simplest model that retained distinct concepts. On the other hand, a seven-cluster model represented the best conceptual and statistical fit with the students' CMap data. Based on comparisons between these results, the researchers suggest that educators may sometimes overlook the self-determined motivations that secondary students have for participating in accelerated programmes, or may not be aware of students' finer-grained reasons for dual enrollment.

Annotated readings

Moon, B., Hoffman, R., Novak, J.D. and Cañas, A. (eds) (2011) *Applied Concept Mapping: Capturing, Analyzing, and Organizing Knowledge*. Boca Raton, FL: CRC Press.

These editors preface their volume with an enthusiastic endorsement, stating that they know of no other method through which the most perplexing problems can so effectively be conceived, analyzed and solved than by using CMaps. Drawing on original 'Novakian' notions of concept mapping, the editors provide a review of its roots and central concepts, and showcase its potential applications. The remaining chapters by contributors give a snapshot of the global expansion that concept mapping has seen since its inception. These chapters demonstrate how CMaps can be used individually or collaboratively to synthesize and visualize large amounts of complex information, and are also useful in comparison to other modeling methods. This is a wide-ranging edited volume.

Kane, M. and Trochim, W. (2007) *Concept Mapping for Planning and Evaluation*. Thousand Oaks, CA: SAGE.

This volume is written by two prominent concept mappers whose areas of expertise relate to organizational learning and programme planning and evaluation. They develop a sequential framework for doing rigorous concept mapping, and demonstrate how CMaps have served as the basis for action in various social domains. The early chapters introduce extensive content on the technical underpinnings of this method and address key issues in the analysis and interpretation of CMaps. The later chapters show detailed examples of the many ways concept mapping can be applied in practice. This book is a more in-depth read.

References

Dare, A., Dare, L. and Nowicki, E. (2017) Concurrent enrollment: Comparing how educators and students categorize students' motivations. *Social Psychology of Education* 20, 195–213. doi:10.1007/s11218-016-9364-8

Derbentseva, N., Safayeni, F. and Cañas, A.J. (2006) Concept maps: Experiments on dynamic thinking. *Journal of Research in Science Teaching* 44, 448–465. doi:10.1002/tea.20153

Fogal, G.G. (forthcoming) Unpacking 'simplex systems': Curricular thinking for L2 writing development. In G.G. Fogal and M.H. Verspoor (eds) *Complex Dynamic Systems Theory and L2 Writing Development*. Amsterdam/Philadelphia, PA: John Benjamins.

Kane, M. and Trochim, W. (2007) *Concept Mapping for Planning and Evaluation*. Thousand Oaks, CA: SAGE.

Moon, B., Hoffman, R., Novak, J.D. and Cañas, A. (eds) (2011) *Applied Concept Mapping: Capturing, Analyzing, and Organizing Knowledge*. Boca Raton, FL: CRC Press.

Novak, J.D. (2010) *Learning, Creating, and Using Knowledge: Concept Maps as Facilitative Tools in Schools and Corporations* (2nd edn). New York: Routledge.

Novak, J.D. and Cañas, A.J. (2006) The origins of concept maps and the continuing evolution of the tool. *Information Visualization Journal* 5, 175–184. doi:10.1057/palgrave.ivs.9500126

Novak, J.D. and Cañas, A.J. (2007) Theoretical origins of concept maps, how to construct them, and uses in education. *Reflecting Education Online Journal* 3, 29–42.

Novak, J.D. and Cañas, A.J. (2008) The Theory Underlying Concept Maps and How to Construct and Use Them. Technical Report, IHMC CmapTools, Institute for Human and Machine Cognition, Boca Raton, Florida. See http://cmap.ihmc.us/docs/pdf/TheoryUnderlyingConceptMaps.pdf (accessed 30 June 2019).

Safayeni, F., Derbentseva, N. and Cañas, A.J. (2005) Concept maps: A theoretical note on concepts and the need for cyclic concept maps. *Journal of Research in Science Teaching* 4, 741–766.

7 Agent-Based Modeling

Overview

In this chapter, we introduce one of the most widely used methods for complexity theory research in the social sciences – agent-based modeling (ABM). As a point of introduction to this method, let us consider global stock markets as an example of a complex system. In this system, individual agents (shareholders) behave (trade shares) in line with their own rules (e.g. buy if the price is expected to increase, sell if the price is expected to decrease). These fairly simple rules are generated from local information (news, rumors, personal opinions or memes) and interaction between agents. Although stock markets are built on these simple rules, when considered as a whole, the markets exhibit complex higher-order patterns: there are nervous price trends and fluctuations, bandwagon effects which see shareholders dump stock or start a buying frenzy, or wait-and-see behavior, leaving the impression that the stock market possesses a will of its own. Parallels in applied linguistics abound.

As our discussion earlier in this book shows, real systems are often too complex and actual manipulation of a system or its parts can present practical challenges due to issues of access or issues of scale (Byrne & Callaghan, 2014). For example, in applied linguistics it would be difficult and slow to understand how language educational policy reform results in changes across institutions and classrooms or how new media and communication trends (e.g. being restricted to 140 characters on a social network platform) affect linguistic innovation if all we had to rely on was observing the institutions, the classrooms or the individuals in question. Other issues that might cause concern include the speed and cost of implementation, and the reproducibility of experimentally intervening in the real world.

In response to this, ABM formulates a simplified representation of a system – which we could call a 'model' – that can provide a set of rules and show *how* different components of a phenomenon interact (Helbing, 2012). Such a model can then be manipulated in various experimental simulations using manageable equations or a computer program. It should be clear from this relative reduction in how systems are represented that ABM is more closely aligned to restricted complexity research, rather than general complexity. However, the power of ABM is in its ability to (a) represent the interacting components and (b) display the emergent properties and dynamic reactions of systems at scale, while (c) simulating various processes and system outcomes (Iba, 2013; Siegfried, 2014). Although ABM contains a quantitative element (i.e. computer simulation; see below), it is included in this part of the book because that quantitative element comes rather late in the process. It is preceded by a substantial effort in model building, which requires a rich understanding of the system typical of a qualitative undertaking.

Readers may wonder what the keywords *agent* and *model* refer to in this research template. One common feature of complex social systems is that they are composed of autonomous 'agents' that interact with each other and with their environment, differ from each other and change over time, and have behaviors that are important to how a system works (Macy & Willer, 2002; Railsback & Grimm, 2012). Agents in ABM are organisms, humans, groups, institutions and any other entity that uses adaptive behavior to pursue a certain goal. Usually, agents' behaviors – though not the resulting system dynamics – are governed by simple rules (Iba, 2013). In this sense, ABM draws on our understanding of agents as those entities capable of exercising independent choice or intentional action that contributes causally to any behavior of the complex system (Hiver & Al-Hoorie [2016]; see also Al-Hoorie [2015]; Larsen-Freeman [2019] for an extended discussion).

Models are purposeful representations of some real system (Helbing, 2010). These may take the form of verbal, symbolic or schematic representations of a system, a process or some other aspect of the real world (Siegfried, 2014). In their most ambitious forms, some models (e.g. neural network models) attempt to model big data and recognize and extract patterns in it. And, while models do not necessarily explain *why* or make predictions, ABM allows researchers to build working models of complex systems from the ground up and, by combining heterogeneous sources and levels of data, find solutions for complex scenarios (Castellani & Hafferty, 2009). Working models help researchers (aka 'modelers') to simulate the dynamic processes and emergent outcomes they would like to understand.

SIEGFRIED (2014: 1) OFFERS A STRONG POSITION ON THE PLACE OF AGENT-BASED MODELING IN RESEARCHERS' LIBRARY OF METHODS:

Simulation is nowadays considered to be the third pillar of science, a peer alongside theory and experimentation. The analysis of many systems, processes and phenomena is often only feasible by developing simulation models and executing them using vast amounts of computing power. Forecasts, decision support and training are further areas that are regularly supported or even made possible by using simulation.

As part of its analytical steps, ABM requires modelers to formulate a model that is a transformation of an empirical situation, specify quantitative values and indicators that connect a model and the target system (i.e. a task called parameterization), then assess, calibrate and scale a model based on existing knowledge, new data or theoretical insights (Siegfried, 2014).

First, the act of formulating a model must be based on researchers' preliminary understanding of how the system works and what its important elements and processes are (Grimm *et al.*, 2014). Among other things, these preliminary ideas might be based on empirical knowledge of the system's behavior, on earlier models built to address similar questions or on existing theories (Macy & Willer, 2002). Unfortunately, models cannot be formulated if there is no prior knowledge of how the system works (Helbing, 2012). Scientists are happy to model many things (including the likelihood of a zombie apocalypse!), but some things really are too complex for the current state of scientific understanding. For example, so far there has been no explicit model of human consciousness, simply because there is little consensus about what human consciousness really is and how it emerges (e.g. Valsiner *et al.*, 2009).

There are also many ways to represent a real complex system in a simplified way. If, for example, a modeler starts out with the very broad objective of modeling the impact of policy change on educational institutions, it would be unclear where to start and what aspects of the real system are important. For this reason, the question(s) being explored through the model must serve as a filter to restrict the number of aspects being modeled (Castellani & Hafferty, 2009). This also illustrates, as we highlighted earlier, that ABM treats complexity in an empirical rather than a paradigmatic way (cf. Jackson *et al.*, 2017). As a practical illustration, with a question such as 'What strategic policies maximize the adoption of educational innovation in language classrooms?', we would know that all aspects of the real system that could be considered irrelevant or insufficiently important for answering this question (but still potentially contributing to the system's overall complexity) should be filtered out (e.g. policymakers' favorite sports teams; the teachers' and students' lunchtime menu preferences). They are ignored in the model, or represented only in a very simplified way (Railsback & Grimm, 2012).

Research Questions

ABM is concerned with multiple levels and their interactions: systems, their agents and their broader contexts (Grimm *et al.*, 2014). ABM looks at both what happens to the system because of what its individuals do, and what happens to the individuals because of what the system does. Additionally, ABM can be used to study questions of how a system's behavior arises from, and is linked to, the characteristics and behaviors of its individual components (Iba, 2013; Siegfried, 2014).

Instead of describing a system only with variables representing the state of the whole system, ABM models its individual agents and their choice architecture (Smajgl & Barreteau, 2014) to explore how system dynamics arise from the ways a system's individual components interact with and respond to each other and their environment. *Choice architecture* here refers to the combination of contingencies and potential directions and pathways for action or movement. Some important questions this approach enables researchers to investigate are:

- How do systems change their behavior due to their agents' interactions?
- How do agents adapt their behavior and interactions due to system-level changes?
- How do agents adjust their behavior in response to their current states, those of other agents and the environment?
- What makes some agents more or less productive for system functioning than some others?
- What makes some interactions in a system more or less beneficial for system-level dynamics than some others?
- How scalable are the drivers of change in systems?
- How do agents' behaviors and interactions provide solutions to system-level problems?
- How do system-level dynamics provide solutions to agent-level problems?
- How does the order in which agents' interactions take place affect system-level change and outcomes?
- How do seemingly functioning systems fail to produce an expected/prior outcome?

Technical Features

So far, we have considered several fundamental ideas: that a model is a purposeful simplification of a complex system for solving a particular question or category of problems; and that ABMs are useful when it is important for a model to account for systems' agents and what they do. Because the assumptions included in a model are experimental, they must be tested and revised systematically (Macy & Willer, 2002). This means modeling takes place in an iterative loop that cycles through first articulating a precise question, assembling hypotheses for key processes, formulating the model and implementing it, and then analyzing, testing and revising that model. With complex models in general, these steps are not trivial or merely intuitive (Grimm *et al.*, 2014). They require careful thought to ensure that the models used are structurally realistic (i.e. not overly simplistic or reductionist) and well calibrated. Let us now explore these stages in greater detail.

Constructing an ABM requires moving systematically from the heuristic part of modeling, in which researchers focus on the problem, data, ideas and hypotheses, to the more formal and rigorous representation of the model. In this sense, ABM could be seen as a type of bottom-up modeling, compared with the more top-down modeling for complexity research (e.g. cellular automata) that expresses phenomena only in numerical terms using differential equations (Iba, 2013; Siegfried, 2014).

At the outset, modelers most often *formulate a question or problem.* This serves as the blueprint for subsequent steps and as a filter for designing a model (Jackson *et al.*, 2017). A clear and concise statement of the question or problem addressed by the model helps to specify what system is being modeled, what the researcher is trying to learn about it and what data will feed into the model. ABM commences with this step because it is impossible to make any decisions about a model – for instance, what should and should not be included and whether its structure makes sense – if it is unclear what the model is for (Helbing, 2012). Knowing a model's purpose is akin to having a roadmap for the rest of the model description: with some idea of the problem a model is designed to solve, there is a much better expectation of what that model should look like. Formulating a productive question is also a major task because it requires a clear focus. Questions that are not focused enough, or are either too simple or too complex, may need to be reformulated once the modeling cycle progresses and this lack of focus becomes apparent (Grimm *et al.*, 2014).

Next, modelers *outline a preliminary conceptual model* by assembling existing hypotheses for the model's essential processes and structures (Railsback & Grimm, 2012). This model is concerned foremost with the processes and structures that are thought to be essential to the question or problem at hand. The preliminary model should articulate its components – i.e. the kinds of things represented in the model – and the variables chosen to characterize them (Iba, 2013; Siegfried, 2014). Agent-based models must specify the following types of components: one or more agents, the phenomenological environment in which the agents exist and interact, the agents' behavioral strategies or rules for interaction, and the global network which the system is embedded in and which affects all agents' interactions. These components are defined by their variable properties or attributes, which is also how the model specifies variations in their states at any time (Byrne & Callaghan, 2014).

Data collection is an important part of this step, and usually several hypotheses are needed to specify what data are essential to the question or problem being addressed (Railsback & Grimm, 2012). Modelers can start top-down and ask questions such as: What processes and structures have a strong influence on the phenomena of interest? Are these factors independent or interacting? Are they affected by other important factors? Whatever technique used to outline the preliminary model, this task has to combine existing knowledge and understanding of the real systems that are being abstracted through this method. For instance, a preliminary model of a language community developed to simulate language use and interactions must draw on data that reference real system information about the agents and their rules for interaction, the environment, etc.

BARRETEAU AND SMAJGL (2014: 244–246) ACKNOWLEDGE THE DIVERSITY OF DATA ELICITATION METHODS AVAILABLE TO EMPIRICAL AGENT-BASED MODELERS

Clearly, model development faces always constraints. There is no situation in which everything a model requires can be sourced from the empirical situation at a reasonable cost. Further, the modelling process is always implemented with a particular focus, which emerges from the modelling goal. This focus translates in a prioritization of some data needs. ... Primary data can be collected by:

Expert knowledge
Literature review
Participant observation
Focus group
Lab experiment
Survey
Expert workshops
Interviews
Databases
Role playing games
Field experiments

Once a preliminary conceptual model has been brainstormed, modelers *articulate a model* that is a detailed and formalized description of the entities in the model, their variables and attributes (Castellani & Rajaram, 2012; Rajaram & Castellani, 2012). Producing and updating this formal model is essential for the entire modeling process. In order for it to be translated unambiguously into computer code in the next step, the model formulation has to be complete and explicit regarding each and every element and aspect of the model (Railsback & Grimm, 2012). Two additional aspects that remain to be specified here are the model's temporal and spatial scales. The temporal scale of a formal model refers to the temporal window that is represented (i.e. the duration of simulation) and how the passage of time is simulated (i.e. using discrete time steps). If the model happens to be spatially explicit, for example in modeling the use of urban space or patterns of physical movement, then the total size or extent of the space must be described. These models can represent spatial information as discrete (i.e. broken into distinct areas within which characteristics do not vary) or continuous (i.e. varying continuously over distance).

The actual *implementation of the model* is often the most technical, usually because it requires software packages that use programming language (e.g. Ascape, EcoLab, MASON, NetLogo, the SACS Toolkit, SWARM, Repast). Implementing a model requires careful prior thought about the model's schedule. A 'schedule' in modeling refers to the sequence of actions the agents in the model are programed to execute, and the order they are executed in (Iba, 2013; Railsback & Grimm, 2012). For example, in order to implement a model that is designed to simulate the intergroup processes within a community, the software algorithm needs a stepwise plan or schedule of various agents interacting and transacting based on the information they have and any updates to the environment or rules under which they are operating. The technical tools used to execute a model require some knowledge of computer code, and while those details are outside the scope of this chapter, accessible sources of information on these open-source software packages can be explored in the annotated references.

A good rule of thumb is to begin this cycle of implementing the model with the simplest model possible, and to gradually develop understanding while iterating through the cycle (Grimm *et al.*, 2014; Jackson *et al.*, 2017). In this way, exploring the consequences of the absolute minimum number of agents and assumptions, and listing other elements and assumptions to be checked as the model is run, allows the model simulation process to suggest what is important as assumptions are updated and parsimony is reached (Siegfried, 2014). This type of iterative simulation of models is particularly useful to investigate the empirically optimum solutions to system behavior and emergent outcomes (Castellani & Rajaram, 2012; Rajaram & Castellani, 2012).

RAILSBACK AND GRIMM (2012: 273–274) ON THE ULTIMATE USE OF AGENT-BASED MODELS FOR RESEARCH:

Understanding is not produced by an ABM automatically; just building a model does not solve the problem it is intended for. Instead, we need to work hard to understand why a model system behaves in a certain way under certain circumstances. The ultimate goal of modeling is to transfer our understanding of the model system to the real system....

Analysis happens throughout the modeling cycle: we analyze early versions of a model and its submodels to improve their formulations and designs, and we do pattern-oriented analysis to develop theory for agent behaviors and to calibrate the model. Modeling and model analysis cannot be separated; we need to analyze and try to understand what a model does all the time.

Many more technical aspects can be added to a model (Grimm *et al.*, 2014; Railsback & Grimm, 2012). Among others these include considerations such as the *execution order*, the decision to randomly shuffle agents' actions or give some agents advantages or disadvantages in the model implementation; *bias*, the decision to program behavioral tendencies into agents' interactions or their choice architecture; *sensing*, the information that agents are given or have, which often determines the ability of those agents to respond and adapt to the environment and to other agents, and how they obtain that information; *updating*, the decision when to recalibrate the environment as agents affect it so that further iterations of the model incorporate a different environment. As implementation variables, these should be seen as additional considerations that might add sophistication and detail to a given model, but they are not meaningful parameters in isolation (Iba, 2013; Siegfried, 2014).

Finally, the model needs *stopping rules* to specify when the model is done or its temporal resolution occurs. For some models the stopping rule comes from the temporal scale by default. If a model is asked to simulate a year-long period of language development for an individual, then the model will halt after the time steps run out. However, other criteria can be used to stop models. For instance, a model can be specified to run until some particular condition occurs or until a certain pattern emerges. This should, obviously, be closely aligned with the question or problem formulated at the outset (Castellani & Hafferty, 2009; Smajgl & Barreteau, 2014).

Example Study

In their paper on the speed of adoption of eco-innovations, Zhang *et al.* (2011) demonstrated how ABM can be used to examine the interdependencies of key players in the automotive industry: manufacturers, consumers and governmental agencies. Their initial assumption was that eco-innovations, such as alternative-fuel vehicles, do not follow a typical diffusion of innovation curve because of long take-off times and discontinuities in overall adoption patterns.

They were curious which mechanisms might increase diffusion of eco-innovations and set out to model the interactions between the agents in this marketplace, each operating under unique optimization goals: consumers are interested in maximizing the utility of an alternative-fuel vehicle but also want to minimize its cost; manufacturers, on the other hand, want to maximize their profits; the priority of governmental agencies is to maximize the social or ecological benefits.

Drawing on consumer preference data, manufacturing cost structure data and environmental change data, the modelers simulated several mechanisms considered important for the rate of adoption of alternative-fuel vehicles: these included technology push, market pull and regulatory push. To this model they added parameter settings for the vehicles produced (e.g. vehicle fuel type, engine power, fuel efficiency, price markup from manufacturing cost) and other information that would add detail to each agent's optimization goals (e.g. regulatory targets, consumers' domain-specific knowledge, word-of-mouth effects).

Simulation results were run until all agents had reached equilibrium toward their optimization goals (i.e. 20–40 model iterations). This model displayed curious interdependencies between manufacturer decision processes and the consumer decision process and showed that demand for eco-innovations such as alternative-fuel vehicles is downward sloping as price increases. The model also supported the idea that technology push is an important mechanism for speeding up the diffusion of eco-innovation. Market pull, in this case, word of mouth, also had a positive impact on the diffusion of eco-innovation by decreasing consumers' preference for fuel-inefficient vehicles. Additionally, word of mouth led to a higher willingness to pay for alternative-fuel vehicles, which demonstrated that the perceived value of eco-innovations increases through word of mouth. Surprisingly, Zhang *et al.*'s (2011) model found that a regulatory push that focuses on regulating the manufacturers' side of things (i.e. government fuel economy mandates) led to a decrease in diffusion of eco-innovation because market share for fuel-inefficient vehicles increased.

This study by Zhang *et al.* (2011) illustrates the utility of ABM for examining the underlying interactions in a system and for achieving a clearer understanding of some of the system-level causal effects of such interactions. While this is only one illustrative example of ABM in action, hundreds more examples can be found – along with the relevant code and accompanying visual output of models – at the OpenABM website (www.comses.net).

Annotated readings

Railsback, S.F. and Grimm, V. (2012) *Agent-Based and Individual-Based Modeling: A Practical Introduction.* Princeton, NJ: Princeton University Press.

This book is designed for the reader with little-to-no expertise in ABM and provides adequate guidance to build and run agent-based models. Using the software platform NetLogo, chapters introduce the reader to modeling concepts and conceptual aspects of how to design ABMs, all the way through how to program and analyze models. Worked examples are provided, which mainly relate to ecological and geographical systems – the two authors' fields of expertise. Each chapter ends with practical modeling exercises, which increase in challenge as the book progresses.

Iba, H. (2013) *Agent-Based Modeling and Simulation with SWARM*. Boca Raton, FL: CRC Press.

Using an impressive variety of illustrative examples, this book introduces the reader to SWARM, a multi-agent simulation library developed at the Santa Fe Institute. Although pre-existing knowledge of either Java or Objective-C programming languages is recommended to apply the models presented, this book is an entertaining read even for those with only a basic understanding of modeling.

Siegfried, R. (2014) *Modeling and Simulation of Complex Systems: A Framework for Efficient Agent-Based Modeling and Simulation*. Wiesbaden: Springer.

Based on the doctoral dissertation of the author, this book reads more like a grand tour of ABM methods and techniques. Early chapters present theoretical background and historical developments, contrasting ABM with closely related templates such as object-oriented modeling and individual-based modeling. The second half of the book outlines the building blocks for a domain-general framework for ABM termed GRAMS – a General Reference Model for Agent-based Modeling and Simulation. This is a book for the intermediate reader.

Smajgl, A. and Barreteau, O. (eds) (2014) *Empirical Agent-Based Modelling: Challenges and Solutions*. New York: Springer.

This edited collection features contributions that showcase examples of ABM in use. These examples are related to topics such as individuals' work-life, social group dynamics, agricultural dilemmas, tourism movements, ecosystem changes, electricity grid use and marketing tactics. While the editors of this volume admit that 'there is no set of rules that holds independent from the modelling situations' (Smajgl & Barreteau, 2014: vii), their aim is to provide a generic framework that more or less standardizes ABM in empirical (i.e. data-driven) situations. This volume would benefit an intermediate to advanced reader.

References

Al-Hoorie, A.H. (2015) Human agency: Does the beach ball have free will? In Z. Dörnyei, P.D. MacIntyre and A. Henry (eds) *Motivational Dynamics in Language Learning* (pp. 55–72). Bristol: Multilingual Matters.

Barreteau, O. and Smajgl, A. (2014) Designing empirical agent-based models: An issue of matching data, technical requirements and stakeholders expectations. In A. Smajgl and O. Barreteau (eds) *Empirical Agent-Based Modelling: Challenges and Solutions* (pp. 239–249). New York: Springer.

Byrne, D. and Callaghan, G. (2014) *Complexity Theory and the Social Sciences: The State of the Art*. New York: Routledge.

Castellani, B. and Hafferty, F. (2009) *Sociology and Complexity Science: A New Field of Inquiry*. Berlin: Springer.

Castellani, B. and Rajaram, R. (2012) Case-based modeling and the SACS Toolkit: A mathematical outline. *Computational and Mathematical Organization Theory* 18, 153–174. doi:10.1007/s10588-012-9114-1

Grimm, V., Augusiak, J., Focks, A., Frank, B., Gabsi, F., Johnston, A., Liu, C., Martin, B.T., Meli, M., Radchuk, V., Thorbek, P. and Railsback, S.F. (2014) Towards better modelling and decision support: Documenting model development, testing, and analysis using TRACE. *Ecological Modeling* 280, 129–139. doi:10.1016/j.ecolmodel. 2014.01.018

Helbing, D. (2010) *Quantitative Sociodynamics: Stochastic Methods and Models of Social Interaction Processes* (2nd edn). Berlin: Springer.

Helbing, D. (2012) *Social Self-Organization: Agent-Based Simulations and Experiments to Study Emergent Social Behavior.* Berlin: Springer.

Hiver, P. and Al-Hoorie, A.H. (2016) A 'dynamic ensemble' for second language research: Putting complexity theory into practice. *The Modern Language Journal* 100, 741–756. doi:10.1111/modl.12347

Iba, H. (2013) *Agent-Based Modeling and Simulation with SWARM.* Boca Raton, FL: CRC Press.

Jackson, J.C., Rand, D., Lewis, K., Norton, M. and Gray, K. (2017) Agent-based modeling: A guide for social psychologists. *Social Psychological and Personality Science* 8 (4), 387–395. doi:10.1177/1948550617691100

Larsen-Freeman, D. (2019) On language learner agency: A complex dynamic systems theory perspective. *The Modern Language Journal* 103 (s), 61–79. doi:10.1111/modl.12536

Macy, M. and Willer, R. (2002) From factors to actors: Computational sociology and agent-based modeling. *Annual Review of Sociology* 28, 143–166.

Railsback, S.F. and Grimm, V. (2012) *Agent-Based and Individual-Based Modeling: A Practical Introduction.* Princeton, NJ: Princeton University Press.

Rajaram, R. and Castellani, B. (2012) Modeling complex systems macroscopically: Case/agent-based modeling, synergetics, and the continuity equation. *Complexity* 18, 8–17. doi:10.1002/cplx.21412

Siegfried, R. (2014) *Modeling and Simulation of Complex Systems: A Framework for Efficient Agent-Based Modeling and Simulation.* Wiesbaden: Springer.

Smajgl, A. and Barreteau, O. (eds) (2014) *Empirical Agent-Based Modelling: Challenges and Solutions.* New York: Springer.

Valsiner, J., Molenaar, P., Lyra, M. and Chaudhary, N. (eds) (2009) *Dynamic Process Methodology in the Social and Developmental Sciences.* Dordrecht: Springer.

Zhang, T., Gensler, S. and Garcia, R. (2011) A study of the diffusion of alternative fuel vehicles: An agent-based modeling approach. *The Journal of Product Innovation Management* 28, 152–168. doi:10.1111/j.1540-5885.2011.00789.x

8 Retrodictive Qualitative Modeling

Overview

This chapter provides an overview of retrodictive qualitative modeling (RQM). RQM is an investigative framework inspired by the conceptual work of social complexivist David Byrne, and first proposed to applied linguistics researchers by Dörnyei (2014). The purpose of RQM is to study how complex, attractor-governed patterns emerge from dynamic, self-organized mechanisms of development. Like many of the research designs that lend themselves particularly well to complexity, RQM can be categorized as a case-based research template that takes complex systems as the case or unit of analysis (Byrne, 2013; van Geert & Steenbeek, 2014). Given this complex unit of analysis, there is a built-in focus on context, temporal change and multicausality in RQM.

At its core, retrodiction is an approach to researching complex dynamic phenomena that starts from an emergent outcome of interest and progresses backward, which might at first sound like an oxymoron, to infer how that reality came about. Tracing backwards from 'what is' to 'what was' explains the prefix 'retro-' in its name (Byrne, 2010). This contrasts other analytic methods with a more variable-centric approach that look forward and attempt to empirically forecast what patterned states will come about or generate forward-pointing accounts of what might happen (Byrne & Callaghan, 2014). RQM reverses this sequence. It begins by identifying the outcomes or attractor states that exist for a domain of interest, and then progresses back to determine the developmental process that brought these about. As an example from the domain of language education, a researcher might begin by observing and identifying salient group or individual learning outcomes in a compulsory class of instructed second language (L2) learners, and then examining through relevant data how those outcomes observed in the instructional setting came to be.

The name retrodictive qualitative modeling is a slight misnomer as it is, in fact, a mixed/multi-method research template, not an exclusively qualitative one, and one that does not rely on formal modeling. However, the logic of RQM is fairly straightforward: that working backward (i.e. retrodicting) from complex, dynamic outcome patterns is necessary to pinpoint the dynamic and situated processes that led to those particular states, and that this can be accomplished with each subsequent research phase building on the design of previous phases. The RQM template, as outlined by Dörnyei (2014), is a step-wise sequence of functional procedures that begins by identifying qualitatively distinct outcomes ('Q') that a system has settled into and then inductively collecting evidence moving backward ('R') to arrive at a model of the developmental process ('M') that brought about these outcomes (Dörnyei, 2014). The aim of RQM is to identify the typical and prominent outcomes of some area of action or topic of interest and then to explore the multicausal processes (also known as 'signature dynamics') that make each of these attractor states and their developmental trajectories unique.

BYRNE (2013: 218) REFLECTS ON WHAT IS NEEDED TO DEVELOP TRANSFERABLE KNOWLEDGE OF A COMPLEX SOCIAL WORLD:

The notion of a single way in which outcomes can be generated has to be abandoned because we must recognize, as the rather strange English expression puts it, there is more than one way to skin a cat. When we intervene in complex systems, we have to recognize that the same outcome may be generated in more than one way. So we have to find methods of identifying causal mechanisms, methods that can cope not only with complex causation, but also with multiple causation.

RQM has found most traction in research related to the psycho-social aspects of language learning and language teaching (Chan *et al.*, 2015; Hiver, 2017). Outside of applied linguistics, some complexity scholars working in various social sciences and their sub-disciplines have recommended this retrodictive framework as the preferred alternative to adopting more mathematical modeling procedures from the parent complexity sciences (see e.g. Byrne, 2009, 2011; Larsen-Freeman & Cameron, 2008). We recommend Dörnyei (2014) as our readers' first source of information on RQM; however, once the underlying logic and its accompanying moves are understood, a passing familiarity with longitudinal data elicitation and analysis would probably be enough to make this template practical for many of our readers.

Research Questions

Prediction is the inference of future observations from current data. Retrodiction, on the other hand, is the extrapolation of present data to observations of the past. In a complex system, emergence often rules out establishing precise future outcomes without referencing the system's past because general laws cannot be observed independent of a specific history (Byrne, 2013). Making matters even more indeterminate is the potential of agency in the social sciences (Al-Hoorie, 2015; Larsen-Freeman, 2019). However, if things are indeterminate, how can any useable knowledge be developed about the complex causal outcomes and processes we observe in the world around us? How can sensible forward-pointing claims be established along the lines of 'if we do this, then that will happen'? Such aspects must, inevitably, be part of a coherent programme of applied linguistics research (Zoltán Dörnyei, 15 January 2016, personal communication).

DÖRNYEI (2014: 89) RECOMMENDS THAT RQM BE SEEN AS A METHOD FOR COMBINING SYSTEMATICITY IN RESEARCH WITH A SENSITIVITY FOR COMPLEXITY:

All is not bad news, though, for the dynamic systems researcher. Although in dynamic systems we cannot predict the behaviour of the system with certainty, the essence of the proposed RQM approach is that we can understand salient patterns – or essential underlying mechanisms – associated with typical system outcomes. And even though we cannot generalise such signature dynamics from one situation to another – or even from one time phase of a situation to the next – the identified patterns are fundamental enough to be useful in understanding the dynamics of a range of other situations. ... RQM offers a research template for deriving essential dynamic moves from idiosyncratic situations in a systematic manner. It is an attempt to generate abstractions that help to describe how social systems work without reducing those systems to simplistic representations – it is therefore an attempt to detect and define higher order patterns that are systematic within and across certain classes of complex systems.

RQM helps us to make progress in resolving this issue by thinking not about causes of change in complex systems first, but about complex outcomes and the nature of effects. Once outcomes and effects are at least partly understood, the way forward, as Byrne (2011) suggests, is to focus backward on the descriptions of systems' development through time or represented as an account of systems' moving into and out of stability as they change across time. Here, the type of research questions that RQM suggests are those focused more on a historical, past-time conception of evidence for the present. Once such evidence is apparent, research can then be extended to the possibility of prospective explanation (i.e. probabilistic predictions) in retrospective historical terms (Byrne & Callaghan, 2014). Example research questions might include:

- What emergent outcomes are possible for a system? Why these and not others?

- What is a system doing right now, and why?
- How did a system come to be what it is right now, where it is right now, and doing what it is right now?
- What sets of similar cases and factor(s) produce different outcomes?
- What sets of different cases and factor(s) produce similar outcomes?
- How has a system adapted and changed itself to reach its current outcome or state?
- How can past trajectories be established?
- What contingencies are at play in system change? What causes combine to produce what effects?
- What causal account can be developed to understand how the system got to where it is?
- What mode of projection into the future can observers rely on?

Technical Features

Retrodiction allows researchers to tell how a system came to be the kind of thing it is now, and can be thought of as a 'mode of inference in which events are explained by postulating (and identifying) the mechanisms which are capable of producing them' (Sayer, 1992: 107). These 'retroductive' techniques, as they are known in the research tradition of other social sciences, originate in the search for complex and contingent causality (Downward & Mearman, 2007). A good number of complex-ivists, though by no means all, would acknowledge that the hunt for a persuasive and nuanced causal account of system outcomes is a necessary objective of research (see also Chapter 3) that aims to both explain observable phenomena and be useful (Byrne & Callaghan, 2014). The dilemma in individual-level, case-focused research is how to generate knowledge from such units of analysis that has potential to be extended beyond that specific case (Lowie & Verspoor, 2019). Using retrodiction as the basis for research design allows scholars to explore what complex systems are and what they do, as well as how they became what they are. This is the goal of RQM, to better represent global outcomes and processes of change through an understanding of how that change is produced.

DAVID BYRNE (2011: 23, 47) MAKES NO BONES ABOUT THE IMPORTANCE OF CAUSAL ACCOUNTS IN HUMAN AND SOCIAL RESEARCH:

If we are interested in cause we have to have an understanding of effect, and effects are to be understood in terms of descriptions of system states in relation to stability or radical change.

Note the unapologetic emphasis on the pursuit of causality outlined here. As Danermark et al have asserted: 'The explanation of social phenomena by revealing the causal mechanisms that produce them is the fundamental task of social research' (2002, p 1). Of course description – the presentation of coherent accounts of what is – is an absolutely necessary precursor of the elaboration of causality, but without some sort of understanding of causality we have no licence for intervention in order to engender change. In other words we need a causal story in order to act. ... When we move into the realm of the social we move into a complex world with multiple and contingent processes of causation, even in relation to clearly defined outcomes.

The initial steps of RQM entail identifying the system outcomes or states that will be the object of investigation (take, for example, an outcome of *democracy*), and purposively sampling individuals or systems (i.e. cases) that are typical of the outcomes or prototypes of a pattern. It is important to remember that these patterned outcomes are finite in number and correspond to the salient attractor states in which a system settles down over time in the state space (Hiver, 2015a).

The next step requires the purposive sampling of systems or cases that are typical of the established outcomes or are prototypes of a pattern (think, for instance, of countries or governments typical of the *democratic* outcome). Data elicitation techniques are then used to explore the outcome of interest, through detailed description of exemplars, and to elaborate on the characteristics of its most prototypical cases (what, for example, makes *democratic* nations unique from other models of governance?). This is often accomplished through combining a range of data sources from conventional focus groups or interviews, to self-report surveys or other observational types of data. Since it is problem oriented in the broadest sense of the word, retrodiction in fact requires a combination of qualitative and quantitative research methods to transcend the use of discipline-specific methods (Downward & Mearman, 2006).

A system's outcomes alone represent only part of the picture, and some would argue not necessarily the most interesting part. This is why identifying and describing the underlying components of the system is only half the job (Hiver & Al-Hoorie, 2016). In the third step of RQM, developmental trajectories are traced through data with a time series element (see Chapter 14) in order to unravel the unique signature dynamics (i.e. the robust causal mechanisms within a system) and build an understanding of how the system ended up in that outcome (e.g. attempt to unravel the process by which a country becomes *democratic*). Finally, once these developmental dynamics are better understood, the phenomenological manifestation of the outcome of interest (i.e. what it looks like and how it impacts other systems) is explored analytically.

BYRNE AND UPRICHARD'S (2011: 112) POSITION, ONE
WE FULLY AGREE WITH, IS THAT RETRODICTION
OF CAUSES CAN PROVIDE A BASIS FOR ACTING AND
INTERVENING IN THE COMPLEX SOCIAL WORLD:

The causal narrative that is sought is one that not only helps to explain
how something came to be as it is, but about the extent to which it is possible to produce desired future change. This may be an ambitious task,
but one that is both worthwhile and possible. It is really rather important
to recognize that a causal narrative is not exclusively textual in a conventional sense. Time series of numbers should be understood as narratives
just as much as any textual form. ... Specifically, useful description for
our purposes are those that help to explain why something and particularly any complex system has come to be the kind of thing it is and not
something other than what it is. In other words, the descriptions achieve
retroductive adequacy; they act as accounts that stand up as explanations
for the state of a system and are based on careful reconstructions of the
history of the system. ... We want to move from retroduction as 'a mode
of inference in which events are explained by postulating (and identifying)
mechanisms which are capable of producing them' (Sayer, 1992, 107) to
retrodiction as a mode of being able to understand what might happen
and how to act in order to change what might happen using knowledge of
how something came to be as it is. Our aim, then, is to think about modes
of inquiry that not only try to explain what has happened, how any system has come to be as it is, but also through informed purposive action,
how to intervene in order to produce a desired future state of a system.

The most well-known scientific work developed based on a logic of
retrodiction is Darwin's *Origin of Species* (Byrne & Callaghan, 2014).
This example may strike our readers as surprising, and yet this scholarly
work was in fact based entirely on a retroductive consideration which
saw Darwin work backwards from an enormous range of qualitative and
descriptive evidence to build an evidence-based case for biological and
ecological system change. Darwin's trajectories were the contingent evolution of species toward the forms he could identify from the observations
of natural history around him or of the fossil record. As this example illustrates, RQM works backward in order to establish configurations and
causal pathways that show parsimonious descriptions of what complex
combinations are at work in guiding systems toward certain outcomes.

Example Study

Hiver (2017) conducted a study of the motivation, performance
and well-being of second/foreign (L2) language teachers that illustrates
how RQM can be used. Hiver wanted to investigate how L2 teachers

maintained their professional equilibrium and instructional effective-ness despite the high-pressure environments they work in and the many conflicting factors their work requires them to deal with. Initial work (Hiver, 2015b) provided evidence that teachers developed a superordi-nate psychological quality – termed 'teacher immunity' – in response to classroom practice-specific conflicts. Drawing on this exploratory work, Hiver showed that teacher immunity develops into dual-natured protec-tive configuration – at times the outcome that emerges may serve a nec-essary safeguarding purpose that allows teachers to remain committed and to thrive, but in other configurations it may threaten the individual's functioning and become a professional liability. Hiver, therefore, set out to examine these two dynamic outcome patterns (i.e. the produc-tive teacher immunity outcome and the maladaptive teacher immunity outcome).

Using RQM, the researcher set out to first identify and analyze the typical and salient outcomes of language teacher immunity. Casing teachers as the complex system in which self-organized change occurs, the following question was the point of departure:

RQ 1: What are the typical outcomes of teacher immunity that emerge in L2 practitioners?

The researcher used a robust two-step identification process by trian-gulating exploratory focus group data (from a variety of teachers and teacher educators) with quantitative questionnaire data of a larger sample of L2 practitioners to validate the outcome categories and charac-teristics both theoretically and phenomenologically. Through this multi-method triangulation, the researcher identified precise teacher immunity archetypes in four emergent categories:

(1) *productively immunized teachers* (i.e. individuals possessing a robust, beneficial form of teacher immunity);
(2) *maladaptively immunized teachers* (i.e. individuals possessing a rigid, counterproductive form of teacher immunity);
(3) *immunocompromised teachers* (i.e. individuals who have not devel-oped any coherent form of teacher immunity);
(4) *partially immunized teachers* (i.e. individuals who have developed half-way features of teacher immunity).

Once these principal archetypes were identified, the researcher then shifted attention to examining the interacting components and the main underlying dynamic patterns of development – or the system's signature dynamics – that produced these observed outcomes. This was done by selecting the three most representative respondents for each outcome and conducting in-depth, retrospective interviews with a time-series element. The research question in focus was:

RQ 2: What were the developmental processes that produced these archetypes of teacher immunity?

Using this somewhat conventional source of data, the researcher was able to trace back (i.e. to retrodict) the global developmental process that all four archetypes followed in a self-organized sequence of four stages – triggering, linking, realignment and stabilization. The researcher's more fine-grained analysis also identified the complex causal mechanisms that led these systems to produce individual trajectories or pathways of development for particular outcomes and archetypes.

Finally, the researcher examined the way in which these emergent outcomes manifested in practitioners' emotions and beliefs, instructional practice, and commitment and persistence within their instructional settings by focusing on this research question:

RQ 3: How do the various outcomes of teacher immunity manifest phenomenologically?

The researcher was able to show that teacher immunity manifested itself in the motivations, cognitions and behavior of various archetypes. Teacher immunity implicitly guided teachers' choices of action and responses to the contextual demands of their teaching. Furthermore, teachers' self-images, their persistence toward goals and their self-efficacy were all tied to specific outcomes of teacher immunity. The researcher thus concluded that teacher immunity enables teachers to withstand conflict, draw on reserves of motivation and sustain productivity in their daily practice.

Annotated readings

Dörnyei, Z. (2014) Researching complex dynamic systems: 'Retrodictive qualitative modelling' in the language classroom. *Language Teaching* 47, 80–91. doi:10.1017/S0261444811000516

This is Dörnyei's original text, based on a plenary presented to applied linguistics scholars, about using this unconventional backward-pointing logic in research designs for studying L2 classrooms. It provides a broad rationale for adopting this logic and should be newcomers' first source of information on RQM in the field. An engaging first-read.

Hiver, P. (2015a) Attractor states. In Z. Dörnyei, P.D. MacIntyre and A. Henry (eds) *Motivational Dynamics in Language Learning* (pp. 20–28). Bristol: Multilingual Matters.

This is a brief and accessible read on the nature of system outcomes – termed 'attractor states' –that are complex and emergent. Because RQM takes settled states and system outcomes as its point of departure, this conceptual chapter provides informative background information that is useful for identifying outcomes and patterns that might be worthwhile researching. No prior knowledge on the topic from complexity and dynamic systems theory (CDST) is assumed in this chapter.

Byrne, D. and Callaghan, G. (2014) *Complexity Theory and the Social Sciences: The State of the Art*. New York: Routledge.

The authors, two social complexivists with a knack for taking big ideas and making them accessible to newcomers to complexity, lay out a fairly comprehensive and technical case for an innovative causal account of phenomena in the social sciences that is based on a critical realist perspective and 'retroductive' evidence. This text includes definitions and historical perspectives, as well as examples from social science research. An authoritative but still reader-friendly source on a range of complexity research topics.

Downward, P. and Mearman, A. (2007) Retroduction as mixed-methods triangulation in economic research: Reorienting economics into social science. *Cambridge Journal of Economics* 31, 77–99. doi:10.1093/cje/bel009

The authors of this paper argue that mixed-methods triangulation can be understood as the methodological manifestation of 'retroduction'. They drill down to the conceptual origins of this logic of inference and situate retroductive methods of complexity research within a critical realist perspective of science. While their background is economics, this paper has lessons for all social sciences. Recommended for the advanced reader in CDST.

References

Al-Hoorie, A.H. (2015) Human agency: Does the beach ball have free will? In Z. Dörnyei, P.D. MacIntyre and A. Henry (eds) *Motivational Dynamics in Language Learning* (pp. 55–72). Bristol: Multilingual Matters.

Byrne, D. (2009) Complex realists and configurational approaches to cases: A radical synthesis. In D. Byrne and C.C. Ragin (eds) *The SAGE Handbook of Case-Based Methods* (pp. 101–112). Thousand Oaks, CA: SAGE.

Byrne, D. (2010) Comparison, diversity and complexity. In P. Cilliers and R. Preiser (eds) *Complexity, Difference, and Identity* (pp. 61–75). Dordrecht: Springer.

Byrne, D. (2011) *Applying Social Science*. Bristol: Policy Press.

Byrne, D. (2013) Evaluating complex social interventions in a complex world. *Evaluation* 19, 217–228. doi:10.1177/1356389013495617

Byrne, D. and Uprichard, E. (2012) Useful complex causality. In H. Kincaid (ed.) *The Oxford Handbook of Philosophy of Social Science* (pp. 109–129). Oxford: Oxford University Press.

Byrne, D. and Callaghan, G. (2014) *Complexity Theory and the Social Sciences: The State of the Art*. New York: Routledge.

Chan, L., Dörnyei, Z. and Henry, A. (2015) Learner archetypes and signature dynamics in the language classroom: A retrodictive qualitative modelling approach to studying L2 motivation. In Z. Dörnyei, P.D. MacIntyre and A. Henry (eds) *Motivational Dynamics in Language Learning* (pp. 238–259). Bristol: Multilingual Matters.

Dörnyei, Z. (2014) Researching complex dynamic systems: 'Retrodictive qualitative modelling' in the language classroom. *Language Teaching* 47, 80–91. doi:10.1017/S0261444811000516

Downward, P. and Mearman, A. (2007) Retroduction as mixed-methods triangulation in economic research: Reorienting economics into social science. *Cambridge Journal of Economics* 31, 77–99. doi:10.1093/cje/bel009

Hiver, P. (2015a) Attractor states. In Z. Dörnyei, P.D. MacIntyre and A. Henry (eds) *Motivational Dynamics in Language Learning* (pp. 20–28). Bristol: Multilingual Matters.

Hiver, P. (2015b) Once burned, twice shy: The dynamic development of system immunity in language teachers. In Z. Dörnyei, P.D. MacIntyre and A. Henry (eds) *Motivational Dynamics in Language Learning* (pp. 214–237). Bristol: Multilingual Matters.

Hiver, P. (2017) Tracing the signature dynamics of language teacher immunity: A ret-rodictive qualitative modeling study. *The Modern Language Journal* 101, 669–699. doi:10.1111/modl.12433

Hiver, P. and Al-Hoorie, A.H. (2016) A dynamic ensemble for second language research: Putting complexity theory into practice. *The Modern Language Journal* 100, 741–756. doi:10.1111/modl.12347

Larsen-Freeman, D. (2019) On language learner agency: A complex dynamic systems theory perspective. *The Modern Language Journal* 103 (s), 61–79. doi:10.1111/modl.12536

Larsen-Freeman, D. and Cameron, L. (2008) Research methodology on language devel-opment from a complex systems perspective. *The Modern Language Journal* 92, 200–213. doi:10.1111/j.1540-4781.2008.00714.x

Lowie, W. and Verspoor, M. (2019) Individual differences and the ergodicity problem. *Language Learning* 69 (s1), 184–206. doi:10.1111/lang.12324

Sayer, A. (1992) *Method in Social Science*. London: Routledge.

van Geert, P. and Steenbeek, H. (2014) The good, the bad and the ugly? The dynamic inter-play between educational practice, policy and research. *Complicity: An International Journal of Complexity and Education* 11, 22–39. doi:10.29173/cmplct22962

9 Social Network Analysis

Overview

In earlier chapters of this book, we proposed that systems are the basic structural building blocks of the complex social world. Many of the methods we introduce in our other chapters are premised on this understanding. Extending this further, networks can be thought of as the architectural superstructure within which any system-in-context is embedded (Kadushin, 2012). A network – the kind we are interested in for social network analysis (SNA) methods – is a multi-node hub made up of interconnected systems, their relationships and the processes that together form the foundational web of the complex social world (Knoke & Yang, 2008). This definition is useful for researchers who aim to study complex and dynamic systems because any system of interest is simply one of many nodes embedded within this interconnected web.

Social network methods were born from the work of social anthropologists and sociologists, circa the early-to-mid 1900s, who developed notions of social structure using creative textile metaphors such as *fabric*, *web*, *intersection*, *texture*, *distance*, *density* and *interwoven relations* (Prell, 2012). These metaphors gradually became formalized in social network theory toward the 1970s as more technical methods and specialist applications emerged from the work of Talcott Parsons, Niklas Luhmann and Jay W. Forrester (Scott, 2017). SNA is now so pervasive that patents even exist related to collecting, analyzing and using network data.

All SNA methods are based on the fundamental assumptions of the importance of relationships between interacting systems or units (Scott & Carrington, 2011). Because of this understanding, SNA requires relational data and expresses its models in terms of relational concepts, information, properties and processes (Yang *et al.*, 2017). As an illustrative example of what we mean by relational data, let us consider a network of multilingual friendships. Each friend is a system in the network with ties to others in the whole. The relationship between two systems is a property of the dyad, a summative value, in this case of two friends, not just one or the other individual. Among other things, these links might be language interactions, behavioral influence, group co-membership, material transactions, transfer of information or personal evaluations of one another (Borgatti *et al.*, 2018). These can all be studied directly with or without reference to the attributes of the individuals involved.

> ### MARSDEN (2005: 8) INTRODUCES THE DIFFERENT SNA DESIGNS DRAWING ON SUCH RELATIONAL DATA:
>
> The broad majority of social network studies use either 'whole-network' or 'egocentric' designs. Whole-network studies examine sets of interrelated objects or actors that are regarded for analytical purposes as bounded social collectives, although in practice network boundaries are often permeable and/or ambiguous. Egocentric studies focus on a focal actor or object and the relationships in its locality. ... The minimal network database consists of one set of objects (also known as actors or nodes) linked by one set of relationships observed at one occasion. ... The matrix representation of this common form of network data is known as a 'who to whom' matrix or a 'sociomatrix'.

In contrast, however, more conventional methods of social research rely mainly on variable analysis through attribute data, and might study questions related to the friends' similarities or differences using such non-relational data. These differences in purpose and emphasis have consequences for the choices that 'networkers' – which is what SNA researchers call themselves – make in choosing a research design, sampling, developing measurements and handling the resulting data. Some of the most central assumptions of social network models and methods are as follows (Kadushin, 2012; Prell, 2012; Wasserman & Faust, 1994):

- individual systems and their behavior(s) are interdependent rather than independent or autonomous;
- relational links between individual systems are interactive pathways through which systems transfer resources (e.g. information, influence) and maintain this interdependence;
- stable (i.e. in equilibrium, but not static or fixed) patterns of relational pathways make up the network structure;
- the network's structural environment provides constraints and opportunities for individual systems' functioning;
- individual systems' functioning feeds back into the relational architecture of the network.

SNA uses visual matrices, information maps and sociograms to represent information about systems and system relationships at the network level. In this regard, they share common elements with concept mapping (see Chapter 6), and some SNA applications add their own sophisticated computational analyses that draw on graph theory. Unlike concept mapping (Chapter 6), however, social network methods focus more broadly on modeling and analyzing the structure (i.e. the networks) that systems exist in and the relational patterns and implications this interconnected network have on systems (see also Mercer, 2015). But like qualitative comparative analysis (Chapter 5) and agent-based modeling (Chapter 6), some SNA applications do require quantitative analyses at later stages though the qualitative element is typically more salient.

Interconnectedness refers to the phenomenological reality of each system being linked and related in some way to all other systems in its global environment (Scott, 2017). Systems are networked if they are bounded together in some phenomenologically real or empirically meaningful way (Carolan, 2014). For example, a social system such as a local community engaged in socio-political activism may be part of a network that includes government institutions, public policymakers and news media drawing attention to these current events. As interconnectedness is an important aspect of complexity and dynamic systems theory (CDST) research, unraveling which systems are networked and how their relationships constitute a coherent whole can form a sophisticated agenda for CDST research drawing on social network methods.

Although SNA's primary emphasis is on the graphic architecture of the systemic networks and their relational structure, multiple levels of analysis are possible. SNA methods place equal importance on what this higher-order structure can reveal about the behavior and functioning of the systems within it (Carolan, 2014). Both levels contain important features that can reveal important structures and processes. This is what SNA scholars refer to as the 'duality of individual and structure' (Hanneman & Riddle, 2005: 90). Given this duality, systemic networks can be used to investigate patterns of interconnectedness and to shed light on system-level issues and model dynamic processes.

Research Questions

We have just seen that SNA has a dual focus on both the structural network that results from 'relations and the implications this structure has on individual or group behavior and attitudes' (Carolan, 2014: 7). As will be clear from the examples in this chapter, SNA is one of the few methods that can be applied equally well to research questions at a variety of levels of analysis (Kadushin, 2012).

At a descriptive level that aims to develop and validate formal models of a network, we could imagine the following questions guiding a line of empirical research:

• Which other systems or actors is a particular system related to in a network?

- Which systems or actors are more influential and less influential within a network?
- What is the nature of the relationships between these systems in the network?
- Based on this network of relations, how does influence spread and information transfer, how are resources exchanged and how does interaction and collaboration come about?
- What structural patterns or architectural features emerge from the relations between systems or actors in a network?
- Given an outcome of interest, at any level, what is the impact of inter-related systems on this phenomenon?
- How do such broad structures change or remain stable over time in a network?

At a more inferential level (in a more general sense) that aims to interpret the utility and outcomes of network models, questions that might lead to productive lines of inquiry include:

- How are networks themselves generated, how do they evolve and how do they exhibit higher-order self-organized outcomes?
- What purpose does, or should, a network serve?
- Can networks be engineered to generate purposefully or are they exclusively spontaneous?
- How do systems within a network adapt and change over time?
- How can change be introduced or control be exerted at the level of links between systems or actors?
- How does overall change come about in networks?
- How do discrete sequences of contact and interaction in dynamic networks influence dynamic processes in the network?
- What does overall network change or change at the system/actor level indicate about the network's functioning?
- What can the existence of two separate networks with similar functioning overall (e.g. similar processes, outcomes), but with key differences in network structure, reveal?
- Conversely, what are the theoretical and practical implications of two networks with similar architectural structure but key differences in the outcomes and processes of network functioning?
- How do sequences of contact and interaction in dynamic networks influence dynamic processes in the network?
- How can temporal changes that impact the functioning and robustness of a network be tracked and forecasted?

These are by no means exhaustive, and nearly any question that relates to associations between multiple systems will be a match with this method (see e.g. Scott & Carrington, 2011).

Technical Features

Earlier in this chapter, we drew a distinction between *relational data* and *attribute data*. Social networks methods use the terms *structural variable* and *composition variable* to refer to these, respectively (Wasserman & Faust, 1994). Let us expand on their relevance to SNA by comparing what these two data types often look like in raw form. In Table 9.1, a case-by-variable dataset presents attribute data of some commonly used demographic variables. These data are of little use for SNA as they contain no relational information (Kadushin, 2012). Instead, network data are either case-by-case data, case-by-affiliation data or some combination of the two. Table 9.2 presents this slightly different picture with case-by-case data. The values shown in this dataset represent the number of friends that each individual has in common with one another – as might be shown on a social networking website/platform.

Relational links can be coded using binaries (e.g. 1 = present; 0 = absent) or values for certain criteria (e.g. intensity, frequency). In this 'simplex' data matrix (Table 9.2) only one relational link is described, but SNA researchers are often interested in multiple kinds of relations that connect systems in a network (aka multiplex data) (Borgatti *et al.*, 2018). A network that represents multiplex data is referred to as a *stacked* network. Multiplex data provide a multifaceted view of how certain relations reinforce or contradict others, though full network data (i.e. maximum information about each system's ties with all other systems) can be difficult and impractical to collect. For this reason, when collecting network data about relations among systems, researchers tend to select only the most relevant possible relations (Hanneman & Riddle, 2005). We return to this later when we take up the issue of boundary specification.

Table 9.1 A data matrix for attribute data

		Variables				
		Age	Gender	Education (years)	Family size	Etc.
Cases	1					
	2					
	3					

Table 9.2 A data matrix for relational data

		Cases				
		1	2	3	4	Etc.
Cases	1	–	3	3	1	
	2	3	–	2	2	
	3	3	2	–	1	
	4	1	2	1	–	

There are several important practical implications of working with relational data, and the first of these relates to the unit of analysis. As we have hinted, in SNA the unit of analysis is not the individual or the local system *per se*, but a unitary collective consisting of a group of individuals or systems and the links between them (Prell, 2012; Yang *et al.*, 2017). SNA develops this information in a representation of points and paths. The points (aka *nodes* or *actors*) represent individuals or systems and their goals or actions. The paths (aka *ties* or *edges*) that run between points tie them together and represent the interactional and causal interdependencies they share. To illustrate this, we could consider a relatively simple sociogram (see Figure 9.1) based on the relational data in the foregoing matrix (Table 9.2) representing a network of friends. In this structure, which is the unit of analysis, each actor represents one friend, and each line linking two nodes is labeled for the number of friends in common. This sociogram can illustrate how information flows from one person to others or how individuals can influence each other based on their shared friendships. In social network theory terminology, the technical term 'actor' helps underscore that with nodes in a network, whatever the system represents (e.g. individuals, communities, groups, organizations, institutions), an element of agency can emerge in complex and often unpredictable ways (Mercer, 2015).

Setting network boundaries for sampling and for data elicitation purposes is an important step if meaningful questions are to be investigated with a network model. Boundary specification entails more than identifying intuitively obvious boundaries of a situation and the systems in context (Carolan, 2014). One common approach to boundary specification, the *positional approach*, is achieved by constructing network nodes based on some *a priori* principle or criterion (Scott, 2017). Others include *event approaches*, based on participation in a given activity, and *relational approaches*, which reflect social connectedness (Marsden,

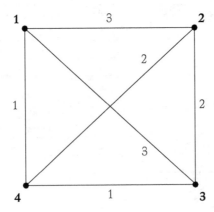

Figure 9.1 Sociogram representing the number of friends shared by individuals

2005). Alternative approaches exist for boundary specification in SNA, all of which attempt to address the need for a theoretically or empirically justified rationale for any including or excluding criteria. These include the *realist approach*, which focuses on actor-set boundaries and membership in the network that is acknowledged by the actors (i.e. systems) in question, and the *nominal approach*, which relies on a theoretically informed choice or is based on the theoretical concerns of the researcher (Wasserman & Faust, 1994).

HANNEMAN AND RIDDLE (2005: 67) WEIGH IN ON THE SOMETIMES BEWILDERING TERMINOLOGY FOR RELATIONS IN SNA:

Social network methods have a vocabulary for describing connectedness and distance that might, at first, seem rather formal and abstract. This is not surprising, as many of the ideas are taken directly from the mathematical theory of graphs. But it is worth the effort to deal with the jargon. The precision and rigor of the definitions allow us to communicate more clearly about important properties of social structures—and often lead to insights that we would not have had if we used less formal approaches.

SNA scholars are in agreement that human and social activities (e.g. learning, creating, teaching, communicating) bring systems into contact with each other – with such contact varying structurally in its value, frequency, duration and direction. These scholars also agree that such interactions are the basis on which relational links are developed between systems (Wasserman & Faust, 1994). With regard to just the dimension of directionality, relations between nodes in a network can be *undirected*, for example between two people standing in the same room who are both receivers; *unidirectional* from one node to another, such as when information is passed on from one entity to another; *symmetric* and mutually reciprocal between nodes, such as when two organizations exchange goods or services; or even *intermediary* in nature when the relationship between two nodes passes first through another node (Kadushin, 2012; Yang *et al.*, 2017). It is clear that many dimensions and forms of relational data can be studied using SNA, and the typography and architecture of each of these relational structures (e.g. in a sociogram) will differ correspondingly.

To illustrate how SNA can help model different relational information, let us consider the concept of *centrality*. Centrality is most often a property of a single node, and it refers to the relational popularity or prominence of a node in the network based on the number of links (aka

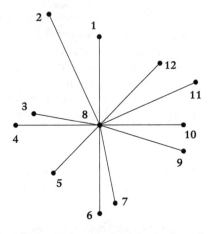

Figure 9.2 Sociogram showing high centrality of a single node

'degrees') it has to other nodes (Everett & Borgatti, 2005). When one node, such as a group leader, is tied to all or nearly all others, that node is said to have high centrality. The opposite would be a node known as an *isolate* that is tied to none, or nearly no others, in a network. Figure 9.2 shows what this might look like in an extreme example of an opinion leader with many followers on social media, none of whom engage in interactions with any others unless the thought leader (node 8) acts as intermediary. The opinion leader could be described as the star attraction within the network (Scott, 2017), and if this were simply one network nested in a larger social media network, we would refer to this sociometric star as a *hub*.

Centrality is not exclusive to individual nodes or actors (Kadushin, 2012); we can also extend this concept to refer to a property of a group of nodes within a network, for instance to model the interactions between colleagues during a meeting or countries in a transnational alliance (Figure 9.3). This network is not only higher in density of relationships, but an additional characteristic is that centrality is distributed and not dependent on a central node when interdependence is balanced throughout such a network. Whereas higher density links result in a more cohesive network – or a cohesive 'cluster' in a portion of the larger network – it is also true that the more distributed the centrality is, the more likely there are to be structural holes, weak ties and isolated nodes (Carolan, 2014; Knoke & Yang, 2008). When this is taken into account, in contrast to the more predictably shaped sociogram (Figure 9.1) representing shared friends, these structures depict very different models of relational information and allow researchers to explore entirely different questions about these systems.

Most networkers think of individuals as being embedded in systems that are embedded in networks that are embedded in other networks

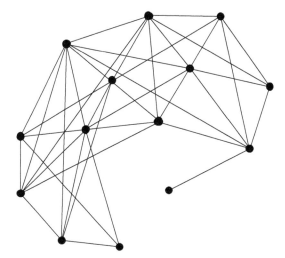

Figure 9.3 Sociogram showing distributed centrality and one isolate

(Borgatti *et al.*, 2018). Network analysts describe such hierarchical or nested structures as *multimodal*. In just one example, say a multilingual setting, individual language users form the first 'mode' embedded within small family groups, a second, in turn, nested in social communities, a third, embedded in nation states and so on. While such multimodal networks hold considerable promise, constructing and making sense of these requires the ability to deal with nested levels of data and analysis. Because of this high bar, many SNA scholars operate under the assumption that their network may constitute a nested structure with other networks, but do not exploit this explicitly for the purposes of research design (Hanneman & Riddle, 2005; Scott, 2017). That is, even though the reality of the human and social world is one where systems reside within other systems that themselves make up larger systems, boundary specification helps make things manageable for the SNA researcher.

Fortunately, SNA is one method of CDST research that has seen adequate, if not widespread, prior use in applied linguistics. A prime example of this is a special issue of the *International Journal of the Sociology of Language*, an early illustration of applying SNA to questions of language development (de Bot & Stoessel, 2002; Wiklund, 2002), language processing (Hulsen *et al.*, 2002), language maintenance (Raschka *et al.*, 2002; Stoessel, 2002) and language competence and use (Smith, 2002). Its most recent applications in the field have been the more formal methods of SNA, for instance in studies on communication perceptions and behaviors (Gallagher, 2019; Gallagher & Robins, 2015).

One exciting recent development from SNA is the study of how networks change over time and the use of simulation to address issues and explore questions in network dynamics. This emergent field, known as dynamic network analysis, uses sophisticated mathematical models – currently still somewhat technical for the non-specialist – to study adaptive and time-dependent networks. Given the promise of these dynamic network analysis methods, it will be interesting to keep a close watch on their applications in fields adjacent to our own and to gauge their utility for studying topics and problems in applied linguistics. Another promising advance with the advent of big data and more powerful and automatized analyses is the ability to model full-network data (aka meta-networks or high-dimensional networks) with thousands of nodes and comprehensive relations in the network. Some visual applications of this can be found simply by running a Google image search of the keywords 'social network analysis'.

Example Study

Gallagher and Robins (2015) designed a study of how networks of communication are constructed in a second language (L2) classroom, and how such relational ties affect learners' willingness to communicate (WTC) in the English for academic purposes (EAP) classroom (see also Gallagher, 2019). Classroom settings such as these present students with many formal and informal opportunities for L2 contact through one-on-one and small-group activities and classroom presentations, and in this context the researchers were interested with whom L2 learners discussed personally important matters. They examined this relational information to compare how networks self-organized between members of the same cultural-linguistic group and among learners with cross-cultural social ties. The researchers hypothesized that learners' L2 WTC would be socially distributed according to relative positions within a social network, and would differ meaningfully between small-group interactions versus large-group interactions.

They sampled 75 EAP students from a pre-sessional (i.e. non-credit bearing) EAP course at a university in England, and reasoned that the EAP course constitutes a relatively well-bounded system of member individuals who interact with each other toward a common goal. Through open recall, students were asked to generate the names of up to 10 individuals with whom they had discussed 'things important to you' in the last two weeks (Gallagher & Robins, 2015: 942). In coding these relational data, intracultural ties were defined as both the respondent and the nominated partner having the same cultural background. Cross-cultural ties were defined as the nominated partner having a cultural background different from the respondent. The researchers also measured respondents' L2 WTC by administering an adapted WTC questionnaire. These multi-item response scales required students to self-report the percentage of time they would choose to initiate L2 communication in various social situations.

Using the XPNet data analysis package, Gallagher and Robins specified the model as having (1) two network tie types simultaneously, in order to look at intracultural versus cross-cultural ties; and (2) directed relations, in which participants nominate or send ties to others directionally. They then specified overall network effects including what baseline tie effects, star effects, triangle effects and two-path effects would look like in their dataset. They chose to further specify interaction effects between network ties and L2 WTC (e.g. sender effects/receiver effects, negative difference effects/positive product effects) in order to examine their research hypotheses. The researchers predicted that:

- L2 WTC would be generally associated with greater network activity;
- large-group L2 WTC would be associated with greater status in the network;
- small-group L2 WTC would be similar across network ties.

Their overall findings showed that group structure was organized predominantly among intracultural ties, but that cross-cultural ties did not appear to demonstrate equivalent self-organizing properties. Along with many detailed findings regarding within-network structure and relational ties (Gallagher & Robins, 2015: 947, 949), their findings illustrate that individuals similar in L2 WTC in one-on-one and small-group settings shared particular intracultural social pockets within the network, and that L2 WTC in large-group and presentation settings was distributed according to popularity/status, though this was limited to participants' intracultural ties. However, they found no support for the notion that participants high in L2 WTC were more active among their network ties in any communication setting.

Annotated readings

Carolan, B. (2014) *Social Network Analysis and Education: Theory, Methods and Applications*. Thousand Oaks, CA: SAGE.

The strength of this book is its ability to relate SNA concepts and practices to the field of educational research. Particularly because it is illustrated with examples and applications on topics adjacent to or least familiar to many in applied linguistics (e.g. communication, group dynamics and group membership, interaction, learning), this book will make much clearer sense than one, say, relating networks to criminology research. It is pitched at a level that is suitable for the intermediate reader and above.

Kadushin, C. (2012) *Understanding Social Networks: Theories, Concepts, and Findings*. Oxford: Oxford University Press.

The accessible style this book is written in may be slightly misleading – it seems almost appropriate for the popular press. However, the level of technical detail is equally impressive, and Kadushin even devotes a chapter to ethics in SNA research. The discussion of terminology and concepts gradually builds up toward 10 master ideas presented in the last chapter, but an impatient reader could just as well begin by reading the coda and then jump back to the start of the book. This book is both a solid introduction to new network-ers and a quality refresher for those already familiar with SNA.

Scott, J. and Carrington, P. (eds) (2011) *The SAGE Handbook of Social Network Analysis*. Thousand Oaks, CA: SAGE.

As regular readers of handbooks about methods or disciplines that we are actively learning about, we authors see them as a one-stop shop for everything we ever wanted to know on unfamiliar topics. This handbook is an excellent illustration, with over 600 pages on fundamental SNA concepts and terms, substantive topics on the many disciplines and thematic areas built on SNA and applications and techniques for every stage and type of SNA research – there is certainly something for every social network analyst at any level of expertise here.

References

Borgatti, S., Everett, M. and Johnson, J. (2018) *Analyzing Social Networks* (2nd edn). Thousand Oaks, CA: SAGE.

Carolan, B. (2014) *Social Network Analysis and Education: Theory, Methods and Applications*. Thousand Oaks, CA: SAGE.

de Bot, K. and Stoessel, S. (2002) Introduction: Language change and social networks. *International Journal of the Sociology of Language* 153, 1–7. doi:10.1515/ijsl.2002.003

Everett, M. and Borgatti, S. (2005) Extending centrality. In P. Carrington, J. Scott and S. Wasserman (eds) *Models and Methods in Social Network Analysis* (pp. 57–76). Cambridge: Cambridge University Press.

Gallagher, H.C. (2019) Social networks and the willingness to communicate: Reciprocity and brokerage. *Journal of Language and Social Psychology* 38 (2), 194–214. doi:10.1177/0261927X18809146

Gallagher, H.C. and Robins, G. (2015) Network statistical models for language learning contexts: Exponential random graph models and willingness to communicate. *Language Learning* 65, 929–962. doi:10.1111/lang.12130

Hanneman, R. and Riddle, M. (2005) *Introduction to Social Network Methods*. See http://faculty.ucr.edu/~hanneman/nettext/Introduction_to_Social_Network_Methods.pdf (accessed 30 June 2019).

Hulsen, M., de Bot, K. and Weltens, B. (2002) Between two worlds. Social networks, language shift, and language processing in three generations of Dutch migrants in New Zealand. *International Journal of the Sociology of Language* 153, 27–52. doi:10.1515/ijsl.2002.004

Kadushin, C. (2012) *Understanding Social Networks: Theories, Concepts, and Findings*. Oxford: Oxford University Press.

Knoke, D. and Yang, S. (2008) *Social Network Analysis* (2nd edn). Thousand Oaks, CA: SAGE.

Marsden, P. (2005) Recent advances in network measurement. In P. Carrington, J. Scott and S. Wasserman (eds) *Models and Methods in Social Network Analysis* (pp. 8–30). Cambridge: Cambridge University Press.

Mercer, S. (2015) Social network analysis and complex dynamic systems. In Z. Dörnyei, P.D. MacIntyre and A. Henry (eds) *Motivational Dynamics in Language Learning* (pp. 73–82). Bristol: Multilingual Matters.

Prell, C. (2012) *Social Network Analysis: History, Theory, and Methodology*. Thousand Oaks, CA: SAGE.

Raschka, C., Wei, L. and Lee, S. (2002) Bilingual development and social networks of British-born Chinese children. *International Journal of the Sociology of Language* 153, 9–25. doi:10.1515/ijsl.2002.007

Scott, J. (2017) *Social Network Analysis* (4th edn). Thousand Oaks, CA: SAGE.

Scott, J. and Carrington, P. (eds) (2011) *The SAGE Handbook of Social Network Analysis.* Thousand Oaks, CA: SAGE.

Smith, L.R. (2002) The social architecture of communicative competence: A methodology for social-network research in sociolinguistics. *International Journal of the Sociology of Language* 153, 133–160. doi:10.1515/ijsl.2002.001

Stoessel, S. (2002) Investigating the role of social networks in language maintenance and shift. *International Journal of the Sociology of Language* 153, 93–131. doi:10.1515/ijsl.2002.006

Yang, S., Keller, F. and Zheng. L. (2017) *Social Network Analysis: Methods and Examples*. Thousand Oaks, CA: SAGE.

Wasserman, S. and Faust, K. (1994) *Social Network Analysis: Methods and Applications.* Cambridge: Cambridge University Press.

Wiklund, I. (2002) Social networks from a sociolinguistic perspective: The relationship between characteristics of the social networks of bilingual adolescents and their language proficiency. *International Journal of the Sociology of Language* 153, 53–92. doi:10.1515/ijsl.2002.005

10 Design-Based Research Methods

Overview

Design-based research (DBR) refers to a group of methods employed over the past few decades by researchers in the learning sciences – an interdisciplinary field focused on the scientific understanding of learning and the design and implementation of learning innovations (Barab & Squire, 2004). This interventionist method was originally intended to bridge research and practice in education, and in this chapter we employ examples that make reference to educational systems. What our readers will also notice is that using mixed methods of data elicitation and analysis to achieve better understanding of the messiness of what transpires in real-world settings, all while treating context as a central part of the story, can be applied across many social and human domains.

Let us first examine the name 'design-based research'. The word 'design' originates from the Latin *designare* which means 'to mark out'. Although for some the word may invoke notions of its industrial and visual applications such as the aesthetics of design (e.g. contemporary architecture), the way it is used in the context of DBR relates to marking out or specifying a sequence of actions taken to deliberately achieve an intended outcome (Collins *et al.*, 2004). In this sense, DBR is a research method that intentionally searches to broaden the focus from a narrower consideration of 'what works' in social settings and instead encourages researchers to develop evidence related to more complex and dynamic questions such as what works for whom, when, in which settings, under what conditions and why (Fishman *et al.*, 2013).

Tracing back the origins of DBR, these methods and their variations (e.g. design-based implementation research) owe their start to the pioneering work of researchers such as Allan Collins (1990) and Ann Brown (1992), among others, who proposed the need for methods able to accommodate a more complex and dynamic view of educational phenomena. This perspective, which draws explicitly from complexity theory, sees learning, cognition, knowing and context as irreducibly part of each other and not as isolated entities or processes (Bell, 2004). These scholars referred to such methodological tools for studying complex systems with emergent properties that arise from the interaction of multiple known and unknown variables as 'design-experiments' (DBR Collective, 2003).

DBR has many parallels with non-complexity and dynamic systems theory (CDST) experimental designs (i.e. randomized control trials, aka RCT). However, rather than attempting to isolate the various factors that impact system change or outcomes of interest as RCT does, DBR embraces the complex nature of systems and their emergent outcomes, taking a more ecological, contextual approach (Tabak, 2004). There are several additional comparisons we might draw. First, while RCT aims to test theory and falsify hypotheses, the aim of DBR is to test and develop theory simultaneously. RCT designs also rely on random samples and systematic comparison of experimental and control groups to obtain evidence of what works, whereas DBR instead attempts to design the environment and conditions necessary in order to achieve local (i.e. context-specific or system-specific) insight into how and why something works – as do field experiments. Finally, although DBR does attempt to generalize, this is closer to the theoretical and analytical generalizing (see Chapter 3 for additional discussion) that relates to transferability and scaling up of research (see e.g. Yin, 2018) than the statistical generalization of RCT (see Chapter 16 for more on statistical significance and experimental designs).

We return to some of these issues in more practical terms later, but here let us touch briefly on a methodological issue that nearly all DBR must grapple with – the question of what makes a particular sequence of actions, intended to deliberately achieve an outcome, successful at a particular time and place (Barab, 2014). This is related to complex causal explanations (see also Chapter 3) and the tension between making an intervention 'work' in a complex setting and the researchers' need for empirical control. The first condition often necessitates changing the design as it unfolds in a way that directly mirrors the dynamic, contingent nature of systems. The second, however, cautions against changing the planned design or research protocol. The compromise adopted by many DBR scholars, as Cobb et al. (2003) propose, is that for any method to fully embrace the complex nature of the systems it studies and their emergent outcomes, it should also adopt a pragmatically adaptive (i.e. emergent) way of operating.

COBB, CONFREY, DISESSA, LEHRER AND SCHAUBLE (2003: 9) OFFER THEIR TAKE ON WHAT DIFFERENTIATES DESIGN-BASED METHODS FROM OTHER EDUCATIONAL RESEARCH METHODS:

Design experiments ideally result in greater understanding of a learning ecology—a complex, interacting system involving multiple elements of different types and levels—by designing its elements and by anticipating how these elements function together to support learning. Design experiments therefore constitute a means of addressing the complexity that is a hallmark of educational settings. Elements of a learning ecology... emphasize that designed contexts are conceptualized as interacting systems rather than as either a collection of activities or a list of separate factors that influence learning. Beyond just creating designs that are effective and that can sometimes be affected by 'tinkering to perfection,' [DBR] explains why designs work and suggests how they may be adapted to new circumstances.

Applied linguistics research spans many specific disciplines, and can speak to many different functions in the research methods it adopts. This is true both in more conventional research as well as research informed by CDST. As with research methods more broadly, there are many functions of DBR (Shavelson *et al.*, 2003). Some of the most common for CDST research include:

- describing (e.g. what are the important characteristics of a system and its functioning?);
- comparing (e.g. does System A function differently than System B in Context Y?);
- evaluating (e.g. how well does a course of action produce a desired outcome in a system?);
- explaining (e.g. to what can we attribute changes in a system's development, and why do processes of development in a system unfold the way they do?);
- predicting (e.g. what might system development look like under a particular set of conditions?);
- developing (e.g. what is an effective way to generate desired change in a system?);
- advising (e.g. how can systems not functioning at their potential be transformed?).

It is likely that in addition to applied linguistics research projects having an overall function or objective, various intermediate stages of the larger project will have their own subsidiary aims. DBR has similar layers but ultimately has a transformative agenda focused on the developing and advising functions of research (Bell, 2004). This means, for example, that if a programme of DBR is designed to *develop* novel ideas for transforming a system, it will most likely first aim to describe, compare and evaluate. By the same token, if a DBR project aims to *advise* on how the conditions for a particular process can be applied across many systems, it will arrive at this objective via describing, comparing, evaluating and so on. In this way, DBR targets these other sub-aims on its way to accomplishing its core objectives of developing and advising for system change and novel outcomes (Collins *et al.*, 2004).

Research Questions

To extend what we have previously said about the objectives of DBR, many of the research questions that can be investigated through DBR are 'big' questions in the sense that they explore for whom, how, when and why something does or does not work in applied settings (Bell, 2004; Penuel *et al.*, 2011). This strikes us as a quintessential transdisciplinary way of going about research. Other questions that DBR can meaningfully address are those geared to theory development. However, rather than grand theories, these are theories of intermediate scope concerned with domain-specific processes and emergent outcomes. This theory development (much like developing grounded theory) can inform further prospective designs through the *developing* and *advising* functions of research (DBR Collective, 2003).

- How can system-level problems be identified and targeted in research?
- What happens to system-level fidelity when unanticipated processes and outcomes are encountered in time and context?
- How are different timescales and feedback loops able to improve our understanding of systems in context?
- How can initial conditions feed into system change iteratively?
- What innovative partnerships can be established to enact system-level change?
- What designs and which agents are necessary for bringing about system-level improvements?
- How can these designs be tailored to the needs and characteristics of particular settings?
- Under what conditions and settings is system change effective?
- How does system-level change unfold across time and in different settings?
- How can the capacity or processes for sustained development be built across contexts and conditions?
- What can iterative cycles of design teach us about the available tools and practical solutions to system-level problems?
- How do iterative cycles of design make the often invisible work of system coordination more visible?
- In what ways can support for local adaptations shape system-level innovation?
- What infrastructures can lead to self-organized transformations in system development and emergent outcomes?

- How can changes implemented at a local level be diffused or scaled up system-wide?

In light of these big questions, Hoadley (2004: 205) cautions that DBR scholars must closely examine the 'systemic validity' of their designs and ensure that the research adequately informs theories, which in turn inform practice. In other words, if systemic validity is what DBR is really after, the inferences drawn from DBR should inform the questions that motivated the research in the first place.

Technical Features

Several key principles of DBR play an important role in how DBR studies are designed and structured (O'Donnell, 2004; Sandoval, 2004). Perhaps the most fundamental of these is that research teams (rather than an individual researcher) form around a persistent problem and commit to using DBR to focus on and solve the problems (Anderson & Shattuck, 2012). This is often done by drawing from multiple stakeholders' perspectives. Practices such as these are not uncommon in applied linguistics research and are growing in some circles associated with methodological innovation (e.g. many labs and multi-site studies). An example of this, for instance in the context of language teacher education, might be to develop a model of the ways in which teacher thought and action creates the conditions for students to develop a deeper understanding of new ideas, and to explain the relations between the types of tasks and teacher practices that can support that learning and the settings in which teachers' develop and refine these instructional practices. In addition, DBR takes place in authentic (i.e. non-laboratory) environments, and chooses to study phenomena within the contexts they naturally occur (Collins et al., 2004; DBR Collective, 2003). This design aspect allows DBR to respond to emergent features of the context.

Further to this point, DBR studies choose to investigate multiple factors that reflect the complexity of systems and their functioning, including contextual variables (e.g. initial conditions, available resources, constraints in place), outcome variables (e.g. self-organized change, emergent patterns, system transformation) and system variables (e.g. adaptivity, coordination, sustainability) (Barab & Squire, 2004). Another guiding principle of DBR is researchers' commitment to a process-oriented, iterative and collaborative design (Cobb et al., 2003). As we have seen from the foregoing research questions, this allows DBR to consider multiple concerns (i.e. for whom, how, under what conditions, why) at multiple timescales, but it requires critical early decisions about the process of iteration, and the choice of what evidence and rationales will form the basis for making changes to designs. It is largely due to this adoption of an iterative design that DBR holds such potential for developing the capacity to sustain change in systems and to scale change up across contexts (Fishman *et al.*, 2013).

THE DESIGN BASED COLLECTIVE (DBR, 2003: 5) ELABORATE THE FUNDAMENTAL TENETS OF DESIGN-BASED RESEARCH:

Educational research that is detached from practice may not account for the influence of contexts, the emergent and complex nature of outcomes, and the incompleteness of knowledge about which factors are relevant. ... We propose that good design-based research exhibits the following five characteristics: First, the central goals of designing learning environments and developing theories or 'prototheories' of learning are intertwined. Second, development and research take place through continuous cycles of design, enactment, analysis, and redesign (Cobb, 2001; Collins, 1992). Third, research on designs must lead to sharable theories that help communicate relevant implications to practitioners and other educational designers (cf. Brophy, 2002). Fourth, research must account for how designs function in authentic settings. It must not only document success or failure but also focus on interactions that refine our understanding of the learning issues involved. Fifth, the development of such accounts relies on methods that can document and connect processes of enactment to outcomes of interest.

A crucial first step when embarking on a DBR study is to clarify the specific purpose of the study and to specify any assumptions about the starting points, pathways of development and prospective endpoints or goals of the system under investigation (Joseph, 2004). Once the research team has articulated these assumptions, the next step is to formulate a design that embodies these in practical settings. This means researchers will mark out a sequence of actions intended to deliberately achieve an intended outcome (Sandoval, 2004).

To illustrate these steps, we might take as our hypothetical purpose an issue such as reversing the rapid decline in language enrollment and investment in language programmes that affects some contexts (American Academy of Arts and Sciences, 2017). In this, as with most other research settings, DBR is conceptualized as a process of generating desired change in a system. For the present example, this may mean finding ways to increase personal participation and support for student learning in this specific domain. With this purpose firmly in mind, the DBR team can begin to draw on actual language student capabilities, instructional histories, analysis of needs, current practices and policy initiatives and other resources as the starting point they intend to build on (Barab,

2014). Once this starting point is more or less clear, the DBR team must also achieve consensus on the ideas or targets that constitute a prospective endpoint for the aim of generating the desired change in the system. What, in other words, constitutes success? Often, though not always, this involves synthesizing the prior research literature to identify central organizing ideas for a domain, and establishing system performance indicators that can demonstrate qualitative change, or newly envisioned outcome patterns (Cobb *et al.*, 2003). This is where the DBR team may refer to the wide-ranging literature on instructed language learning and the conditions necessary for optimal language development, while also benchmarking the level and type of change the system would be expected to undergo. The researchers would use this opportunity to attend to the conditions needed to support student learning in the classroom and to maximize perceptions of value for continued language learning. They would also plan the processes they intend to test and revise iteratively to raise personal participation in language learning. Finally, the research team will need to generate multiple forms of data, not simply for logistical reasons, but to document system change as they proceed and to develop a complex understanding of the ecology of learning (Fishman *et al.*, 2013).

Once a study has been planned and structured, DBR employs mixed methods for data collection and analysis (see also Chapter 18). One review (Anderson & Shattuck, 2012) of the most cited DBR studies over a single decade showed that the research tools employed in most empirical DBR studies are mixed, and that the results of both qualitative and quantitative measurements are presented. DBR is built on a kind of applied pragmatism that closely mirrors what we have argued about transdisciplinary approaches to CDST research (see Chapter 3) and typically involves mixed methods using a variety of research tools and techniques (Collins *et al.*, 2004). Anderson and Shattuck (2012: 17) argue that DBR is 'largely agnostic when it comes to epistemological challenges to the choice of methodologies used', and that by operating from this more problem-oriented approach 'it is perfectly logical for researchers to select and use differing methods, selecting them as they see the need'.

Along with this openness to mixed multi-methods, DBR expects researchers to generate an extensive and longitudinal dataset. It is this type of dataset that supports a systematic yet complex analysis of the phenomenon under investigation (Cobb *et al.*, 2003). In practice, DBR entails collecting and curating a range of data sources (O'Donnell, 2004). In a language education setting, for instance, this might include integrating data sources such as samples of ongoing student work or products of student learning from tasks and other instructional materials, responses to interviews and diary prompts, notes from observation protocols, interactional patterns and classroom discourse and ratings on other more quantitative measurements (e.g. surveys or assessments), to name just a few (Barab, 2014).

As we have highlighted, the design of DBR is iterative in the sense that data feed into subsequent cycles of design. However, the extensive longitudinal dataset generated from a DBR study is often analyzed retrospectively in order to provide a situated and dynamic account of the processes and outcomes under investigation, and to ensure that resulting claims are valid and grounded in evidence (Tabak, 2004). As part of this process, from the earliest stages of DBR, researchers must be explicit about the criteria for and types of evidence that will be used to make particular types of inferences (Penuel *et al.*, 2011). This enables teams of researchers to submit their analyses and conclusions for monitoring and scrutiny by other scholars. A retrospective analysis can also be contrasted with the analyses conducted during the ongoing iterations as a way of providing coherence to these effects (i.e. the modified aspects) of the study. This comparison of levels of analysis has the added benefit of framing a study as a prototypical case of some broader phenomena and making it possible to anticipate outcomes in future designs.

Of course, DBR scholars stress that design research is 'not... a euphemism for "anything goes" research' (DBR Collective, 2003). DBR's strengths (e.g. Shavelson *et al.*, 2003: 25) lie in its ability to help researchers confront real-world complexities and demands, co-construct knowledge of emergent systems and their functioning, test and develop theories in the 'crucible' of ecological settings and promote and adopt innovations that can sustain adaptive change under these conditions.

Example Study

As mentioned earlier in this chapter, DBR has seen use primarily in educational settings. Naturally, our example study relates to this domain. Parker *et al.* (2013) conducted an interesting DBR study of a high-enrollment college-preparatory class: Advanced Placement (AP) US Government and Politics. The problem they aimed to address was the mismatch between rapidly climbing enrollments in such AP classes and students' alarming failure rates on the high-stakes end-of-course AP tests. The researchers were also concerned with the scope of such courses featuring mile-wide and inch-deep coverage, and the tendency of these classes to disregard current thinking and evidence on how learning occurs. These cumulative issues had resulted in a wave of criticism being leveled at the quality and rigor of the AP classes in question. The researchers' ambitious aims in this DBR study were to (a) deepen students' conceptual learning and capacity for adaptive transfer in this advanced course, (b) help students achieve the same or higher scores on the AP test, (c) encourage greater engagement and success for a wider range of AP students and (d) develop a course architecture that is sustainable and scalable by design.

These scholars first specified their design principles, and applied these through a collaborative project-based intervention to the AP course at two high schools (Schools A and B) in a suburban school district. Several research questions were chosen by Parker *et al.* (2013) to guide the analyses used in this study:

- RQ 1: Can a project-based AP course be created in which students do as well or better on the AP test than students in a traditionally taught AP course?
- RQ 2: Will students demonstrate a deeper level of knowledge as assessed by a complex scenario test?
- RQ 3: Will students report greater engagement in their learning experience, inside and outside the classroom?

Over the year-long course, qualitative and quantitative data were collected from these high schools and compared with two traditionally taught high schools (Schools C and D) in a neighboring state. This resulted in a sample of 289 students comprising 12 classes and 5 teachers. Quantitative data were the official AP exam and a complex scenario test, which required application of knowledge, administered toward the end of the course. For the qualitative measures, a sample of students in each of the classrooms was interviewed individually three times during the course, and following the administration of both tests, each of the classes was interviewed in a large-group format.

Regarding the first research question, results indicated that both classes with a non-traditional project-based format achieved higher scores on the AP test compared with the traditionally taught classes ($d = 0.25$). Furthermore, significantly more students at the project-based Schools A (47.7%) and B (16.8%) achieved a high pass ($d = 0.78$), making them eligible for college credit, than traditional students at Schools C and D (5.7%).

With regard to the second research question, the project-based students in School A (a high-achieving school overall) scored significantly higher on three of the four dimensions of the complex scenario test as compared with students in the traditional courses ($d = 0.50$); those in School B (a moderately achieving school) did not perform significantly differently from students in the traditional courses. These findings suggest that some of the project-based students understood the course content more deeply to the point that they were able to apply it in a novel situation to solve a complex problem.

Finally, the qualitative data revealed that many students in the early stages of the design experiment found project work frustrating, arguing that they felt they had insufficient background information and preferred to stick to a more conventional course structure. In later stages, once students were oriented to a new way of doing AP, they began comparing the course's project-based approach with the straightforward efficiency of test-prep teaching and learning. In contrast to the purpose and pedagogy of traditional AP courses, the project work seemed to be obscure, indirect or even pointless to some students. While many students reported finding such constructivist learning refreshing and enjoyable, the quasi-repetitive project cycling and sustained inquiry in this course also appeared to intensify the difference in students' minds between learning for understanding and learning for test performance.

Annotated readings

The Design-Based Research Collective (DBR) (2003) Design-based research: An emerging paradigm for educational inquiry. *Educational Researcher* 32, 5–8. doi:10.3102/0013189X032001005

In this brief paper, 10 pioneering scholars of DBR lay out a clear rationale for a method sensitive to change and the complexities of real-world contexts. They argue that intentional design is central in efforts to create usable knowledge and advance empirical understanding of what works in complex settings, for whom, under what circumstances, how and why. This is a straightforward introduction for the uninitiated.

Collins, A., Joseph, D. and Bielaczyc, K. (2004) Design research: Theoretical and methodological issues. *Journal of the Learning Sciences* 13, 15–42. doi:10.1207/s15327809jls1301_2

These scholars outline the goals and applications of DBR and how it is related to other methodologies. Using various examples, once more related to the learning sciences, they then illustrate how DBR is carried out. Following from these examples, they conclude by providing broad guidelines for conducting DBR. Readers will find this a descriptive and practical paper.

Tabak, I. (2004) Reconstructing context: Negotiating the tension between exogenous and endogenous educational design. *Educational Psychologist* 39, 225–233. doi:10.1207/s15326985ep3904_4

In this article, Tabak critically examines what she terms a 'design-stance' in research. Drawing as others do from educational research, she illustrates some characteristics that can inadvertently threaten the efficacy of DBR. She proposes that when design and intervention are central to the research process (as they are in DBR), context is crucial for constructing rich and veridical accounts of how complex systems function and change.

Bell, P. (2004) On the theoretical breadth of design-based research in education. *Educational Psychologist* 39, 243–253. doi:10.1207/s15326985ep3904_6

The premise of this paper is the notion that important things can be learned about the nature and the conditions of system change and functioning by attempting to deliberately engineer and sustain innovation in everyday settings. Bell writes fairly lucidly on how this would work in the context of educational research, but his ideas are applicable to much wider domains. This is a theoretically advanced article.

References

American Academy of Arts and Sciences (2017) America's languages: Investing in language education for the 21st century. See https://www.amacad.org/sites/default/files/pu blication/downloads/Commission-on-Language-Learning_Americas-Languages.pdf (accessed 5 August 2019).

Anderson, T. and Shattuck, J. (2012) Design-based research: A decade of progress in education research? *Educational Researcher* 41, 16–25. doi:10.3102/0013189X11428813

Barab, S. (2014) Design-based research: A methodological toolkit for engineering change. In R.K. Sawyer (ed.) *The Cambridge Handbook of the Learning Sciences* (pp. 151–170). Cambridge: Cambridge University Press.

Barab, S. and Squire, K. (2004) Design-based research: Putting a stake in the ground. *Journal of the Learning Sciences* 13, 1–14. doi:10.1207/s15327809jls1301_1

Bell, P. (2004) On the theoretical breadth of design-based research in education. *Educational Psychologist* 39, 243–253. doi:10.1207/s15326985ep3904_6

Brown, A.L. (1992) Design experiments: Theoretical and methodological challenges in creating complex interventions in classroom settings. *Journal of the Learning Sciences* 2, 141–178. doi:10.1207/s15327809jls0202_2

Cobb, P., Confrey, J., diSessa, A., Lehrer, R. and Schauble, L. (2003) Design experiments in education research. *Educational Researcher* 32, 9–13. doi:10.3102/0013189X032001009

Collins, A. (1990) *Toward a Design Science of Education*. New York: Center for Technology in Education.

Collins, A., Joseph, D. and Bielaczyc, K. (2004) Design research: Theoretical and methodological issues. *Journal of the Learning Sciences* 13, 15–42. doi:10.1207/s15327809jls1301_2

DBR Collective (2003) Design-based research: An emerging paradigm for educational inquiry. *Educational Researcher* 32, 5–8. doi:10.3102/0013189X032001005

Fishman, B.J., Penuel, W.R., Allen, A.-R., Cheng, B.H. and Sabelli, N. (2013) Design-based implementation research: An emerging model for transforming the relationship of research and practice. *National Society for the Study of Education Yearbook* 112 (2), 136–156.

Hoadley, C. (2004) Methodological alignment in design-based research. *Educational Psychologist* 39, 203–212. doi:10.1207/s15326985ep3904_2

Joseph, D. (2004) The practice of design-based research: Uncovering the interplay between design, research, and the real-world context. *Educational Psychologist* 39, 235–242. doi:10.1207/s15326985ep3904_5

O'Donnell, A.M. (2004) A commentary on design research. *Educational Psychologist* 39, 255–260. doi:10.1207/s15326985ep3904_7

Parker, W.C., Lo, J., Yeo, A.J., Valencia, S.W., Nguyen, D., Abbott, R.D., Nolen. S.B., Bransford. J.D. and Vye, N.J. (2013) Beyond breadth-speed-test: Toward deeper knowing and engagement in an advanced placement course. *American Educational Research Journal* 50, 1424–1459. doi:10.3102/0002831213504237

Penuel, W.R., Fishman, B.J., Cheng, B.H. and Sabelli, N. (2011) Organizing research and development at the intersection of learning, implementation, and design. *Educational Researcher* 40, 331–337. doi:10.3102/0013189X11421826

Sandoval, W.A. (2004) Developing learning theory by refining conjectures embodied in educational designs. *Educational Psychologist* 39, 213–223. doi:10.1207/s15326985ep3904_3

Shavelson, R.J., Phillips, D.C., Towne, L. and Feuer, M.J. (2003) On the science of education design studies. *Educational Researcher* 32 (1), 25–28. doi:10.3102/0013189X032001025

Tabak, I. (2004) Reconstructing context: Negotiating the tension between exogenous and endogenous educational design. *Educational Psychologist* 39, 225–233. doi:10.1207/s15326985ep3904_4

Yin, R.K. (2018) *Case Study Research and Applications: Design and Methods* (6th edn). Thousand Oaks, CA: SAGE.

Part 3
Quantitative Methods

11 Panel Designs

Overview

Panel designs, a form of longitudinal research are an important tool from which complexity and dynamic systems theory (CDST) researchers can draw. Unfortunately, this tool seems to be underappreciated in applied linguistics. Very few empirical investigations have utilized panel data, relative to the pervasiveness of one-shot cross-sectional research. This is ironic considering that language learning is more concerned with change rather than stability. This is why Larsen-Freeman (2015) has argued that 'language acquisition' is a misnomer, and should be relabeled 'language development'.

Longitudinal research is a rather broad field and subsumes various approaches including panel designs. In essence, panel data refers to the situation where data are collected from the same individuals (or other units, e.g. schools) over time. This hints at why this type of research is uncommon. It involves additional issues related to feasibility, design, analysis and patience that cross-sectional researchers do not have to worry about.

Panel designs are also distinct from repeated cross-sectional designs. In a repeated cross-sectional design (including time series analysis; see Chapter 14), the researcher measures the same variables on *different* individuals over time. For example, the researcher might be interested in comparing the attitudes toward computer-assisted language learning (CALL) in 2000, 2005, 2010, 2015 and 2020. In a panel design, however, the researcher measures the same variables on the *same* individuals over time. Therefore, the researcher would have to track down the same individuals on these five data collection waves in order to obtain a clearer picture of their developmental patterns. Panel analysis offers more flexibility in examining change dynamics than the standard pretest–post-test–delayed post-test design. The canonical panel approach can also be contrasted with time-series analysis (see Chapter 14), which involves the measurement of several variables from a few individuals – or even one individual – on many more data collection waves (e.g. over 50) (Menard, 2002).

SINGER AND WILLETT (2003: 9–10, ORIGINAL EMPHASIS) ON THE UNIQUE INSIGHTS LONGITUDINAL PANEL DATA CAN PROVIDE:

To model change, you need longitudinal data that describe how each person in the sample changes over time. We begin with this apparent tautology because too many empirical researchers seem willing to leap from cross-sectional data that describe differences among individuals of different ages to making generalizations about change over time. Many developmental psychologists, for example, analyze cross-sectional data sets composed of children of differing ages, concluding that outcome differences between age groups—in measures such as antisocial behavior—reflect real change over time. Although change is a compelling explanation of this situation—it might even be the *true* explanation— cross-sectional data can never confirm this possibility because equally valid competing explanations abound. Even in a sample drawn from a single school, a random sample of older children may differ from a random sample of younger children in important ways: the groups began school in different years, they experienced different curricula and life events, and if data collection continues for a sufficient period of time, the older sample omits age-mates who dropped out of school. Any observed differences in outcomes between grade-separated cohorts may be due to these explanations and not to systematic individual change. In statistical terms, cross-sectional studies confound age and cohort effects (and age and history effects) and are prone to selection bias.

Note that because of the rich insights that could be obtained from panel data, different statistical applications have been developed to deal with various situations. Example applications that could be applied to panel data include latent growth curve modeling (see Chapter 12) and multilevel modeling (see Chapter 13). The reader should therefore ideally have some familiarity with multiple regression and causal modeling. A helpful introduction is provided by Kline (2016) and a more advanced treatment is found in Russo (2009). In this chapter, we focus on one specific application of panel data, namely *cross-lagged panel data*.

Research Questions

Cross-lagged panel design can help answer various questions related to (the plausibility of) a causal relationship among the variables of interest, including

- Is there evidence for a causal relationship among the variables?
- Is there evidence for reciprocal causality among the variables?
- Is this pattern of relationship consistent over data collection waves, or does it change with time?
- Is this pattern consistent for different subgroups underlying the data?

Cross-lagged panel design is typically applied with two variables or two data collection waves – though it can accommodate more variables and waves. Furthermore, as discussed in more detail later, this design cannot provide unequivocal evidence for causality. Instead, it highlights the plausibility of causality, and should ideally be used in combination with other empirical and theoretical considerations.

Technical Features

Experiments are the typical approach to arrive at causal inference, but this approach is unfeasible in many situations, such as when researchers cannot manipulate conditions at will. This is often the case, for example, when investigating language learning in naturalistic settings. It is also the case when multiple complex interactions exist between variables over time. An alternative approach is cross-lagged panel design. Panel design helps clarify the short- and long-term dynamics and the plausibility of causal interrelationships among factors, including intra-individual change over time. Thus, panel design deals with both change and interconnectedness, two key criteria for CDST-appropriate methods.

As an illustration of panel design, consider the example of a researcher interested in the question of whether it is higher second language (L2) motivation that leads to higher L2 achievement, or if it is the opposite. After collecting the data at two intervals, the cross-lagged researcher would conduct an analysis examining whether motivation predicts achievement after controlling for the previous level of achievement, and whether achievement predicts motivation after controlling for the previous level of motivation. This process can be represented with two arrows crossing each other (hence cross-lagged; see Figure 11.1). (See Chapters 3 and 16 for more on causality.)

From Figure 11.1, we can compute a total of six correlations: between Motivation 1 and Achievement 1 (called *synchronous correlation*), between Motivation 1 and Motivation 2 and between Achievement 1 and Achievement 2 (both called *autocorrelations*) and finally between Motivation 1 and Achievement 2 and between Achievement 1 and Motivation 2 (the cross-lagged correlations in the model). The basic model in Figure 11.1 can be extended to include more variables and more time points, depending on the research question. Including more than two time points leads to more accuracy and confidence in the results (Singer & Willett, 2003).

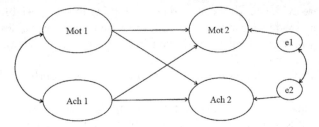

Figure 11.1 The basic structure of a two-wave cross-lagged panel design (Ach = achievement, Mot = motivation)

Figure 11.1 also points to another advantage of cross-lagged panel design, namely the investigation of reciprocal causality. Sometimes, the direction of causality is unambiguous. For example, as a field-specific illustration, it would be justifiable to argue for unidirectional causality in the relationship between first language (L1) and accentedness or between gender and attitudes (in that the former causes the latter, rather than vice versa). In many real-life situations, however, reciprocal causality is more likely. In the example in Figure 11.1, it is more likely that motivation and achievement influence each other synergetically over time, which empha-sizes the CDST notion of interconnectedness, rather than one uniformly influencing the other. Panel design can test this hypothesis empirically and estimate the magnitude of this reciprocal relationship over the dif-ferent waves measured (Finkel, 1995).

In many situations, causal inference is a complex issue. In the context of cross-lagged analysis, a number of assumptions need to be satisfied before causal interpretations can be confidently made, such as lack of measurement error (which can be ameliorated with latent variables), lack of unmeasured third variables (or the *third variable problem*, which is typically solved through experimental manipulation) and choosing an appropriate time lag for the effect to materialize (Finkel, 1995; Kenny, 2005). Because some of these assumptions (especially the third variable problem) may not be satisfied in actual research, some methodologists have cautioned against overinterpreting the results and recommended treating them as suggestive (Shadish *et al.*, 2002).

Nevertheless, intentional experimental manipulation by the researcher is not the only way to rule out the possibility of an unmeasured third variable. In certain situations, the researcher may be able to locate a useful *instrumental variable*. An instrumental variable is found in situ-ations 'where the forces of nature or government policy have conspired to produce an environment somewhat akin to a randomized experiment' (Angrist & Krueger, 2001: 73). In the foregoing example, one might argue that the relationship between motivation and achievement could be spu-rious; there may be an 'omitted variable' that could cause both. A critical reader, for example, might wonder whether it could have simply been the use of effective learning strategies that influenced both variables. Those who use effective strategies achieve better results and also feel satisfied and report higher motivation. Critical readers may be able to think of a range of potential explanations for associations obtained from observational data. Even if these omitted variables could be specified in advance, there would typically be too many to include in any single study. However, if we happen to find an instrumental variable, we might be able to shed some light on causality. For example, imagine that the textbook publisher used by the hypothetical learners in this study decided to publish a second, colorful edition. Let's also imagine that the second edition has no additional content apart from its colorfulness. If Motivation 2 (see Figure 11.1) increases after introducing the second edition, we may safely argue that the association between Motivation 2 and Achievement 2 would be causal. In short, the use of instrumental variables requires an opportunistic researcher. Such instrumental variables can shed rare and unique insight that might not be readily available under typical circumstances. To date, such *natural experiments* (see e.g. Dunning, 2012; Gerber & Green, 2012; Rutter, 2007) have been underutilized in the applied linguistics literature.

Example Study

Geerlings *et al.* (2015) attempted to investigate the relationship between ethnic self-identification and heritage language use. Geerlings *et al.* noted that research into this topic was scarce and conflicting. They report results suggesting that minorities in the United States tend to move toward more identification with American society, while other research suggests that ethnic identity is strengthening over time. Different theories also tend to support different predictions. As Geerlings and colleagues review in detail, some theories expect that language socialization at an early age would lead to preference for heritage language and identity, while others argue that the desire to validate one's identity is what leads to preference for heritage language use in order to make oneself unique. A third set of theories maintain that these two directions are not mutually exclusive.

Geerlings and colleagues analyzed data from 5262 American adolescents (female = 2687) collected over two waves (1992 and 1996). Some of these participants came from Asian backgrounds (e.g. Vietnam, Cambodia), while others came from Latin American backgrounds (e.g. Mexico, Colombia). The researchers were also able to account for other important background variables, such as time lived in the United States, heritage language proficiency and whether both parents share the same background. The researchers additionally utilized multilevel modeling (repeated measures nested within individuals; see Chapter 13) to handle their data.

These analyses showed that the results for the two subsamples (Asian and Latin American) were different. For Latin Americans, both cross-lagged effects were significant. That is, heritage language use preference predicted ethnic self-identification, and ethnic self-identification also predicted heritage language use preference. Thus, there was evidence for reciprocal causality. This was not the case for Asians, however. For Asian adolescents, language preference predicted ethnic self-identification, but not vice versa. Causality was unidirectional for this subsample.

Annotated readings

Ruspini, E. (2002) *Introduction to Longitudinal Research*. London: Routledge.

Just as the title suggests, this book offers an introduction to various issues related to longitudinal research, including terminology, characteristics, data collection and analysis, and problems associated with different longitudinal approaches. Plenty of examples are given throughout.

Menard, S. (2002) *Longitudinal Research* (2nd edn). Thousand Oaks, CA: SAGE.

This is another introductory book on longitudinal research. It is one of the 'little green book' series. Despite being very brief, the book delves into various issues that are discussed in much detail.

Shadish, W.R., Cook, T.D. and Campbell, D.T. (2002) *Experimental and Quasi-Experimental Designs for Generalized Causal Inference*. Belmont, CA: Wadsworth, Cengage Learning.

This is arguably one of the classic texts in research design. Chapter 12 deals with causal models and includes a short but clear discussion on cross-lagged analysis and its potential limitations and elaborates on instrumental variables.

Finkel, S.E. (1995) *Causal Analysis with Panel Data*. Thousand Oaks, CA: SAGE.

This short book is devoted to various issues in panel data including cross-lagged designs. It tends to be somewhat technical by discussing the different equations used to estimate different models, thus giving the reader an 'under the hood' look.

Angrist, J.D. and Krueger, A.B. (2001) Instrumental variables and the search for identification: From supply and demand to natural experiments. *Journal of Economic Perspectives* 15 (4), 69–85. doi:10.1257/jep.15.4.69

This is an accessible article that provides an introduction to instrumental variables, including definition, interpretation and pitfalls. It also offers a useful list of exemplar studies that have utilized instrumental variables over the years.

Glenn, N.D. (2005) *Cohort Analysis* (2nd edn). Thousand Oaks, CA: SAGE.

This book goes into detail discussing the various issues researchers face when dealing with cohorts. It has a useful section on data requirements and availability.

Andreß, H.-J., Golsch, K. and Schmidt, A. (2013) *Applied Panel Data Analysis for Economic and Social Surveys*. Heidelberg: Springer.

In this book, the authors discuss managing and analyzing panel data for different outcome variables. Stata applications are provided.

Longhi, S. and Nandi, A. (2015) *A Practical Guide to Using Panel Data*. Thousand Oaks, CA: SAGE.

This is a book exclusively on panel data and its different applications. Stata applications are provided with a focus on sociological research topics.

Baltagi, B.H. (2013) *Econometric Analysis of Panel Data* (5th edn). Chichester: Wiley.

A mathematically oriented treatment of the subject. This volume is more appropriate for advanced readers familiar with the central issues of panel designs.

References

Angrist, J.D. and Krueger, A.B. (2001) Instrumental variables and the search for identification: From supply and demand to natural experiments. *Journal of Economic Perspectives* 15 (4), 69–85. doi:10.1257/jep.15.4.69

Dunning, T. (2012) *Natural Experiments in the Social Sciences: A Design-Based Approach*. Cambridge: Cambridge University Press.

Finkel, S.E. (1995) *Causal Analysis with Panel Data*. Thousand Oaks, CA: SAGE.

Geerlings, J., Verkuyten, M. and Thijs, J. (2015) Changes in ethnic self-identification and heritage language preference in adolescence: A cross-lagged panel study. *Journal of Language and Social Psychology* 34 (5), 501–520. doi:10.1177/0261927x14564467

Gerber, A.S. and Green, D.P. (2012) *Field Experiments: Design, Analysis, and Interpretation*. New York: Norton.

Kenny, D.A. (2005) Cross-lagged panel design. In B.S. Everitt and D.C. Howell (eds) *Encyclopedia of Statistics in Behavioral Science* (Vol. 1; pp. 450–451). Hoboken, NJ: John Wiley & Sons.

Kline, R.B. (2016) *Principles and Practice of Structural Equation Modeling* (4th edn). New York: Guilford Press.

Larsen-Freeman, D. (2015) Saying what we mean: Making a case for 'language acquisition' to become 'language development'. *Language Teaching* 48 (4), 491–505. doi:10.1017/S0261444814000019

Menard, S. (2002) *Longitudinal Research* (2nd edn). Thousand Oaks, CA: SAGE.

Russo, F. (2009) *Causality and Causal Modelling in the Social Sciences: Measuring Variations*. Dordrecht: Springer.

Rutter, M. (2007) Proceeding from observed correlation to causal inference: The use of natural experiments. *Perspectives on Psychological Science* 2 (4), 377–395. doi:10.1111/j.1745-6916.2007.00050.x

Shadish, W.R., Cook, T.D. and Campbell, D.T. (2002) *Experimental and Quasi-Experimental Designs for Generalized Causal Inference*. Belmont, CA: Wadsworth, Cengage Learning.

Singer, J.D. and Willett, J.B. (2003) *Applied Longitudinal Data Analysis: Modeling Change and Event Occurrence*. Oxford: Oxford University Press.

12 Latent Growth Curve Modeling

Overview

In this chapter, we review latent growth curve modeling (LGCM). LGCM can be seen as one application of panel data (Chapter 11), and as the longitudinal version of structural equation modeling (SEM). Many applied linguists are already familiar with SEM to some extent, as it has become increasingly popular in recent years. However, SEM is primarily concerned with cross-sectional data. In order to handle longitudinal data and change over time, applied linguists frequently use conventional approaches such as pretest–posttest designs and repeated measures analysis of variance (ANOVA). However, these conventional approaches offer a rather limited view of the data, particularly given the complexity and dynamic systems theory (CDST) focus on continuous system change and interconnectedness. This chapter will illustrate some of the various applications and interesting insights that applied linguistics researchers can obtain from the data using LGCM.

The term *latent* in the context of LGCM refers to the notion that the observed temporal trajectory in the data analysis is assumed to be a manifestation of an underlying process. Typically, we are more interested in this underlying process that gave rise to the observed trajectory. Therefore, our interest in the observed repeated measures is secondary; we use them to estimate the unobservable (latent) trajectory. This allows us to then describe the time trajectory and subsequently attempt to explain it by incorporating explanatory variables into the model (Bollen & Curran, 2006).

As an illustration, consider the case of reading ability in a classroom instructional setting. Reading ability may increase over time with appropriate instruction. When we measure reading at different time points, we end up with a trend. LGCM assumes that this trend is an (imperfect) representation of an underlying reading ability. LGCM then attempts to estimate the developmental pattern of this ability. This is also exactly how SEM deals with latent variables. In SEM, researchers typically use several observed indicators to estimate a latent variable. The latent variable is considered a more precise measure than the simple mean of these indicators because the latent variable takes into account the reliability of its indicators.

Another important advantage of LGCM is that it allows researchers to model the overall trajectory of all cases, as well as the individual trajectory of each case. The latter pertains to inter-individual variability, which could be seen as one of the concerns that CDST research attempts to address. In fact, Curran and Willoughby (2003) advance the argument that LGCM combines characteristics of the variable-centered approach and the person-centered approach, two sharply divergent views to development. The variable-centered perspective (also called nomothetic) emphasizes the overall mean trajectory of all cases. The person-centered perspective (called idiographic), on the other hand, emphasizes the unique and idiosyncratic trajectories of each individual. LGCM is able to draw from both approaches to shed rich light on applied linguists' data. It can model a distinct trajectory for each case, a mean trajectory for all cases, as well as the variability around this mean.

Because LGCM is an extension of SEM, the reader should ideally already be familiar with SEM. This includes familiarity with topics such as software, terminology, parameters and identification, and path diagram conventions. Helpful introductions to these SEM topics can be found in Byrne (2012) and in Kline (2016).

Research Questions

Using LGCM, the researcher can ask a number of new and interesting questions. Examples include:

- When does a given process start (intercept)? What is the initial state of development?
- Is there significant variability around this initial state? Is there inter-individual variability?
- Is there change over time (slope)? Is this change linear or nonlinear? Does it reach a plateau at some point? Is there intra-individual variability?
- Is there inter-individual variability in intra-individual change?
- What is the overall trend (of change through time)? Is it increasing or decreasing?
- How rapid is this change? How steep is it?
- Does the initial state predict the steepness of change?
- Do two or more subgroups in the data differ in their trajectories? If so, how?
- What explains inter-individual variability in initial states? What explanatory variables can account for initial states?

- What explains intra-individual variability in development? What explanatory variables help account for the rate of change over time?
- What explains inter-individual variability in intra-individual variability? Is it possible that there are distinct subgroups underlying the data causing this variability?
- Is the rate of change (slope) in one variable related to the rate of change (slope) in another variable?

At first, this list of questions might seem bewildering. This is no surprise. Conventional statistics (e.g. pretest–posttest designs and repeated measures ANOVA) can hardly start to tackle many of these complex questions about changes through time. Although multiple regression may address some of these questions, LGCM offers much more flexibility.

Take as an example the last point in the previous list. An example of this research question might be whether reading ability – to extend the foregoing illustration – is related to the amount of effort expended over time. At face value, this might sound like a question that can be handled via a simple Pearson correlation. However, notice that our question here is longitudinal. Is the *change* in reading scores related to the *change* in effort? A procedure like Pearson's correlation deals with one-shot cross-sectional data and is unable to account for such longitudinal matters.

Technical Features

Figure 12.1 presents a visual representation of a basic LGCM of reading development based on data hypothetically collected over four annual waves. The two main components are the *intercept* and the *slope*. The intercept represents the initial state of development while the slope represents the rate of change over time. The four boxes are the actual measurements taken from learners at the four annual waves. Below each box, there is a time-specific error term that takes into account the reliability of the measurement.

With the exception of the four reading measurements, the other components in Figure 12.1 are shown in ovals. Conventionally, an oval shape implies that the component is inferred rather than directly measured. In Figure 12.1, the only components actually measured are the four reading scores. This is also why the arrows are pointing toward the four boxes. This means that the observed reading scores are assumed to be caused by the underlying developmental process (represented by the intercept and the slope) and by some measurement error. The double-headed curved arrow linking the intercept and the slope is the covariance, a measure of the association between two variables. A positive covariance would indicate that individuals starting with higher reading scores at the intercept also have a steeper rate of growth over time – something akin to an

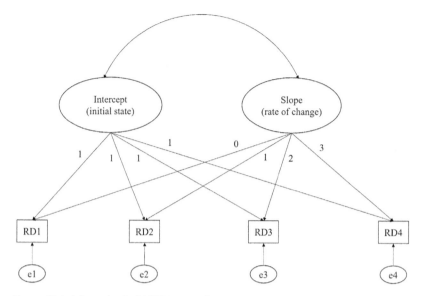

Figure 12.1 A hypothetical LGCM example

advantage for high achievers. On the other hand, a negative covariance would suggest that a low reading score at the start would lead to steeper growth – students with lower initial grades catch up with other students. Sometimes, the means and the variances of both the intercept and the slope are also shown in the figure.

An interesting part in Figure 12.1 is the numbers next to the arrows. For the intercept, all arrows have a value of 1. This is because this value only represents the initial state (sometimes called the constant). The slope, on the other hand, represents growth and therefore it has a value of 0 at the first reading score – there is no growth yet. Growth then increases with each reading score. In this example, the growth is linear (1, 2, 3). However, if the growth is nonlinear, as it may well be, we would need an additional slope with appropriate values such as the squares of those in the original slope (e.g. 1, 4, 9). If our data collection missed a year, the figure would then have the values 0, 1, 2, 4 to indicate that the third year is missing.

As previously mentioned, Figure 12.1 represents a basic version of LGCM. The researcher may need to add additional components depending on the research question. For example, researchers may measure reading at more than four waves. The more data collection waves the researcher has, the more accurate their estimation of the underlying trajectory will be. In any case, LGCM requires a minimum of three waves of data collection. With two waves only, there is no way to tell whether the trend is linear or nonlinear, and many of the assumptions of interconnectedness and continuous change would not be readily detectable.

Another consideration with LGCM is that the researcher can add additional variables. The foregoing example is sometimes called an *unconditional model*. When a researcher adds predictors to it, it is called a *conditional model*. LGCM can accommodate predictors whether they are stable or changing over time. Examples of time-varying predictors might include attitudes to learning, motivation for learning or the development of a certain linguistic feature (e.g. third person singular –s) in a learner's oral production. These variables can change from one data collection wave to another, and therefore they need to be re-measured at each wave. In contrast, time-invariant predictors need to be assessed once. Examples might include gender (typically), first language and amount of exposure to the language before the study. What is interesting is that LGCM allows the researcher to use these predictors to explain both an initial state and development over time, thus treating both of them as dependent variables to be accounted for.

Another interesting application of LGCM is *mixture modeling*. Here, we assume that we have distinct groups underlying our data, and each group has a different developmental trajectory. This application closely reflects what may be a complex and dynamic reality of the situation under study and can be very useful in many contexts – such as to understand inter-individual variability – although some methodologists have cautioned against overusing this feature (see following quote by Nagin & Tremblay [2005]). A further useful feature of LGCM is the possibility of using *piecewise modeling*. This applies to the situation where a developmental trajectory has distinct phases. For example, if a trajectory shows growth for some time, then a plateau and finally a decline, we can split this trajectory into three separate temporal chunks. Each segment of this pattern would then be treated separately for analytical purposes.

NAGIN AND TREMBLAY (2005: 882–883) ON THE DANGERS OF REIFYING A STATISTICALLY BASED GROUP:

We forthrightly acknowledge that the risk of reification is particularly great when the groups are identified using a statistical method. The group's reality is reinforced by the patina of scientific objectivity that accompanies statistical analysis and by the language used to describe the statistical findings (for example, 'group 1, which comprises x percent of the population, is best labeled')....

The tendency to reify groups has important risks. One is in the conduct of public policy. If a group is small and its behavior is socially undesirable, such as committing crimes, reifying the group as a distinct entity – rather than as an extreme on a continuum – may provoke draconian responses to the behavior, by creating the impression of a bright line of separation between 'them' and 'us.' Human history is replete with tragic instances in which a fictional group-based separation is the first step in dehumanizing a 'them.' Two other risks are not inherently insidious but still important. One is that reifying creates the impression that groups are immutable, a risk we discuss later. It may also trigger a quixotic quest for assessment instruments designed to assign individuals to their true trajectory group...

We have to add that this approach is not uncontroversial. Some complexivists have expressed concerns about the reification of variables, particularly latent variables. According to Byrne (2002: 117), such expressions refer to 'a set of procedures which I have always considered to be wrongheaded and dangerous – those which interpret measured "variables" as indicators of "real" latent "variables" – reification squared and, in the case of structural equation modelling, cubed'. An additional issue is described by Michell (2003, 2008) as a potentially self-perpetuating error of assuming that all variables are quantifiable, despite the empirical possibility that certain attributes are non-quantitative in nature. Such mindless reifying of objects highlights a 'preference for the [methodological] artifice of simplicity' (Larsen-Freeman & Cameron, 2008: 1) in much of applied linguistics research.

On the other hand, there is the argument that being non-existent in real life does not render an idea completely useless. Thus, even if a latent variable does not exist in the real world, it may still have important analytical uses in understanding, predicting and dealing with various issues in the real world. The same principle applies to what we have learned from the 'circle' even though there might not be a perfect circle in the universe – as Hume (1921/1748: 23) put it, 'Though there never were a circle or triangle in nature, the truths demonstrated by Euclid [will] for ever retain their certainty and evidence'.

Example Study

Walker *et al.* (1996) conducted a study that can help explain some important benefits of using LGCM. These researchers wanted to examine the relationship between the amount of care given and caregiving satisfaction among a particular population: daughters caring for their elderly mothers. This question, as we have highlighted immediately above, is longitudinal and necessitates appropriate methods. Noting that the then-available results were mixed, Walker and colleagues speculated that the conflicting results might be due to the statistical methods that had been used and their failure to account for variability within the samples investigated.

Walker *et al.* recruited 130 daughters caring for their elderly mothers. The researchers asked the daughters about the amount of care they gave to their mothers and about their level of satisfaction, as well as some background information (particularly residence with the mother and duration of care to-date). In other words, the primary outcome variable in this study was *satisfaction*, while the explanatory variables were amount of *caregiving* and other background characteristics (co-residence and duration of care). The researchers collected their data four times with about a year gap between each data collection wave. The researchers had nine hypotheses – some of which relate to initial states while others to the nature of change over time:

Hypothesis 1: There is individual variability in change in satisfaction over time. This means that some daughters will report increased satisfaction over time, others decreased, while some others may remain the same.

Hypothesis 2: The overall trend of caregiving will increase over time, as mothers grow older.

Hypothesis 3: Despite the variability proposed in Hypothesis 1, the overall trend of satisfaction will decrease over time.

Hypothesis 4: The initial level of caregiving will be positively influenced by co-residence. That is, daughters who live with their mothers in the same place will provide more care.

Hypothesis 5: The longer one had been giving care (i.e. prior to commencing the research), the lower one's initial level of satisfaction.

Hypothesis 6: Those giving the highest care in Wave 1 will also experience the lowest initial satisfaction.

Hypothesis 7: Parallel to Hypothesis 5, the longer one had been giving care, the greater the decline in satisfaction over time.

Hypothesis 8: Parallel to Hypothesis 6, those giving the highest care in Wave 1 will also show the steepest decline in satisfaction.

Hypothesis 9: The sharper the increase in caregiving, the steeper the decline in satisfaction.

As these various hypotheses show, Walker *et al.* were able to ask rich questions about their phenomenon of interest using data that were collected over four time points (representing over four years' worth of data). In addition to their primary outcome variable (satisfaction), the researchers were able to ask questions involving amount of care, co-residence and duration of caregiving. Their questions addressed the relationships among these variables both in terms of their initial states (intercept) and their interactive change over time (slope). While their study was not explicitly framed in CDST terms, these convey the precise flavor of questions on which CDST research focuses.

In their article, Walker *et al.* showed that some of their hypotheses were supported while some were not (see their article for a complete discussion of the results). Figure 12.2 presents a simplified version of Walker *et al.*'s results. For example, contrary to Walker *et al.*'s expectations, duration of care was not related either to initial (0.007) or to change (0.001) in satisfaction. Both values were too small in magnitude and did not reach statistical significance. In contrast, co-residence did show a larger association that was statistically significant.

When it comes to the relationship between amount of care and satisfaction, Walker *et al.* also found some interesting results. The relationship between initial care and initial satisfaction was negative (−0.541), suggesting that caregivers who were providing the highest care at the beginning of the study showed the lowest initial satisfaction. Similarly, change in amount of care was negatively associated with change in satisfaction (−0.638), suggesting that those who had to increase their care at a higher rate experienced a steeper decline in satisfaction over time. Figure 12.2 also shows a diagonal arrow from initial care to change in satisfaction (0.090). This suggests that initial care, on its own, was not associated with the rate of change in satisfaction. Only change in amount of care over time was associated with the rate of change in satisfaction.

Although this study was not conducted by applied linguists, its relevance is not hard to appreciate. Many questions in applied linguistics lend themselves to longitudinal investigations. We might be interested, for instance, in the development of the proficiency of learners, either globally or in relation to a more specific linguistic feature, such as

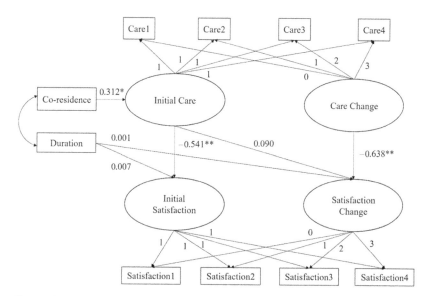

Figure 12.2 A simplified version of Walker *et al.*'s results (Note: *p < 0.05, **p < 0.01)

accuracy in oral production or the use of certain morphological inflec-
tions. LGCM allows the researcher to examine how that feature develops over time and to what extent its developmental trajectory is related
to other explanatory variables, whether time varying or time invariant.
Again, the researcher could examine the relationship of these explanatory variables both in relation to the initial state of proficiency and to its
rate of change over time.

LGCM can also be used in experimental research. The typical
approach in experimental investigations in applied linguistics is to
use a pretest–posttest design, and perhaps an additional delayed post-
test. However, the researcher could learn much more from their data
using LGCM. For example, instead of one experimental treatment, the
researcher might wish to utilize two (or more) complex experimental
treatments: the researcher may introduce a pedagogical intervention
to improve a certain aspect of proficiency, and simultaneously another
environmental treatment to improve learner satisfaction. The researcher
can now examine how change in satisfaction (for those who do show an
increase in it) is related to change in proficiency over time. The analysis could then look at the relationship both with initial states and with
rate of change over time. The model will also be able to accommodate
other explanatory variables, time varying and time invariant, that are
relevant to the research question(s). It is therefore clear that LGCM has
the potential to broaden the repertoire of tools at the disposal of applied
linguists which in turn can expand the research questions they are able
to investigate.

Annotated readings

Burchinal, M.R., Nelson, L. and Poe, M. (2006) IV. Growth curve analysis: An introduction
to various methods for analyzing longitudinal data. *Monographs of the Society for
Research in Child Development* 71 (3), 65–87. doi:10.1111/j.1540-5834.2006.00405.x

This is a useful overview of assumptions that need to be satisfied in the analysis of longitudinal data. This article also compares the characteristics of LGCM with those of other
approaches available (univariate and multivariate repeated measures ANOVA, hierarchical linear models and growth mixture model methods). It also surveys some popular
software programs used for these methods.

Lowry, P.B. and Gaskin, J. (2014) Partial least squares (PLS) structural equation modeling (SEM) for building and testing behavioral causal theory: When to choose it and
how to use it. *IEEE Transactions on Professional Communication* 57 (2), 123–146.
doi:10.1109/TPC.2014.2312452

This is a reader-friendly introduction to key concepts in SEM, which the authors describe
as a *second-generation* (G2) technique. The authors compare G2 techniques to correlation,
regression and difference of means tests like *t*-tests and ANOVA (all called G1). James
Gaskin has also developed an Excel Stats Tools Package, which can conveniently calculate
many important measures required for SEM. It is available to download for free from

www.statwiki.kolobkreations.com. Gaskin also has a YouTube channel with many useful videos that anyone interested in how to conduct SEM should watch (www.youtube.com/user/Gaskination/playlists).

Byrne, B.M. (2012) *Structural Equation Modeling with Mplus: Basic Concepts, Applications, and Programming.* New York: Routledge.

This book is primarily concerned with SEM, but the author devotes one chapter to the application of LGCM. The chapter first offers a brief overview and then a step-by-step guide to analyzing data using Mplus. Byrne has written parallel books based on other software as well, including AMOS, EQS and LISREL.

Preacher, K.J., Wichman, A.L., MacCallum, R.C. and Briggs, N.E. (2008) *Latent Growth Curve Modeling.* Los Angeles, CA: SAGE.

This is one of the popular 'little green book' series published by SAGE. It deals with many issues related to LGCM and clarifies terminology. It also surveys the various models for which LGCM can be implemented. The last chapter in the book is devoted to comparing LGCM and multilevel modeling.

Singer, J.D. and Willett, J.B. (2003) *Applied Longitudinal Data Analysis: Modeling Change and Event Occurrence.* Oxford: Oxford University Press.

This is an important book dealing with different longitudinal approaches. One chapter titled 'Modeling Change Using Covariance Structure Analysis' deals specifically with LGCM, even though the chapter title does not give that away. This book tends to be somewhat mathematically oriented.

Duncan, T.E., Duncan, S.C. and Strycker, L.A. (2006) *An Introduction to Latent Variable Growth Curve Modeling: Concepts, Issues, and Applications* (2nd edn). Mahwah, NJ: Lawrence Erlbaum.

This is a book-length comprehensive treatment of the subject. The authors also provide the syntax of their examples for different software programs. This book and its treatment of the method tends to be rather advanced.

Bollen, K.A. and Curran, P.J. (2006) *Latent Curve Models: A Structural Equation Perspective.* Hoboken, NJ: Wiley.

This is one of the definitive texts in this area, written by two authorities on SEM and LGCM. This is another book for advanced readers who really would like a deep-dive into the method.

Winter, B. and Wieling, M. (2016) How to analyze linguistic change using mixed models, growth curve analysis and generalized additive modeling. *Journal of Language Evolution* 1 (1), 7–18. doi:10.1093/jole/lzv003

This article provides a useful tutorial for language researchers on mixed models, growth curve analysis and generalized additive models, all of which are well suited to analyzing non-linear change over time. The authors additionally provide the R code of their examples so that readers can use it for their own analyses.

References

Bollen, K.A. and Curran, P.J. (2006) *Latent Curve Models: A Structural Equation Perspective*. Hoboken, NJ: Wiley.

Byrne, B.M. (2012) *Structural Equation Modeling with Mplus: Basic Concepts, Applications, and Programming*. New York: Routledge.

Byrne, D. (2002) *Interpreting Quantitative Data*. London: SAGE.

Curran, P.J. and Willoughby, M.T. (2003) Implications of latent trajectory models for the study of developmental psychopathology. *Development and Psychopathology* 15 (3), 581–512. doi:10.1017/S0954579403000300

Hume, D. (1921/1748) *An Enquiry Concerning Human Understanding*. Chicago, IL: Open Court.

Kline, R.B. (2016) *Principles and Practice of Structural Equation Modeling* (4th edn). New York: Guilford Press.

Larsen-Freeman, D. and Cameron, L. (2008) *Complex Systems and Applied Linguistics*. Oxford: Oxford University Press.

Michell, J. (2003) The quantitative imperative: Positivism, naive realism and the place of qualitative methods in psychology. *Theory and Psychology* 13 (1), 5–31.

Michell, J. (2008) Is psychometrics pathological science? *Measurement* 6, 7–24.

Nagin, D.S. and Tremblay, R.E. (2005) Developmental trajectory groups: Fact or a useful statistical fiction? *Criminology* 43 (4), 873–904. doi:10.1111/j.1745-9125.2005.00026.x

Walker, A.J., Acock, A.C., Bowman, S.R. and Li, F. (1996) Amount of care given and caregiving satisfaction: A latent growth curve analysis. *The Journals of Gerontology: Series B* 51B (3), P130–P142. doi:10.1093/geronb/51B.3.P130

13 Multilevel Modeling

Overview

This chapter provides an overview of multilevel modeling (MLM), and to do so let us begin by contextualizing how such an approach is useful in a complex social world. Scholars in the social sciences have long recognized that our world is a multilayered structure of influence (Bronfenbrenner, 1979). For example, in the domain of healthcare, patients in different hospitals would most likely receive somewhat different treatments, as each hospital features different doctors, nurses and other staff, has different facilities, follows different procedures, etc. This fact can affect the outcomes of each hospital. Unique environments can similarly be found in different institutions such as corporations, banks and prisons (not that we have firsthand experience with the latter). Even in agriculture, farm animals and plants can be influenced by the particular farm they happen to be raised on, thus affecting their well-being and the products obtained from them.

Such multiple layers of influence apply equally well to educational institutions. Schools can and do create distinct environments for their students depending on many factors, such as the demeanor of the principal and administrators, adherence to rules and regulations and many other socialization processes. Many experienced teachers would agree that the social environment can be quite different from one school to another, and even from one class to another in the same school. This environment is not just an outcome of the backgrounds of students or their abilities before joining the school. These differences that are tangible in the environment can also exist even if the students did not choose their environment (e.g. they happened to be assigned to classes in a random fashion due to some local regulations) through the socialization processes that take place after such an assignment occurs.

These examples illustrate clustering under higher-level units. In the context of MLM with random effects, this clustering is called *nesting*. A student, for instance, can be nested within a class within a school within a neighborhood. Each of these higher-level units encompasses the lower-level units and can have a downward effect on them. The complexity and dynamic systems theory (CDST) parallel for this would be the notion of nested systems that are hierarchical in nature. MLM is an effective method to examine such nested systems and to model and partition the variance attributable to each of these levels.

MLM with random effects can be thought of as an application of panel data (Chapter 11), and as a particular extension of multiple regression. Therefore, as a primer to the method this chapter deals with, the reader should have a reasonable grasp of issues related to multiple regression, such as coefficients, covariates, dummy variables and R^2. Accessible introductions can be found in Allison (1999) and in Miles and Shevlin (2001). A detailed treatment of the assumptions required to conduct regression is provided by Berry (1993).

Research Questions

MLM is a flexible procedure that allows the researcher to ask various questions. Imagine a researcher in an educational setting interested in examining school achievement. This researcher could collect longitudinal data (i.e. repeated measures) from students over time. The researcher may also decide to collect these data from different schools. In this example, insights could be obtained from the repeated measures (Level 1), from student characteristics such as gender and motivation (Level 2) and from school characteristics such as public versus private (Level 3). Example research questions could be (Rasbash, 2008):

- Is there intra-individual change over time (mean)?
- How variable is the intra-individual progress (variance)?
- Are there inter-individual variables (e.g. gender, motivation) that can predict change over time? Do males progress faster or slower?
- Are there inter-individual variables (e.g. gender, motivation) that can predict variability in change over time? Is the progress of individuals of certain characteristics (e.g. females) more uniform overall?
- Is there more progress in some schools in comparison to others (Level 3)?
- Can this progress be explained by certain student characteristics (e.g. gender, motivation)?
- Can this progress be explained by certain school characteristics (e.g. public vs. private)?
- Can this progress be explained by an interaction between student characteristics and school characteristics? Do females progress faster in private schools, for example?
- Is there variability in progress across different schools?
- Can this variability be explained by certain student characteristics (e.g. gender, motivation)?

- Can this variability be explained by certain school characteristics (e.g. public vs. private)?
- Can this variability be explained by an interaction between student characteristics and school characteristics? Are males more variable in public schools, for example?
- How much of the variance is accounted for by each of the three levels? Does each higher level add significantly to the variance explained by the lower levels?

As many of these research questions illustrate, an important feature of MLM is its ability to model not only the mean of the attribute in question, but also its variability. MLM also allows the researcher to include explanatory variables (which MLM also calls covariates) at different levels of analysis. These explanatory variables might be time invariant (e.g. gender) or time varying (e.g. motivation). For additional research questions that researchers could investigate with MLM, see Tabachnick & Fidell (2013: 789–791).

Technical Features

In some contexts, MLM is more a necessity than a luxury. If the data set has clusters (e.g. students sampled from a number of classes), students from the same class would likely be more similar to each other than students coming from different classes. This creates dependence within the data. However, the standard analysis of variance (ANOVA) and regression models rest on the independence assumption, violation of which can inflate the Type I error rate. MLM can also handle this dependence and adjust for it so that standard errors and significance tests are more accurate.

Thus, an important feature of MLM is that it explicitly takes context into account. This is, of course, one of the main lessons of CDST that informs compatible research methods – the other being dynamic change (see e.g. our discussion in Part 1 of the book). Instead of treating all participants equally, it matters from which class and which school each student originates. In fact, MLM is sometimes called *contextual analysis* (Diez Roux, 2002; Iversen, 1991). MLM can deal with open systems without the need to 'control, restrict, or remove the effects of outside contextual influences' (Luke, 2004: 2). Disregard of contextual factors can lead to inappropriate conclusions (Hox, 2010), conceptually and methodologically. For example, the researcher might fall into the *ecological fallacy*, in which conclusions made with aggregated data are applied at the individual level (see e.g. Larsen-Freeman, 2006). Conversely, transporting conclusions from individual analysis to the group level may result in the *atomistic fallacy* by ignoring emergent outcomes.

> ### ROBSON AND PEVALIN (2016: 6–7) ON THE IMPORTANCE OF TAKING THE COMPLEXITY OF THE BIGGER PICTURE INTO ACCOUNT:
>
> Your models should always be theory-driven, and the best model choice is one that corresponds to a sound theoretical rationale. One that is often overlooked is the general theoretical arguments around how the social world is portrayed. Education researchers, such as Bronfenbrenner (1977, 2001), have argued that the outcomes of individuals, particularly children, cannot be understood without taking different contexts into perspective. His ecological systems approach identifies a number of different contexts to be taken into consideration in terms of how they work independently and together to create the environments in which children live. By looking at data collected from individuals, we are focusing on the micro-level (i.e. individual) effects of specific characteristics on outcomes of interest, but it is more likely the case that these micro-level effects vary significantly across larger units at the meso (school or community) and macro (municipal or national) levels. The micro and the macro (and the micro and meso) interact. This theoretical perspective is most readily tested with statistical techniques that recognize these important distinctions.... The popularity of theories that focus exclusively on the individual or solely on higher levels (groups, firms, nations) is being overshadowed by approaches that try to mix the two and presumably give a more accurate depiction of the complexity of the social world.

An important concept in MLM is whether coefficients are *fixed* or *random*. When a higher-level variable (e.g. schools) represents all units of analysis (i.e. our interest is all schools in a region and we have already sampled all of them), the coefficient is called fixed. On the other hand, if the schools in our data set are only a sample of the schools of interest rather than the whole population, then the coefficient is called random. MLM makes certain adjustments to the analysis depending on whether these schools represent the whole population or just a sample from it. In MLM terminology, there is also a distinction between fixed and random intercepts, and fixed and random slopes (see e.g. Robson & Pevalin [2016] for a discussion).

Levels can occur not only in nature, but also as researcher-imposed structures. As an illustration, consider the following scenarios:

* Repeated measures or panel design: Multiple observations may be nested within the individual, such as accuracy of language use over time. Here, the individual is not the lowest level of analysis.

- Multivariate data: We may wish to measure more than one aspect from each individual, such as both accuracy and fluency of their language production. Again, the individual here is a higher-level unit.
- Multistage survey designs: A researcher may divide the population of interest into units (say, 100 regions or cities) and then sample from some of these units only (say, 30) in order to minimize costs.
- Interventions: The treatment may be administered at the group level (e.g. class) as opposed to the individual level (the student). This is very common in applied linguistics research where interventions are frequently administered to intact classes.

An interesting advantage of MLM is that it is also versatile enough to handle data that are missing at random. In fact, this approach even allows the researcher to deliberately drop some measures. For example, a researcher investigating second language (L2) learning outcomes may have a rather extended language test, but time constraints may make administering the whole test impractical. In this case, the researcher may decide that there is a set of core items that all participants must respond to (e.g. about vocabulary) and other items related to other aspects (e.g. grammar, reading and listening). Here, the researcher could administer the core items, and then administer each of the other aspects to different participants. In other words, each participant responds to the vocabulary part plus one randomly selected aspect.

Returning to the concept of systems' nestedness and accompanying hierarchies, another advantage of MLM is its ability to handle different types of complex hierarchies. Life is not always as neat as we would like it to be. In some cases, we may have a *strict hierarchy*, such as students within classes within schools. Here, each student belongs to one class, and each class belongs to one school. However, there are cases where this hierarchy does not hold:

- Cross-classified structures: Imagine that we wish to investigate the relationship between student performance at school and later at university. We may find that students from the same schools go to the same universities (see Figure 13.1a). However, it is more realistic to expect students from the same school to go to different universities. In Figure 13.1b, Students 5 and 6 went to University 2 instead of University 1. The reverse occurred for Students 7 and 8. Note that, in both cases, the student is still the lowest level of analysis.
- Multiple membership structures: Imagine that we wish to examine the relationship between student characteristics and teacher characteristics. We may find that each student has one teacher (Figure 13.2a). However, it is more likely that more than one teacher is responsible for teaching the students (or some of them). As shown in Figure 13.2b, Student 1 has only one teacher. However, Student 2

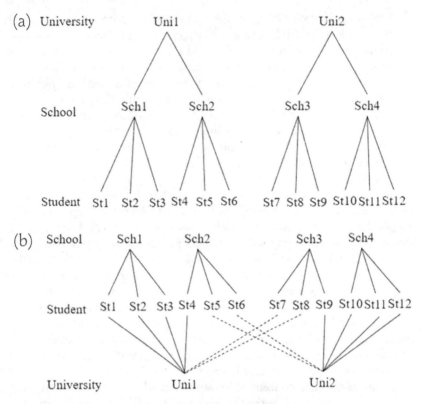

Figure 13.1 Strict hierarchy versus cross-classified structures

has two teachers. Student 6 even has three teachers. MLM can also model the proportion allocated to each teacher. For Student 2, the two teachers have an equal share of the teaching load. For Student 6, however, the share is split into 40-20-20.

MLM can handle all these complex structures. It can also handle structures where there is a combination of cross-classification and multiple membership. Therefore, many researchers prefer to avoid the term hierarchical modeling to describe MLM because the structures that MLM can handle are not limited to strict hierarchies.

Example Study

A study by Trautwein and Lüdtke (2007) provides some insights into the utility of MLM. Trautwein and Lüdtke observed that, despite the growing number of studies on homework, the relationship between homework and academic achievement is still controversial. Trautwein and Lüdtke argued that homework is a complex issue that involves interactions among student, peer, classroom and family factors, all of which

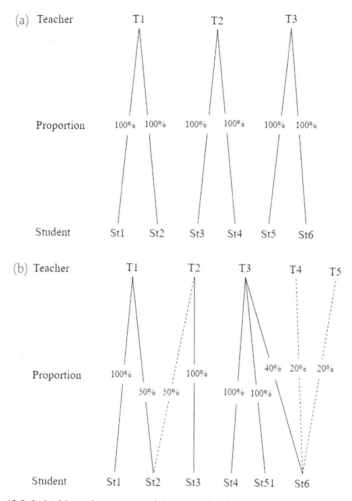

(a) Teacher   T1   T2   T3

Proportion   100% 100%   100%   100%   100% 100%

Student   St1   St2   St3   St4   St5   St6

(b) Teacher   T1   T2   T3   T4   T5

Proportion   100%   100%   40% 20% 20%
                    50% 50%   100% 100%

Student   St1   St2   St3   St4   St51   St6

Figure 13.2 Strict hierarchy versus multiple membership structures

may play a role in how a student performs on their homework assignments and benefits from them. Trautwein and Lüdtke also thought that homework commitment may differ among different school subjects – a plausible conjecture. The researchers therefore set out to examine this complex homework–achievement link.

Trautwein and Lüdtke conducted a study on homework in six different school subjects (German, English, history, biology, mathematics and physics). They administered a questionnaire to 511 Grades 8 and 9 students asking them about the time and effort they allocated to doing their homework in each of the six school subjects, as well as some other motivational and demographic variables and a test of basic cognitive abilities. Therefore, school subject was Level 1 in this study, and the student was Level 2. The students came from 42 classes and from the three major tracks in the German educational system (academic, intermediate and lower), and therefore these two variables (class and track) represented Level 3.

Trautwein and Lüdtke used MLM to test a number of hypotheses:

- *Level 1 (intra-individual differences in school subjects):*
  Hypothesis 1: Students will report putting more effort into homework in subjects where their expectancy beliefs (i.e. doing it successfully) are high.

  Hypothesis 2: Students will report putting more effort into homework in subjects where their value beliefs (utility and cost) are high.

  Hypothesis 3: Students will report putting more effort into homework in subjects where their perceived homework quality (being interesting) is high.

  Hypothesis 4: Students will report putting more effort into homework in subjects where their perceived teacher control (knowledge of compliance) is high.

  Hypothesis 5: The effects of perceived homework quality will be partly mediated by the homework motivation variables (expectancy and value).

  Hypothesis 6: The more the parents consider homework important in a school subject, the more effort the student will put into that subject.

  Hypothesis 7: In contrast to Hypothesis 6, the same will not be true for the amount of actual help parents provide for homework in each subject.

- *Level 2 (inter-individual differences across students):*
  Hypothesis 8: The higher the student conscientiousness, the higher the homework effort overall.

  Hypothesis 9: The more supportive the parent–child communication, the higher the homework effort overall.

  Hypothesis 10: The higher the student grade, the less the homework effort overall.

- *Interaction between subject and student levels:*
  Hypothesis 11: Conscientiousness will interact with perceived homework control, in that the effect will be weaker in students high in conscientiousness but stronger in those low in it.

- *Time on homework as a dependent variable:*
  Hypothesis 12: At the subject level, homework motivation will not be a good predictor of homework time, as the mere time spent on homework is not a good reflection of quality.

Hypothesis 13: At the subject level, prior achievement will be a non-significant or negative predictor of homework time.

Hypothesis 14: At the student level, conscientiousness will be a non-significant or negative predictor of basic cognitive abilities.

Hypothesis 15: Due to the complexity of time on homework, the variables in the model will be able to explain more of the variance in homework effort than in homework time.

Thus, Trautwein and Lüdtke were able to ask rich questions related to different levels. At each level, there were also various variables that were hypothesized either to show or not show a relationship. Most of these hypotheses were supported by the results (see their article for a complete presentation of these results). For example, when it comes to homework effort, the researchers found that 53% of the variance in homework was explained by intra-individual differences while 47% was explained by inter-individual differences. When it comes to homework time, 67% of the variance was attributable to intra-individual differences, 31% to inter-individual differences and 2% to the class level.

This example gives an illustration of how MLM allows the researcher to build a complex model. The researcher does not have to limit themselves to a few variables, but can include a larger set of variables at different levels of analysis. MLM also allows the researcher to examine cross-level interactions, which can provide truly unique insights into the phenomena under investigation.

From a CDST perspective, it is highly unlikely that events are completely independent, and we cannot know what the relationships will be at one level of analysis from the relationships that exist at another. Ignoring this fact may lead to inaccurate inferences drawn from empirical data unless the variability is explicitly partitioned and accounted for in attempting to explain those complex phenomena. MLM allows a researcher to do just that at a high level of sophistication.

Annotated readings

Robson, K. and Pevalin, D.J. (2016) *Multilevel Modeling in Plain Language*. Los Angeles, CA: SAGE.

This is a very accessible introductory book to MLM. Just as the title indicates, the authors do an excellent job of explaining MLM concepts in simple terms. Perhaps this book should be the first resource for readers interested in learning more about this topic.

Diez Roux, A.V. (2002) A glossary for multilevel analysis. *Journal of Epidemiology and Community Health* 56 (8), 588–594. doi:10.1136/jech.56.8.588

One of the challenging aspects of MLM is getting a grasp of the terminology used in this area. Because of this, MLM can be confusing at first. Diez Roux provides a helpful glossary to the most common terms used.

LEMMA (Learning Environment for Multilevel Methodology and Applications) virtual learning environment, Bristol University. http://www.bristol.ac.uk/cmm/learning/online-course/

This is a free online course on MLM and different topics and applications that fall under MLM. This course was prepared by experts in this area and includes practical examples using different software packages.

Peugh, J.L. (2010) A practical guide to multilevel modeling. *Journal of School Psychology* 48 (1), 85–112. doi:10.1016/j.jsp.2009.09.002

The author of this paper provides a step-by-step guide to building different types of MLM models. While it assumes some fundamental background knowledge, it provides helpful practical examples. The appendix also includes the SAS and SPSS syntax of these models.

Singer, J.D. and Willett, J.B. (2003) *Applied Longitudinal Data Analysis: Modeling Change and Event Occurrence.* Oxford: Oxford University Press.

This book is concerned with longitudinal data more generally, and some chapters are concerned with MLM more specifically. This book tends to be a fairly advanced treatment of the topic, and we would recommend it to those generally familiar with conventional modeling methods.

Goldstein, H. (2011) *Multilevel Statistical Models* (4th edn). Chichester: Wiley.
Hox, J.J. (2010) *Multilevel Analysis: Techniques and Applications* (2nd edn). New York: Routledge.
Rabe-Hesketh, S. and Skrondal, A. (2012) *Multilevel and Longitudinal Modeling Using Stata* (3rd edn). College Station, TX: Stata Press Publication.
Hox, J.J. and Roberts, J.K. (eds) (2011) *Handbook of Advanced Multilevel Analysis.* New York: Routledge.

This is a set of rather advanced texts we have found useful for delving into details of various issues related to MLM. Interested readers may consult them as a primer on best practices after getting to grips with the foundations of MLM from the other sources we recommend.

Preacher, K.J., Wichman, A.L., MacCallum, R.C. and Briggs, N.E. (2008) *Latent Growth Curve Modeling.* Los Angeles, CA: SAGE.

The last chapter in this book offers a useful comparison of multilevel modeling and latent growth curve modeling.

References

Allison, P.D. (1999) *Multiple Regression: A Primer.* Thousand Oaks, CA: Pine Forge Press.
Berry, W.D. (1993) *Understanding Regression Assumptions.* Newbury Park, CA: SAGE.
Bronfenbrenner, U. (1979) *The Ecology of Human Development: Experiments by Nature and Design.* Cambridge, MA: Harvard University Press.

Diez Roux, A.V. (2002) A glossary for multilevel analysis. *Journal of Epidemiology and Community Health* 56 (8), 588–594. doi:10.1136/jech.56.8.588

Hox, J.J. (2010) *Multilevel Analysis: Techniques and Applications* (2nd edn). New York: Routledge.

Iversen, G.R. (1991) *Contextual Analysis*. Newbury Park: SAGE.

Larsen-Freeman, D. (2006) The emergence of complexity, fluency, and accuracy in the oral and written production of five Chinese learners of English. *Applied Linguistics* 27 (4), 590–619. doi:10.1093/applin/aml029

Luke, D.A. (2004) *Multilevel Modeling*. Thousand Oaks, CA: SAGE.

Miles, J. and Shevlin, M. (2001) *Applying Regression & Correlation: A Guide for Students and Researchers*. London: SAGE.

Rasbash, J. (2008) *Module 4: Multilevel Structures and Classifications*. LEMMA VLE, University of Bristol, Centre for Multilevel Modelling. See http://www.bristol.ac.uk/cmm/ (accessed 30 June 2019).

Robson, K. and Pevalin, D.J. (2016) *Multilevel Modeling in Plain Language*. Los Angeles, CA: SAGE.

Tabachnick, B.G. and Fidell, L.S. (2013) *Using Multivariate Statistics* (6th edn). Boston, MA: Pearson.

Trautwein, U. and Lüdtke, O. (2007) Students' self-reported effort and time on homework in six school subjects: Between-students differences and within-student variation. *Journal of Educational Psychology* 99 (2), 432–444. doi:10.1037/0022-0663.99.2.432

14 Time Series Analysis

Overview

The approaches discussed in Chapters 11–13 assume that the same units are followed over time. However, there are occasions when the researcher is able to collect data over time, but not from the same units. Examples include measures obtained from nationwide samples over several years. A distinct feature of time series analysis (TSA) is that it typically involves a large number of time-ordered, equally spaced observations. This allows the researcher to handle hundreds or even thousands of data points collected over time. Thus, an added advantage of TSA over latent growth curve modeling (Chapter 12) is its ability to easily handle many more data collection points – though it typically uses fewer variables. Obviously, this is a very useful tool for complexity and dynamic systems theory (CDST) researchers, who are often interested in a rich understanding of the developmental aspects of the phenomena under study.

Given sufficient data collection points, it becomes possible to forecast, probabilistically, how the variables are likely to behave in the future, and to speculate about how they might have behaved in the past (Ostrom, 1978). This feature gives us a valuable means of theory building, testing and development. Without discounting anything we have said about how CDST values openness to context, the importance of initial conditions, interconnectedness, soft-assembly and nonlinear change and self-organization, the ability to make predictions is certainly one of the most important ways to put a theory to the test empirically. Put differently, as the saying goes 'the proof of the pudding is in the eating'.

> *KANTZ AND SCHREIBER (2003: 48) ON THE ROLE OF PREDICTION IN NONLINEAR TSA:*
>
> In this book we are concerned with the detection and quantification of possibly complicated structures in a signal. We want to be able to convince others that the structures we find are real and not just fluctuations.

The most convincing argument for the presence of some pattern is if it can be used to give an improved prediction. It is a necessary condition for a theory to be compatible with the known data but it is not sufficient. In order to become accepted, a theory must successfully predict something which can be verified subsequently. In time series analysis, we can take this requirement of predictive quality quite literally.

TSA essentially involves the collection of numerous observations and plotting them in a time series plot. The data are then analyzed in a way that is different from standard regression analysis. This analysis differs because of the problem of *autocorrelation* of error terms. That is, in many statistical procedures, observations are expected to be randomly selected from a population. However, autocorrelation happens when the data are collected over time, and the data can no longer be treated as random. Just as with the CDST principles of interdependence and complex causality, instead each data point becomes very similar to the one just before it and the one just after it (also called serial dependence in TSA). This similarity violates the assumption of non-autocorrelation in regression and in many other statistical procedures, and inflates significance tests. Consequently, if TSA did not take this principle into account, researchers would get significant results when they should not (Ostrom, 1978).

There are different methods of TSA (see e.g. Montgomery *et al.*, 2008). Two popular methods are time series regression analysis and Box–Jenkins time series (Ostrom, 1978). Time series regression analysis operates in a way similar to structural equation modeling: the researcher specifies certain predictions in advance and then uses the data to test these predictions. Box–Jenkins time series, on the other hand, is empirically based. This means that Box–Jenkins time series looks at the data and then develops a model describing them inductively. Other varieties involve the researcher deliberately manipulating some variables in order to investigate the effectiveness of an intervention. This is sometimes referred to as interrupted time series (see Chapter 16 on single-case designs).

The topic of TSA is notorious for its heavy reliance on technical details and mathematical notation. It is hard to find a book on this method that a beginner can readily open and learn about TSA without encountering complex equations on almost every page – which might be discouraging to some readers. However, in this chapter, as in the rest of the book, we try to offer a conceptual introduction to TSA that is accessible and that does not involve a single equation. Expert TSA users might therefore find this chapter too basic, or even simplistic at times, if they come to it expecting a treatment of the equations (e.g. nonlinear differential equations) that underlie TSA. However, we aim to explain particular terms to the readers that are associated with TSA as a starting point for further reading. At the end of this chapter, as we have done in other chapters, we refer interested readers to a number of annotated readings that provide further technical detail.

Research Questions

TSA allows the researcher to investigate a number of interesting questions related to making forecasts and predictions of complex and dynamic phenomena. Some of the topics mentioned in the following research questions might be unfamiliar to some readers, but they will be discussed later in this chapter.

- Based on the present data, to what extent can we forecast how the data may look in the future?
- Based on the present data, to what extent can we speculate how the data might have looked in the past?
- How far into the future (or past) does the available data allow us to make predictions (or retrodictions)?
- In addition to the point estimate, what is the horizon, or interval, forecast (see later)?
- What is the trend of the data? Is it linear or nonlinear?
- What is the nature of the data fluctuation? Is it stationary, seasonal, cyclical or just random?
- Is there evidence for causality in the pattern? Are there variables that 'Granger-cause' this pattern (see later)?

As these examples illustrate, the questions revolve around two main purposes: identifying the nature of the data sequence and making forecasts based on what is known from the data. However, we must make it clear early in this chapter that predictions and projections are rarely if ever deterministic in real life (Bisgaard & Kulahci, 2011). More realistically, the model should be stochastic (i.e. probabilistic) and in this way is actually CDST-compatible. This is because there are always potential influences that are unknown – and perhaps unknowable in advance – that introduce an element of randomness into the analyses. Instead, TSA users can obtain a *prediction interval* and calculate the probability that an observation will fall within that interval.

Technical Features

TSA can be used when the phenomenon of interest lends itself to repeated waves of data collection. The researcher should be able to go back to the phenomenon to study it and take measurements over time, or have access to a database that already has this type of data. For example, a researcher might investigate the development of certain aspects of a learner's second language (L2), such as the use of a particular grammatical structure, code-switching tendencies or the T-unit length in L2 discourse.

After collecting the time series data, the researcher can visually plot them to examine the developmental trajectory of the data. Alternatively, the researcher can calculate the correlations among the different data points (called correlograms of autocorrelation and partial autocorrelation in TSA). The resulting shape may turn out to be stationary, seasonal, cyclical or random. These different types are explained with examples as we progress through this section.

Imagine that a school library has statistics about its monthly users. Figure 14.1 shows a hypothetical example of library users during a 10-year period. This pattern is called stationary because it tends to have a constant mean, variance and autocorrelation throughout. Despite some fluctuations, it is clear that the average number of users tends to be somewhere between 60 and 70 most of the time. Such a stationary trend makes forecasting future trends relatively easy and straightforward. A popular method used for this purpose is called Auto-Regressive Integrated Moving Average (ARIMA, Box & Jenkins, 1976).

Now imagine that our school library also has time series data for the book-borrowing record of its L2 learners. Figure 14.2 plots this hypothetical data. As can be seen, it is clear that the borrowing trend has increased over this 10-year period. If we look at the borrowing trend within each year, we will also notice a cyclical pattern. Learners show the most interest in borrowing books during the middle of each year.

From inspection of this trend, we might speculate on the borrowing record pre-2005 and post-2015. We might, for instance, forecast the amount of demand in a specific month in the near future. This is a point forecast. Alternatively, we can develop a horizon forecast, predicting for

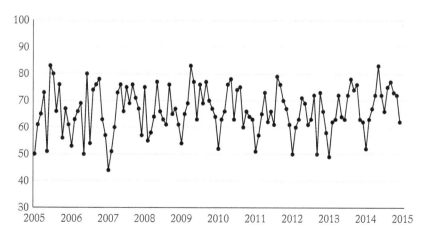

Figure 14.1 Hypothetical data showing a stationary trend of library users

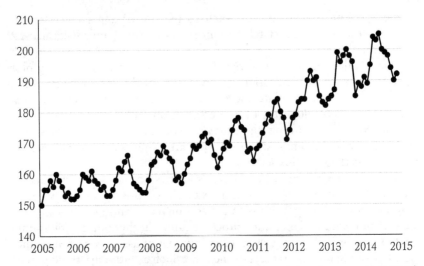

Figure 14.2 Hypothetical school library borrowing record showing a seasonal trend

example the pattern of several months (i.e. the time horizon in question). We would expect the borrowing record to follow a similar pattern with the middle of the year still being the period of highest demand. Statistical procedures have been developed within TSA to formalize forecasts such as these. Off-the-shelf technologies for gathering intensive data have improved in recent decades, and advances in software packages have made these new analytic techniques increasingly available to researchers: common statistical packages (e.g. MATLAB, R, SAS, SPSS and STATA) have modules that can accommodate such forecasting.

We may additionally hypothesize that the increasing trend has to do with the fact that the school library has been accepting more and more students in recent years. Based on this hypothesis, then, we would anticipate that the trend will continue to increase as the school library continues to increase its student intake. This is an example of Granger causality (see the example study later for an illustration).

Now let's consider the number of books acquired by this hypothetical school library over the years (Figure 14.3). This time, the pattern is less straightforward than the previous ones. The book acquisition record does seem to show a trend, but it is not as regular as the borrowing record (Figure 14.2). Here, we see the first three years representing one pattern, then the next four years showing that acquisition plummeted (perhaps due to a fiscal crunch) and then the last years recovering. In the time series literature, this is called a cyclical trend. Unlike the seasonal trend in Figure 14.2, the cyclical trend has no fixed period (e.g. repeating the cycle each month, year and so on). We might try to forecast acquisition in subsequent years, but if the reason for plummeting acquisition figures is a crisis in educational funding, it would be hard to tell in advance

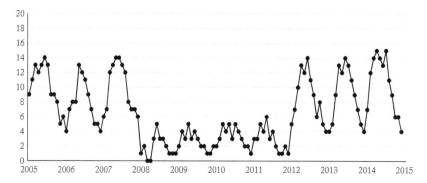

Figure 14.3 Hypothetical book acquisition data showing a seasonal trend

when this is going to happen. We might have an idea of how the figure might be, but not when exactly.

Now, let's take a look at the number of books damaged during this period. Unlike the previous situations, Figure 14.4 does not show a clear trend. The mean keeps changing throughout the period. Sometimes no books are damaged, but sometimes 20 are damaged (quite a few!). The variance is also changing; the variation is sometimes wide and at other times narrow. This apparently random pattern makes it hard to make forecasts. Still, it might be possible to see a trend during the last three years, where the pattern seems to be decreasing. If this is the case, then the most useful part of the plot for forecasting purposes may be the graph of past time trends.

Analysis of time series involves a variety of statistical procedures (see e.g. Hill & Lewicki, 2006). One example is *smoothing*. Smoothing involves a process of averaging adjacent data points so that we come up with what is commonly referred to as a *moving average* to represent the developmental trajectory of the phenomenon in question. The analysis

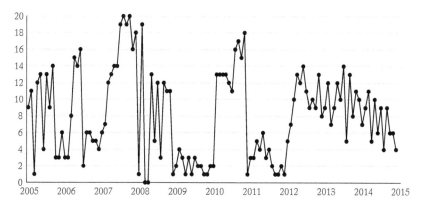

Figure 14.4 Hypothetical record of damaged books showing a random pattern

may also reveal that the data exhibit *additive* or *multiplicative* seasonality. Additive seasonality indicates that a trend increases by a certain number. For example, if our school library acquires a few new books every month, but acquires 20 additional books in September, we have an additive pattern (i.e. we add 20 books to the total number). On the other hand, if the school library has enough funds to acquire an additional 20% of its current number of books in September, then we have a multiplicative pattern (i.e. we multiply the current number by 0.2). These two patterns lead to different trajectories and, consequently, different projections. Over time, additive patterns maintain a linear trend. Multiplicative patterns become nonlinear (or exponential).

A pattern that has been frequently observed by time series researchers has come to be known as *damped trend*. This trend exhibits, through a stochastic process, a proportional decrease over time. For instance, our school library might realize that the 20% increase in book acquisition was too ambitious, and so they may decide to have an increase of 18% in the next cycle. After that, the increase might drop to 16% and so on. The trajectory therefore appears to be 'damped' over time, and this is a common pattern of development in systems responding to negative feedback (see Chapter 2 on this issue).

BISGAARD AND KULAHCI (2011: 22) ON THE IMPORTANCE OF DATA VISUALIZATION:

In most cases, graphical and mathematical modeling go hand in hand. Careful graphical scrutiny of the data is always the first and often crucial step in any statistical analysis. Indeed, data visualization is important in all steps of an analysis and should often be the last step as a 'sanity check' to avoid embarrassing mistakes. We need to develop a 'feel' for the data and generate intuition about what we are dealing with. Such 'feel' and intuition come from hands-on work with and manipulation of the data. Statistical graphics is perhaps the most important means we have for learning about process behavior and for discovering relationships. Graphics is also important in data cleaning. However, graphical data analysis of time series data is not necessarily obvious and trivial. It requires skills and techniques. Some methods and approaches are better than the others. There is an art and a science to data visualization... Data always includes peculiar patterns. Most are worth careful scrutiny. Of course, some patterns may be unimportant. But in many cases, outliers and strange patterns indicate something important or unusual and in some cases may be the most important part of the entire dataset. Therefore, they should not easily be glanced over or dismissed. As Yogi Berra of the New York Yankees said at a press conference in 1963, 'You can observe a lot by watching.' This is particularly true with time series data analysis!

Example Study

An important area of inquiry in TSA is how to investigate causality (Chapter 3 presents a more detailed exposition of the topic). Understanding patterns through pure descriptive approaches as well as forecasting patterns to a satisfactorily accurate level are certainly desirable features of TSA. However, TSA will become even more useful if it can additionally shed light on the underlying mechanisms of the obtained pattern and, particularly, what might have caused it. This is key to CDST research, much of which aims to understand the interaction of complex causal mechanisms in context that led to a particular outcome. In TSA, such applications are well known, and for instance Sir Clive Granger (1969) demonstrated how causal inference can be obtained for one time series using another prior time series, which won him a Nobel Prize.

Marazzo *et al.* (2010) applied time series and Granger causality – named after the Nobel laureate – to understanding the issue of air transport demand in Brazil. The authors argued that air transport is one of the most vital domains in any nation. Understanding current demand for air transport and anticipating future increases in that arena are essential for budgetary plans and for its immense economic impact. Marazzo and colleagues obtained their data from the Brazilian market and applied a range of time series analyses. They found that there is a high annual growth rate in air traffic, predicting that – at this rate – the capacity of major Brazilian airports will be fully utilized at some point. This forecast has important applications, both immediately and over a longer time horizon, as it could help officials make strategic plans and better utilize the nation's available resources.

Importantly, Marazzo *et al.* (2010) wanted to understand what factors might have contributed to this growth in air transport demand, and specifically the contribution of economic growth (gross domestic product [GDP]). To investigate this, the researchers applied Granger causality to examine the relationship between air transport demand and GDP between 1966 and 2006. Their article presents in some detail the statistical equations they used. We do not introduce these here as the sheer unfamiliarity of this mathematical notation might make some readers feel a bit overwhelmed. At a conceptual level, however, the task was rather straightforward: In order for the hypothesis that GPD causes air transport demand to be supported, Granger causality requires that prior levels of GPD improve the prediction of air transport demand, compared to the prediction obtained from prior levels of air transport demand only. After analyzing the relationship between these two time series trends, Marazzo and colleagues found that GPD is a plausible candidate to explain the observed growth rate in air transport demand. In fact, their analysis revealed that GPD requires about two years to reach its maximum effect on air transport demand. This provides one particular illustration of the CDST notion of complex causal conditions having a delayed effect and a non-proportional effect over time.

Annotated readings

StatSoft Inc. (2013) *Electronic Statistics Textbook*. Tulsa, OK: StatSoft. See http://www.statsoft.com/Textbook/Time-Series-Analysis (accessed 30 June 2019).

As mentioned earlier in this chapter, the reader should expect to encounter some technical details even in the introductory texts in this topic. It might therefore be a good idea to start with an online text that is available for free. This book has one chapter on TSA, and from it the reader can get a more detailed overview of this area.

Bisgaard, S. and Kulahci, M. (2011) *Time Series Analysis and Forecasting by Example*. Hoboken, NJ: Wiley.

Bisgaard and Kulahci acknowledge that it is hard to find an easy-to-read textbook on TSA, which was their motivation for writing this book. Readers will find this book relatively easy to follow, though it is not entirely devoid of technical equations. The authors also have an interesting chapter on visualizing time series and its dos and don'ts.

Montgomery, D.C., Jennings, C.L. and Kulahci, M. (2008) *Introduction to Time Series Analysis and Forecasting*. Hoboken, NJ: Wiley.

This is a mildly technical text that presents a detailed overview of TSA methods. The authors also present practical examples using three software packages: Minitab, JMP and SAS.

Schelter, B., Winterhalder, M. and Timmer, J. (eds) (2006) *Handbook of Time Series Analysis: Recent Theoretical Developments and Applications*. Weinheim: Wiley-VCH.

This is a collection of chapters on rather advanced topics in TSA. These topics include nonlinear dynamical models, deterministic and probabilistic forecasting and graphical modeling of dynamic relationships.

Kantz, H. and Schreiber, T. (2003) *Nonlinear Time Series Analysis* (2nd edn). Cambridge: Cambridge University Press.

This book specializes in nonlinear TSA. It deals with advanced topics including chaotic data and noise, ergodicity and strange attractors, and coupling and synchronization of nonlinear systems.

Box, G.E.P. and Jenkins, G.M. (1976) *Time Series Analysis: Forecasting and Control*. Oakland, CA: Holden-Day.

This is an important book in TSA. The authors deal with what were then groundbreaking models such as autoregressive moving average models and their statistical estimation. Box and Jenkins' treatment of these issues is definitely targeted at an advanced audience.

References

Bisgaard, S. and Kulahci, M. (2011) *Time Series Analysis and Forecasting by Example.* Hoboken, NJ: Wiley.

Box, G.E.P. and Jenkins, G.M. (1976) *Time Series Analysis: Forecasting and Control.* Oakland, CA: Holden-Day.

Granger, C.W.J. (1969) Investigating causal relations by econometric models and cross-spectral methods. *Econometrica* 37 (3), 424–438. doi:10.2307/1912791

Hill, T. and Lewicki, P. (2006) *Statistics: Methods and Applications: A Comprehensive Reference for Science, Industry, and Data Mining.* Tulsa, OK: StatSoft.

Kantz, H. and Schreiber, T. (2003) *Nonlinear Time Series Analysis* (2nd edn). Cambridge: Cambridge University Press.

Marazzo, M., Scherre, R. and Fernandes, E. (2010) Air transport demand and economic growth in Brazil: A time series analysis. *Transportation Research Part E: Logistics and Transportation Review* 46 (2), 261–269. doi:10.1016/j.tre.2009.08.008

Montgomery, D.C., Jennings, C.L. and Kulahci, M. (2008) *Introduction to Time Series Analysis and Forecasting.* Hoboken, NJ: Wiley.

Ostrom, C.W. (1978) *Time Series Analysis: Regression Techniques.* Beverly Hills, CA: SAGE.

15 Experience Sampling Method

Overview

In his review of the origins of the experience sampling method (ESM), Mihaly Csikszentmihalyi (2014) highlights the long-existing tension between subjective and objective approaches to studying human and social phenomena. The former approaches, which are often more qualitative in nature, privilege subjective experience and personal meaning, while more quantitative approaches tend to recognize the more rigorous results of controlled experimentation as valid. He argues that since human experience and the quality of that experience is of interest to all of the social sciences, the human and social disciplines can only become fully fledged sciences if they find a way to investigate life in all its complexity, drawing equally on subjective and objective approaches (cf. Mehl & Conner, 2012).

To relate this explicitly to complexity and dynamic systems theory (CDST), both recent (LeDoux, 2002) and more historical points of view (James, 1890/2013) stress the need to take two factors into account: first that individual experience is complex and idiosyncratic, and second that it is structurally dynamic, undergoing relentless change. This is why experience sampling methodologists recognize the importance of considering experience as a unitary complex, emerging from the interplay between emotions, motivations and cognitions, and not uniquely from physiological input (Bolger *et al.*, 2003; Feldman Barrett & Barrett, 2001).

By its very design, experience sampling data are complex and dynamic (Brose & Ram, 2012). In intact settings (e.g. at work, at home with one's family, in a classroom and within social institutions) where there is some degree of familiarity with a well-defined complex system or developmental question of interest, collecting such *in situ* and time-dense data can genuinely be one of the more CDST-compatible ways of studying the temporal and phenomenological aspects of human functioning and behavior (Deboeck, 2012).

With this agenda in mind, the main methodological challenge shifted to developing a reliable measurement of temporal experience and the accompanying events by combining a focus on lived experience with methodologists' attempt to use the tools of empirical investigation – including available designs, data elicitation techniques and statistical analyses (Csikszentmihalyi & Larson, 1987). Thus, the ESM was devised in response to this challenge and has turned out to be, as Hektner *et al.* (2007: 6) suggest somewhat tongue-in-cheek, 'a nomothetic contamination of [an] ideographic approach'.

What does such an approach look like in practice? The most characteristic feature of ESM is that it prompts individuals to respond to data elicitation stimuli at regular intervals (e.g. to indicate their affective state or level of alertness throughout the day each time they are signaled to do so) (Reis & Gable, 2000). Such repeated measurements result in a type of data that allow researchers to model distinct processes of change for individuals because time is the primary axis that makes the data meaningful and coherent (Bolger & Laurenceau, 2013). As a classic example, the very first published report using ESM, conducted by Csikszentmihalyi and two of his graduate students Reed Larson and Suzanne Prescott (Csikszentmihalyi *et al.*, 1977), was a study of how adolescents spend their waking hours and how these activities change over the course of a week. ESM is, therefore, a means of collecting information about both the context and the content of human life. 'Much like a newspaper reporter gathers information on the who, what, where, and when, ESM provides a record of the... landscape of daily life' (Hektner *et al.*, 2007: 125).

However, beyond simply cataloguing which activities people engage in, where and with whom, it is the affect, cognitions and motivations accompanying such samples of experience that provide a window into the quality of that experience (Mehl & Conner, 2012). Put differently, what people do in the naturally occurring contexts of everyday life can reveal a great deal of the complexity underlying human thought, feeling and development because it captures these various interconnected elements and interactions that bring about qualitatively distinct outcomes (e.g. concentration, learning, commitment, understanding, enjoyment, friendship and success) (Bolger *et al.*, 2003).

Although there are aspects of this method and with the study of lived experience that resonate with mixed-method approaches (a point we address later in this chapter), ESM in practice includes a density of data points collected longitudinally over a defined time span at the individual level. This means that ESM, like many other quantitative methods in this part of the book, produces an abundance of data that also presents analytic challenges including dealing with missing data, creating strategies to summarize meaningful events within the data stream and dealing with the effect of autocorrelation in a time series. For these reasons, we include it in the more quantitative part of this book.

Research Questions

Hektner *et al.* (2007: 12) propose that there 'are few important questions... that cannot benefit from the systematic sampling of experiences'. Other scholars (e.g. Bolger & Laurenceau, 2013; Mehl & Conner, 2012) have expressed the same sentiment. Using ESM data, researchers can take various avenues as they investigate complex situations, emergent outcomes and dynamic patterns of development.

On very large scales of time and context, one of the main foci of ESM relates to individual–environment interactions. Questions that lend themselves well to this line of investigation include:

- How are particulars of human behavior, functioning or performance (e.g. learning, communication, language use) shaped by interactive environmental influences?
- What situational constraints and interplays are there for such behavior or activity and for the social interaction it entails?
- What is the role of individuals within functioning systems and in modifying a social environment?

With an emphasis on individuals and how emotional, motivational and cognitive components coexist and contribute to their experience, other more micro-level questions suggest themselves:

- How do individuals experience qualitatively distinct situations (e.g. being in a second language [L2] classroom, a study-abroad context), activities (e.g. expending effort, allocating attention, interacting communicatively) and outcomes (e.g. success, failure, excitement, interest, understanding)?
- In such settings, what complex links can be uncovered between individual thoughts, feelings and actions?
- How do such links fluctuate through time?
- What are the most prominent representations of individuals' experience of salient events (e.g. learning, interacting)?
- In a given setting, what outcomes emerge that are more or less stable across individuals?
- How do individuals differ from one another in their experience of similar situations, and how do such experiences and outcomes change through time?
- For particular target-related behavior (e.g. accomplishing something, completing a task), what processes of change are part of these experiences?

At a more group level of analysis, questions related to person-to-person interactions and the interpersonal dynamics inherent in human and social systems become more apropos:

- What type of interaction rules or parameters exist between individuals who make up a meaningful system?
- How do such co-adaptive exchanges manifest and influence system behavior/system change?
- What are the characteristics and outcomes of such interpersonal interactions?
- How do these interactions and their specifications change over time?

Technical Features

Although it is a method that originated in the study of psychological phenomena, ESM has potential for any discipline committed to exploring the interaction between individuals, contexts and processes such as learning, development or human behavior more generally (Trull & Ebner-Priemer, 2014). This method spotlights fluctuations within these processes at one or more timescales of choice by asking individuals to provide a response at a precise time block to questions that are tailored to the interests and goals of the researcher. We elaborate on how this works below.

The way ESM undertakes sampling experience – which is also where it gets its name – consists of asking individuals to provide systematic self-reports either at regular intervals (e.g. interval-contingent sampling), when they are signaled (i.e. signal-contingent sampling) or following a particular event of interest such as after every meal (i.e. event-contingent sampling) (Goetz et al., 2016). In the most commonly used technique, individuals provide a response to these stimuli whenever a signaling device prompts them to respond. In previous decades, this depended largely on participants carrying electronic beepers or pagers (similar to those that doctors carry) (Conner Christensen et al., 2003); however, such signals can now be fully automated and sent to any one of the latest smart devices or wearables using compatible apps (e.g. RealLife Exp, developed by LifeData LLC) or as a 'push' reminder to one's phone messaging service (see Kubiak & Krog [2012] for one review). The signal is a cue to complete a self-report questionnaire at that precise moment, and intervals can be scheduled as regularly or infrequently as is appropriate to the research scope and the time window (Feldman Barret & Barret, 2001). Some variations include every 5 or 10 minutes in an hour-long period, between every stand-alone activity in a group meeting or project, every two hours over a day-long period or three times a day over a week.

As a domain-specific illustration, we could imagine a study designed to explore the structure of L2 classrooms as well as students' subjective experience in them by prompting them to respond every 5 or 10 minutes in the lesson. Drawing on such repeated sampling data, an ESM design could explore participants' real-time quality of experience in classrooms while involved in different instructional configurations and examine the link between that experience and variations in ongoing attention, interest or performance related to specific instructional practices or conditions.

Participants can be prompted to respond on a wide variety and a large number of measures. With this flexibility in mind, ESM is best suited to measuring dimensions of immediate episodic experience (e.g. how do you feel about your performance right now?) that tend to be context dependent, rather than more global (e.g. how do you generally feel about your ability to perform?) or retrospective (e.g. the last time you performed?) dimensions (Bolger & Laurenceau, 2013). Although any question format currently used in self-report data can be adapted for ESM – including a range of open- or closed-ended questions – these should be designed to capture participants' momentary perceptions or responses. Such questions make up what is termed the *experience sampling form* (ESF). An ESF might include prompts focused on the physical setting (e.g. location, time of day) and social context (e.g. number and description of others sharing the moment), as well as actions, thoughts, intensity of feelings and any other relevant self-appraisals (Hektner *et al.*, 2007; Reis & Gable, 2000).

To extend the L2 classroom illustration, we might imagine students being asked to respond at each interval to semantic differential scales about their mood (e.g. alert–drowsy, relaxed–anxious, confused–clear, involved–detached), Likert-style items indicating their opinion about how challenging, important, satisfying or interesting they found the classroom task (e.g. *strongly agree* to *strongly disagree*) or free response items indicating what they were doing and why, who they were with and what they were thinking about as they were signaled.

While ESFs are usually designed to be completed in no more than minutes or even seconds, these should be tailored to the purpose and scope of the research (Conner Christensen *et al.*, 2003). Of course, the intervals used in the sampling schedule must also be designed with the length of the ESF in mind. In a study where the ESF is in very short form (e.g. it can be completed in under a few seconds), respondents can be signaled much more frequently; however, if it takes participants more than a couple minutes to complete the ESF, the frequency of sampling needs to be reduced in order to lessen the demand on respondents (Bolger & Laurenceau, 2013).

MIHALY CSIKSZENTMIHALYI (2014: 24) ON THE 'RESEARCH ALLIANCE' BETWEEN PARTICIPANTS AND THE ESM RESEARCHER:

Obtaining [ESM] data requires some care and concern. The Experience Sampling Method is a means for communicating with people about their daily lives, a transaction requiring what Offer and Sabshin (1967) have termed a research alliance—a mutual understanding about the procedures and ends of the study. (Jokes about our being FBI agents suggest the potential for misunderstanding.) Most participants find that the procedure is rewarding in some way, and most are willing to share their experience. However, cooperation depends on their trust and on their belief that the research is worthwhile. Before we begin, we explain to each person the purpose of our research—that we are interested in learning about daily experience. With adolescents, it has proved useful to be a little more personal; we say, 'We're interested in your story, whatever it might be.' ... At the conclusion, we sit down with each person and review the week to discuss how it went and to share the sampling that has been obtained of their experience.

It should be clear by comparison that methods which rely entirely on naturalistic observation of behavior (e.g. participant observation) obtain more limited information about the activities of individuals and the contexts where these occur (Bolger *et al.*, 2003; Shiffman *et al.*, 2008). Experience sampling, as in our foregoing hypothetical example, can be seen as adding a further dimension to this by tapping into the ways in which individuals actually experience those activities and contexts. And, unlike most traditional self-report techniques, it does not rely on a single assessment but gathers repeated measurements across many occasions. By doing this, ESM combines the ecological validity of naturalistic behavioral observation with the non-intrusive nature of diaries and the rigor and precision of psychometric techniques (Csikszentmihalyi, 2014: 23).

In order to make better sense of the data that are collected, they are coded along various external and internal attributes or 'coordinates of experience' (Hektner *et al.*, 2007: 63). External coordinates of experience here refer to aspects such as the time, date and location of the response, as well as the specifics of the activity and who one was with at the time of responding. These coding schemes – often but not always qualitative – can be derived from the data in a more bottom-up way or they may be established categorizations that are clearly defined before data collection. The degree of specificity in coding such external attributes will depend largely on the research questions and the purpose of the research. In either case, these codes tend to be fairly elaborate and descriptive, and are often subcategorized in a codebook for the sake of systematicity.

On the other hand, internal coordinates are measures that are assessed primarily quantitatively, such as via semantic differential or Likert-type rating scales. Examples include respondents' reported levels of concentration, involvement and attention during a particular activity. Compared with external coordinates, these quantitative data pose fewer problems as they can be analyzed in a rather straightforward manner.

However, coding aspects of internal experience that are assessed using an open-ended format can be a little more tricky (Bolger & Laurenceau, 2013). In these cases, data often come in the form of participants' thoughts at the time of the response. Many studies initially code open-ended responses to activity and thought using more fine-grained codes and then collapse these codes into more functional categories (for an illustration see Mehl & Conner [2012]). As these analyses progress, such codes tend to be aggregated into larger categories; in such cases, intercoder agreement is an important consideration. It goes without saying that assigning codes and raw scores to data, and any subsequent formatting, queries and analyses will most likely take place within a data analysis software package. There are numerous such platforms for both qualitative and quantitative analyses.

HEKTNER ET AL. (2007: 81–82) ON WHETHER ESM IS QUALITATIVE, QUANTITATIVE OR BOTH:

The sheer volume of numbers produced by an ESM study lends itself well to some complex statistical analyses. Aspects of personality manifested in daily life, such as self-esteem, can be measured by multiple items over multiple time points across multiple contexts. Thus the utility of ESM for quantitative research on human lives and conditions can hardly be overstated.

Yet ESM can also be a valuable qualitative research tool, letting us know, in the participants' own voices, what they are doing, thinking, and feeling, and how they are perceiving their social and physical environment.... This two-pronged example is not meant to imply that qualitative researchers should design their own qualitative ESM and quantitative researchers should focus only on numeric rating scales and percentages. In fact, ESM is best used when both the qualitative and quantitative information it provides is brought to bear on a broad question.

Of course, ESM is by no means a perfect method, and it too must grapple with practical implementation issues (Goetz *et al.*, 2016). Perhaps the biggest drawback we hinted at earlier is the heavy demand that such regular responses to the data elicitation stimuli (i.e. the questions or items) impose on respondents. This can be a factor that discourages potential participants, lowers overall completion rates and causes data quality to deteriorate as time passes. Csikszentmihalyi (2014) reports that in published ESM research, respondent ages range from 10 to 85 years, and that depending on the setting and the backgrounds of the individuals recruited (e.g. blue-collar workers, grade school students, retirees) a completion rate of 70%–85% is decent.

Another major drawback is the question of obtrusiveness, that is whether the repeated measurement procedure has an excessive influence on the phenomena being measured (Shiffman *et al.*, 2008). Given the complex and dynamic view of human experience underlying ESM, we might well ask whether there are substantial reactive effects of this method of data elicitation on individuals' experience. In addition, existing concerns about the objectivity of what people say about themselves (i.e. self-report data) apply. After all, even ESM data are susceptible to participant biases such as individuals selectively editing their responses due to social desirability. However, by adopting sound tools for measurement and prudent designs, such threats to the validity of ESM can be minimized and these concerns alleviated.

A final challenge concerns the sheer amount of data generated from such time-series measurements. A sample of 20 individuals responding to 15 items/questions four times per day for a week ($20 \times 15 \times 4 \times 7$) would generate 8400 data points. With some reviews showing that the average ESM study lasts between 1 and 2 weeks and averages 8–12 signals per day (Reis & Gable, 2000), 10 times this amount of data is not uncommon.

Example Study

Thomas Goetz and his colleagues in Germany and Canada (Goetz *et al.*, 2013) designed an ESM study to focus on the discrete emotions experienced in educational settings. They began with an interesting question ('Do girls really experience more anxiety in mathematics?') and attempted to answer it by comparing ESM state assessment of emotions and self-perceptions with 'classical' trait assessment of these constructs. Their objective in this study was not only to shed new light on gender differences in math anxiety, but to contrast *in situ*, state-level reports reflecting 'real' experiences and trait-level reports that are affected more by subjective beliefs.

Despite similar grades, an unfortunate finding in the academic emotions literature is that girls typically report lower academic self-concept and greater anxiety in mathematics compared to boys. Goetz *et al.* hypothesized that this discrepancy would be evidenced only on trait measures (i.e. those more influenced by enduring self-perceptions) but may not be observed on the ESM measures of *in situ* math anxiety.

They randomly selected a sample of 2 to 4 high-school students from each of 41 classrooms ($n = 111$ students) who first completed self-report measures of trait mathematics anxiety, academic self-concept and achievement in a standardized questionnaire. Over the next two weeks, *in situ* math anxiety was assessed via ESM during each math class at randomized times. A personal digital assistant (PDA) signaled participating students an average of five times per class.

Using hierarchical linear modeling, the researchers conducted multilevel analyses (see Chapter 13) at three levels: measures nested within students, and students nested within classrooms. For trait math anxiety, their findings replicated previous research showing that female students report higher levels of math anxiety than male students. However, no gender differences were observed for any ESM measures of in-class (i.e. state-level) math anxiety. Thus, the ESM data were able to show a more complex picture of emotions situated in the classroom over time than the cross-sectional data alone could show.

The ESM adopted by Goetz *et al.* (2013, 2016) also allowed the researchers to examine the following emotional features:

- the duration of emotions experienced;
- affect instability and reactivity (i.e. extreme changes in emotional experiences);
- affective pulse (i.e. the frequency and type of change in the emotional intensity);
- affective spin (i.e. the degree of qualitative shifts in emotional experiences).

Annotated readings

Bolger, N. and Laurenceau, J.-P. (2013) *Intensive Longitudinal Methods: An Introduction to Diary and Experience Sampling Research*. New York: Guilford Press.

This in-depth volume provides a genuinely applied look at longitudinal designs and data analyses – of which ESM is a main example. The chapters set out key definitions and address issues related to the choice of study design and research questions, best practice in constructing a longitudinal dataset – including sampling considerations and analyses of power – and practical discussion of within- and between-subjects analyses. Example studies, sample datasets and accompanying output for analyses (e.g. in SPSS, R and Mplus) complement these chapters.

Csikszentmihalyi, M. (ed.) (2014) *Flow and the Foundations of Positive Psychology: The Collected Works of Mihaly Csikszentmihalyi*. New York: Springer.

Selected chapters in this collection provide a methodological overview of the origins, uses, strengths and pitfalls of ESM. At times retrospective in focus, at others more hands-on, this collection of papers should be background reading for anyone interested in conducting ESM research.

Hektner, J., Schmidt, J. and Csikszentmihalyi, M. (2007) *Experience Sampling Method: Measuring the Quality of Everyday Life*. Thousand Oaks, CA: SAGE.

This excellent introduction to experience sampling is broken into three parts: part one tells the story of the foundations and purpose of experience sampling, part two touches on the methodological issues specific to experience sampling and part three puts meat on these methodological bones by sharing specific illustrations and findings from ESM studies that have accumulated within social science research.

Mehl, M.R. and Conner, T.S. (eds) (2012) *Handbook of Research Methods for Studying Daily Life*. New York: Guilford Press.

This handbook, inspired by Csikszentmihalyi's work in ESM, features the combined expertise and methodological know-how of over 50 scholars within this collection of methods. In a surprisingly lively style, contributions range from the theoretical and conceptual rationale for such methods, to study design considerations and methods of data collection, data analytic methods and practical applications from an impressive number of disciplines and topical perspectives.

References

Bolger, N. and Laurenceau, J.-P. (2013) *Intensive Longitudinal Methods: An Introduction to Diary and Experience Sampling Research*. New York: Guilford Press.

Bolger, N., Davis, A. and Rafaeli, E. (2003) Diary methods: Capturing life as it is lived. *Annual Review of Psychology* 54, 579–616. doi:10.1146/annurev.psych.54.101601.145030

Brose, A. and Ram, N. (2012) Within-person factor analysis: Modeling how the individual fluctuates and changes across time. In M.R. Mehl and T.S. Conner (eds) *Handbook of Research Methods for Studying Daily Life* (pp. 459–478). New York: Guilford Press.

Conner Christensen, T.S., Feldman Barrett, L., Bliss-Moreau, E., Lebo, K. and Kaschub, C. (2003) A practical guide to experience-sampling procedures. *Journal of Happiness Studies* 4, 53–78. doi:10.1023/A:1023609306024

Csikszentmihalyi, M. (ed.) (2014) *Flow and the Foundations of Positive Psychology: The Collected Works of Mihaly Csikszentmihalyi*. New York: Springer.

Csikszentmihalyi, M. and Larson, R.W. (1987) Validity and reliability of the experience sampling method. *Journal of Nervous and Mental Disease* 175, 526–536.

Csikszentmihalyi, M., Larson, R.W. and Prescott, S. (1977) The ecology of adolescent activities and experiences. *Journal of Youth and Adolescence* 6, 281–294. doi:10.1007/BF02138940

Deboeck, P.R. (2012) Modeling nonlinear dynamics in intraindividual variability. In M.R. Mehl and T.S. Conner (eds) *Handbook of Research Methods for Studying Daily Life* (pp. 440–458). New York: Guilford Press.

Feldman Barrett, L. and Barrett, D.J. (2001) An introduction to experience sampling in psychology. *Social Science Computer Review* 19, 175–185. doi:10.1177/089443930101900204

Goetz, T., Bieg, M., Lüdtke, O., Pekrun, R. and Hall, N.C. (2013) Do girls really experience more anxiety in mathematics? *Psychological Science* 24, 2079–2087. doi:10.1177/0956797613486989

Goetz, T., Bieg, M. and Hall. N. (2016) Assessing academic emotions via the experience sampling method. In M. Zembylas and P.A. Shutz (eds) *Methodological Advances in Research on Emotion and Education* (pp. 244–258). New York: Springer.

Hektner, J., Schmidt, J. and Csikszentmihalyi, M. (2007) *Experience Sampling Method: Measuring the Quality of Everyday Life*. Thousand Oaks, CA: SAGE.

James, W. (1890/2013) *Principles of Psychology (Vol. 1)*. New York: Henry Holt.

Kubiak, T. and Krog, K. (2012) Computerized sampling of experiences and behavior. In M.R. Mehl and T.S. Conner (eds) *Handbook of Research Methods for Studying Daily Life* (pp. 124–143). New York: Guilford Press.

LeDoux, J. (2002) *Synaptic Self: How Our Brains become Who We Are*. New York: Viking Penguin.

Mehl, M.R. and Conner, T.S. (eds) (2012) *Handbook of Research Methods for Studying Daily Life*. New York: Guilford Press.

Reis, H.T. and Gable, S.L. (2000) Event-sampling and other methods for studying everyday experience. In H.T. Reis and C.M. Judd (eds) *Handbook of Research Methods in Social and Personality Psychology* (pp. 190–222). New York: Cambridge University Press.

Shiffman, S., Stone, A.A. and Hufford, M.R. (2008) Ecological momentary assessment. *Annual Review of Clinical Psychology* 4, 1–32. doi:10.1146/annurev.clinpsy.3.022806.091415

Trull, T. and Ebner-Priemer, U. (2014) The role of ambulatory assessment in psychological science. *Psychological Science* 23, 466–470. doi:10.1177/0963721414550706

16 Single-Case Designs

Overview

Between-group design is a name sometimes used to describe the conventional approach of comparing an experimental group to a control group. The advent of inferential statistics cemented the position of group-based design in many disciplines (Barlow *et al.*, 2009; Kazdin, 2011). Most of the credit for these early advances goes to Sir Ronald A. Fisher (1890–1962), who laid the foundations of modern statistics almost single-handedly and without thoroughly studying his contemporaries or predecessors (Hald, 2007). His genius is partly attributed to his poor eyesight as a child. According to Salsburg (2001), Fisher's doctors banned him from reading by artificial light because of his nearsightedness. His tutor had to teach him mathematics in the dark, and so Fisher had to rely on his imagination to learn the lessons. This helped him develop a geometric sense of mathematics, allowing him to arrive at conclusions without elaborating intermediate steps. The conclusions were obvious to him, but other mathematicians had to spend years trying to figure out the proofs. Leading statisticians also acknowledged his contributions, including the inventor of the Student's *t*-test, William Sealy Gosset (1876–1937), who said that 'Fisher really worked out the complete mathematics' (cited in Salsburg, 2001: 28).

The Fisherian revolution came at a price, however. Fisher's most fruitful years were those he spent at Rothamsted Agricultural Experimental Station, UK (see Salsburg, 2001). Fisher studied crop variation extensively to examine the effects of factors such as soil quality and rain quantity. As Barlow *et al.* (2009) explain, this is the origin of some terminology such as split plot analysis of variance (ANOVA). Most importantly, 'Much as in the study of individual differences, the fate of the individual plant is irrelevant in the context of the yield from the group of plants... if the yield is better *on the average* than a similar plot treated differently' (Barlow *et al.*, 2009: 7, original emphasis). Although this rationale may work fine in agronomy, applying it to humans raises a number of concerns – some of which are ethical, as discussed later in this chapter, but most obviously regarding the complexity and dynamic systems theory (CDST) view of complex patterns and dynamic processes of change. Furthermore, the elegance of inferential statistics accompanying between-group designs has contributed to the marginalization of an alternative option, single-case designs.

Single-case designs (also called single-subject and within-subject) does not rely on the conventional approach of calculating the mean of an experimental group and comparing it to that of a control group. Instead, a single-case study typically uses the individual as his/her own control during the developmental trajectory (though somewhat different designs exist as well; see later). Inference, therefore, is based on comparing before versus after, not control versus experimental. It is useful for intervention research, and it allows for within-study replication of effects. The unit of analysis does not have to be an individual; it can be a collective such as a class or a school. Finally, contrary to what its name might suggest, a single-case study *can* include more than one case. It is just that each case is analyzed separately.

ALAN KAZDIN (2011: 393–394, ORIGINAL EMPHASIS) ON THE UNIQUE INSIGHTS OF SINGLE-CASE DESIGNS TO THE INDIVIDUAL:

I would like to add to the special strengths one that is laced with empathy, concern for others, and the priorities of our daily lives. I noted how single-case designs can evaluate groups (e.g., in classrooms or schools, the community at large), but let us return to the focus on the individual. A unique strength of single-case designs is providing a way to evaluate change and impact of interventions on a particular person. This is very important, as many of us have experienced or will experience in life. For many questions that guide our everyday life, we care very much about the individual. It is interesting to us personally and intellectually to ask about the group data. For example, we hear about a new treatment (e.g., for obesity, diabetes, blood pressure, or hair loss). Does it work? Is a change in the treatment associated with real change or is it another one of those bait-and-switch television ads that says 'clinical evidence shows' (that does not mean randomized controlled trials) where we see two models, one cast as 'before' and one cast as 'after' receiving/taking the intervention?

I note the obvious, namely, that we owe so many advances in clinical work (e.g., psychological and medical science) to between-group research methods to help underscore the point about individuals. In our daily lives it is about individuals—ourselves, our loved ones, and about friends, and not about group data. As an illustration, my annual physical exam could easily turn into a methodological brawl....

MY PHYSICIAN: 'You probably ought to have that medical test in about 5 years, just to make sure you don't have… [reader—insert your favorite serious disorder—my physician rotates several variations of cancers, heart disease, and diabetes].'
ME: 'That sound *serious*; maybe I should have the test now.'
My P: 'Actually the data (he means group) show that you probably do not need that medical test because the rate of that problem is pretty low at your age right now and for most people does not pick up for a few more years.'
ME: 'Just speaking generally, is it possible that I am one of the cases in the group that gets that disease on the early side?'
MY P: 'Yes, of course, but not very likely.'
ME: 'I would really like the test, because what happened to the big group might not be what happens to me. Also, the test does not hurt (I am a medical coward) and the information could help with one of my personal priorities (staying alive).'
My P: 'Uh—you are probably fine without it, but in 3 or 4 years it would be pretty important. Well, I see that my next appointment is here—God willing, let's continue this discussion at your next physical.'

Research Questions

The primary purpose of single-case designs is to investigate the effectiveness of treatments in a way that is fully concerned with a situated and dynamic understanding of how such outcomes are reached. Typically, the researcher wishes to affect an improvement in participants. This is why this approach has been used extensively in intervention research, including clinical treatment and special needs education, as well as various applied fields such as education and psychology.

The researcher identifies the problem and then introduces a certain treatment systematically in order to investigate its effect on that problem. In this sense there are parallels with other complex interventionist methods such as design-based research (see Chapter 10). The problematic behavior is ideally operationalized in multiple ways so that the researcher can obtain a more comprehensive picture of the effect of the treatment. Example research questions include:

- How variable is the outcome? What shape does it have over time?
- Do different individuals follow the same developmental pattern?
- When an intervention is introduced, what effect does it have on this pattern?
- Does this effect vary from individual to individual? If so, how?
- Is the effect persistent after withdrawing the treatment?

- Does the effect replicate over time?
- Does the effect apply to different operationalizations of the outcome?

This brief overview shows the contrast with time series analysis (Chapter 14), which is typically used as a descriptive procedure. Single-case designs, however, were developed specifically to go further than description to intervention. This overview also shows the contrast with cross-lagged modelling (Chapter 11), which is typically limited to a few data collection waves. Single-case research is highly amenable to interventions that last for an extended period of time.

Technical Features

Randomized controlled trials are currently the gold standard in quantitative research (Kazdin, 2011; Shadish *et al.*, 2002). However, as previously mentioned, a number of concerns have been raised by proponents of single-case designs about randomized controlled trials and their reliance on significance testing (Barlow *et al.*, 2009; Chassan, 1979):

(1) A study employing the conventional experimental design usually requires only a few more improvements in the experimental group to make the difference significant. For example, a typical study with 30 participants in each group requires that the experimental group contains only 8 more improvements to reach significance (e.g. 23 out of 30 improvements in the experimental group vs. 15 out of 30 in the control group, $p = 0.032$, two-tailed, equal variance assumed or not). If only 7 experimental participants improve in this example (i.e. 22 out of 30), the results fail to reach significance ($p = 0.065$). Thus, a significant result may mean that only a small number of participants have improved due to the treatment and, worse, just one participant may make the difference between a significant and non-significant result.
(2) These 8 participants whose improvement is associated with the treatment are diffused within the total 23 improvements in the experimental group. Significance testing cannot distinguish them from those 15 whose improvement might be due to other factors, just as in the control group. Therefore, although we can conclude that at least eight participants have benefited from the treatment, we typically do not go further and locate these few individuals. Instead, researchers simply conclude that the treatment was effective.
(3) When the study compares two treatments and the outcome shows no significant difference in improvement, the typical conclusion is that the two treatments are equally effective. However, there might still be considerable variations in the characteristics of the individuals who have responded favorably to each treatment. Significance testing cannot tell us whether this is the case.

(4) If the result does reach significance in this case, the obvious conclusion is that one treatment is more effective than the other. However, the other treatment might have been effective with a subsection of the second group, but their small number does not allow statistical significance.

(5) The treatment under question could have, ironically, made some individuals *deteriorate* in response. Because of the nature of the averaging procedure, we cannot recognize this pattern. Even if researchers implement a pretest and examine the dataset case by case, the design still does not permit the unequivocal conclusion that an observed deterioration is actually due to the treatment (i.e. it could be a natural deterioration just like what happened in the control group).

As an illustration of the last point, consider the example of a randomized controlled trial testing the effectiveness of an experimental drug. If the experimental group shows more improvement on average than the control group, we may conclude that the drug is effective. However, this still does not rule out the possibility that this drug has actually made some experimental patients deteriorate (e.g. certain types of patients do not react well to this particular drug). Remember also that in the control group, researchers might additionally expect to see some deterioration. The design of this experiment does not allow observers to form positive or negative conclusions about the effects of the experimental drug unequivocally. The deterioration of some experimental patients may be due to the drug or to natural causes just like any other patient in the control group. This is a serious blind spot in the design of randomized controlled experiments, which are considered the gold standard in science today.

What is somewhat obvious is that most of the weaknesses listed above come from the fact that between-group designs rely principally on averaging. Single-case designs, on the other hand, can help avoid these issues and forestall these typical concerns. They can also help alleviate potential ethical consequences, an example of which can be seen in studies concluding that certain instructional approaches are effective while they decrease the desire to engage in learning or raise anxiety in a subgroup of the sample.

Therefore, one of the first steps in a study utilizing a single-case design is to determine the appropriate unit of analysis. Typically, it is the participant. A number of participants may be analyzed separately, and the exact number of participants may be small (e.g. one or two learners). The sample could also be much larger, though in some cases this can cause practical constraints. The advent of accessible technology (e.g. videotaping, smartphone apps) can greatly help in addressing these practical constraints. In many cases, the researcher would need to collect detailed data over many days from each participant individually (e.g. during class). In some other cases, the unit of analysis may be a collective (e.g. a whole class). This is still considered 'single'-case if the goal is to arrive at an overall class improvement, though admittedly some individual-level information might be lost in this process.

Two of the most popular designs used by single-case researchers are the *A-B-A-B design* and the *multiple baseline design*. The A-B-A-B design is rather intuitive. In the first phase, the researcher collects descriptive data about the dependent variable of interest (say student engagement) repeatedly until a baseline is established. Once the researcher obtains a good picture of how stable the baseline is, the treatment (e.g. flipped classroom) is then introduced and the researcher continues collecting data. In the third and fourth phases, the treatment is withdrawn and then reinstated (see Figure 16.1).

The rationale behind the last two phases (withdrawing and reinstating the treatment) is that it functions as a within-study replication of the effect. It also demonstrates that the change occurs when and only when the treatment is present. This design permits the researcher to obtain much stronger internal validity than with the conventional pre–post design despite, ironically, requiring far fewer participants. In fact, this design has been described as 'the most convincing means of demonstrating the functional relationship between behavioral phenomena and their controlling conditions' (Bandura, 1969: 243).

One obvious limitation to this design is that it is not always possible, or desirable, to withdraw the treatment. In educational research, for example, it may not be appropriate to withdraw a treatment that

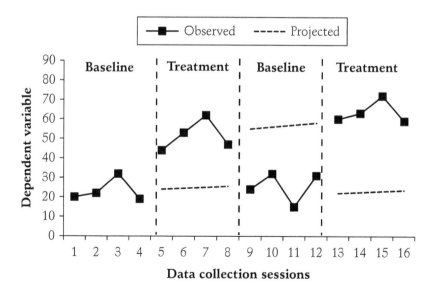

Figure 16.1 Hypothetical A-B-A-B design data showing a clear treatment effect

has benefited learners, even if that is possible. In response to this limitation, single-case researchers developed an alternative design, the *multiple baseline design* (Figure 16.2). In this design, the researcher divides the participants into different groups, and each group receives the treatment at a different time. In order to conclude that the treatment is effective,

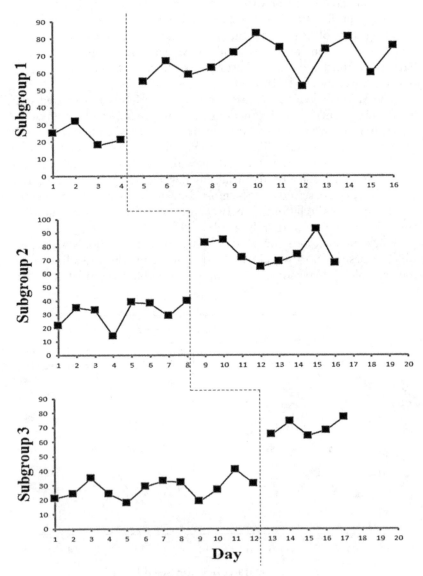

Figure 16.2 Hypothetical multiple baseline design data showing a clear treatment effect

improvement must be observed upon the introduction of treatment in each group.

The above example of a multiple baseline design shows a treatment taking place *across participants*. However, the researcher can also choose to apply the treatment on the same participants to completely eliminate group comparisons. That is, the treatment could alternatively take place *across behaviors*, where slightly different treatments address different aspects (e.g. fluency vs. accuracy). For example, the treatment could first be modeled to improve fluency and, after some time, it is remodeled to improve accuracy. In order for the treatment to be considered effective, these two variations need to show improvement on fluency and accuracy, respectively, shortly after being introduced. Similarly, the treatment may also take place *across settings*, such as different school subjects, again on the same participants. Just like the A-B-A-B design, these variations of the multiple baseline design also involve within-study replication, which raises the internal validity of the results.

In addition to internal validity, another clear advantage of single-case designs is that it requires the researcher to collect large amounts of data. In contrast to pre–post designs, this large amount of data not only enhances observers' confidence in the results, but it also provides a richer portrait of change and progress over time. These are clearly part and parcel of doing research from a CDST perspective. The researcher would be able to more clearly see shifts and changes taking place during the study. As a result, the researcher has the chance to change and adapt the study design, if needed, in explicit acknowledgement of the complexity and messiness of real life. Given these characteristics, single-case designs correspond with some features of design-based research (see Chapter 10). The strength of such possibilities is that the researcher no longer has to be a passive observer for the sake of objectivity.

Evaluation of the effectiveness of the treatment may involve visual inspection or statistical analysis. In visual inspection, the researcher simply looks at the graph (e.g. Figure 16.1) and determines whether there is an effect. The effect would be a lack of overlap between the observed pattern and the projected pattern. Some researchers have dubbed the case 'a slam-bang success' where there is clearly no overlap between these two patterns (Gilbert *et al.*, 1975: 45). However, because visual inspection may not always be straightforward, a number of statistical procedures have been developed as a robust complement to visual inspection (see Kazdin, 2011: Appendix; Shadish, 2014).

Example Study

Christle and Schuster (2003) designed a study with the objective of improving mathematics achievement in a classroom setting using a single-case design. The researchers reviewed a growing literature demonstrating a positive link between active class participation and student achievement. That is, students who participate more during lessons tend to achieve at a higher level. However, Christle and Schuster also argued that one common strategy that teachers use in class is the *one-student-participating-at-a-time method*, where the teacher asks a question and then students raise their hands to answer. The researchers argued that this method favors high-achievers since they tend to raise their hands more and consequently have more participation opportunities.

In an attempt to provide equal opportunities to students, Christle and Schuster tested the effectiveness of *response cards*. A class of 24 fourth-grade students were given individual cards and were asked to write down their answers in response to the teacher's question. Instead of raising their hands to answer, then, the students raise their cards up so that the teacher can walk around and see the different answers. This approach would therefore give each student the chance to respond to the question and show their answers to the teacher.

The researchers applied an A-B-A design (the fourth B condition was dropped due to scheduling conflicts). The A conditions adopted the traditional hand-raising (HR) method, while the B condition used response cards. Before the study, the researchers selected five students who represented different levels found in that class to analyze their performance.

Here, we present the results from one participant, Emily. As shown in Figure 16.3, Emily hardly participated in either the first or the second HR conditions. In contrast, she had the chance to actively participate in the response card (RC) condition. This behavior was also reflected on her quiz scores taken at the end of each condition: 87, 93 and 63, respectively. Christle and Schuster showed that the other four participants also had very similar results. The researchers concluded that this method is a much more effective alternative as it allows all students to show their

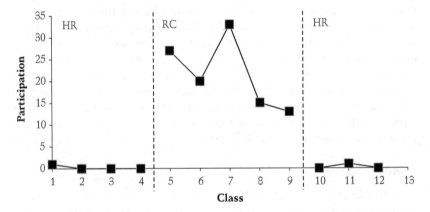

Figure 16.3 Results of Emily adapted from Christle and Schuster (2003) (HR = hand-raising condition, RC = response cards condition)

responses to the teacher. The teacher, in turn, can efficiently check all answers and determine whether re-explanation is necessary. By applying this single-case design, Christle and Schuster were able to offer a novel take on the association between active classroom participation and student achievement by focusing on learners individually rather than averaging the scores of different learners.

Annotated readings

Rizvi, S.L. and Nock, M.K. (2008) Single-case experimental designs for the evaluation of treatments for self-injurious and suicidal behaviors. *Suicide and Life-Threatening Behavior* 38 (5), 498–510. doi:10.1521/suli.2008.38.5.498

This is a short and concise primer of the different single-case designs. It may be the ideal first reading for an absolute beginner in this area.

Kazdin, A.E. (2011) *Single-Case Research Designs: Methods for Clinical and Applied Settings* (2nd edn). Oxford: Oxford University Press.

This is a book-length, detailed treatment by Alan Kazdin, a former president of the American Psychological Association and an authority in this area. The author deals with issues related to measurement quality and other considerations when conducting single-case research. The book also discusses other single-case designs not described in this chapter. The appendix summarizes the various statistical analyses available for single-case researchers.

Barlow, D.H., Nock, M. and Hersen, M. (2009) *Single Case Experimental Designs: Strategies for Studying Behavior Change* (3rd edn). Boston, MA: Allyn & Bacon.

Another authoritative book in this area. This volume deals in detail with the rationale of single-case research, the different design options and statistical tests available.

Kennedy, C.H. (2005) *Single-Case Designs for Educational Research*. Boston, MA: Pearson/Allyn & Bacon.

In contrast to the above-mentioned books, this one is concerned with single-case designs in educational research more specifically.

Shadish, W.R. (2014) Statistical analyses of single-case designs: The shape of things to come. *Current Directions in Psychological Science* 23 (2), 139–146. doi:10.1177/0963721414524773

This article addresses somewhat advanced issues related to statistical analyses of single-case data. These include effect sizes, multilevel models and Bayesian analysis. Recommended for the advanced reader.

Sidman, M. (1960) *Tactics of Scientific Research: Evaluating Experimental Data in Psychology*. New York: Basic Books.

Although it was published decades ago, this book is still an important text that lays the philosophical foundations of this largely marginalized area.

Mellow, J.D., Reeder, K. and Forster, E. (1996) Using time-series research designs to investigate the effects of instruction on SLA. *Studies in Second Language Acquisition* 18 (3), 325–350. doi:10.1017/S0272263100015059

This source presents an example study from the second language (L2) field. The authors argue for the need for interrupted time series analysis in the domain of L2 instruction and review some empirical results as an illustration.

References

Bandura, A. (1969) *Principles of Behavior Modification*. London: Holt, Rinehart & Winston.

Barlow, D.H., Nock, M. and Hersen, M. (2009) *Single Case Experimental Designs: Strategies for Studying Behavior Change* (3rd edn). Boston, MA: Allyn & Bacon.

Chassan, J.B. (1979) *Research Design in Clinical Psychology and Psychiatry* (2nd edn). New York: Halsted.

Christle, C.A. and Schuster, J.W. (2003) The effects of using response cards on student participation, academic achievement, and on-task behavior during whole-class, math instruction. *Journal of Behavioral Education* 12 (3), 147–165. doi:10.1023/a:1025577410113

Gilbert, J.P., Light, R.J. and Mosteller, F. (1975) Assessing social interventions: An empirical base for policy. In C.A. Bennett and A.A. Lumsdaine (eds) *Evaluation and Experiment: Some Critical Issues in Assessing Social Programs* (pp. 39–193). New York: Academic Press.

Hald, A. (2007) *A History of Parametric Statistical Inference from Bernoulli to Fisher, 1713–1935*. New York: Springer.

Kazdin, A.E. (2011) *Single-Case Research Designs: Methods for Clinical and Applied Settings* (2nd edn). Oxford: Oxford University Press.

Salsburg, D. (2001) *The Lady Tasting Tea: How Statistics Revolutionized Science in the Twentieth Century*. New York: Freeman.

Shadish, W.R. (2014) Statistical analyses of single-case designs: The shape of things to come. *Current Directions in Psychological Science* 23 (2), 139–146. doi:10.1177/0963721414524773

Shadish, W.R., Cook, T.D. and Campbell, D.T. (2002) *Experimental and Quasi-Experimental Designs for Generalized Causal Inference*. Belmont, CA: Cengage Learning

17 Idiodynamic Method

Overview

Many available methods rely primarily on averaging data from a number of units (e.g. individuals). These methods provide a hypothetical average that aims to represent the central tendency of the units and group-level variability. This may be fine for some purposes, but complexity and dynamic systems theory (CDST) research often requires a deeper understanding of the processes involved in the phenomenon under study. From this perspective, individual idiosyncrasies are not noise to be eliminated in favor of a single, neat average. This notion is known as the *ergodicity problem*. When the units of a group are strongly similar to each other, then we have an ergodic ensemble, where generalization from the individual to the group is justifiable. However, this condition is more often than not absent in data. This phenomenon has been explicitly observed and problematized in studies going back more than a decade (e.g. Larsen-Freeman, 2006), which Lowie and Verspoor (2018) highlight well.

> *WANDER LOWIE AND MARJOLIJN VERSPOOR (2019) ON THE ERGODICITY PROBLEM:*
>
> Basically, the ergodic principle states that we cannot generalize group statistics—especially when we deal with human beings—to the individual, and vice versa, unless the group is an ergodic ensemble. That is why we need two lines of research in applied linguistics: group studies and single-case studies.

When the CDST researcher zooms in on one learner, for example, an important consideration is the timescale of the investigation. The timescale of a process can range from seconds to minutes to days to months to years. When it comes to investigating seconds and minutes, things can become challenging. The researcher would need a tool to collect accurate, real-time data on this learner's intra-individual variability during, say, a specific language task that lasts just minutes or even seconds (see also Chinn & Sherin, 2014).

The idiodynamic method was developed for this purpose (MacIntyre, 2012). It aims to uncover fluctuations over time and the possible reasons underlying them. Therefore, the idiodynamic method allows the CDST researcher to subject the phenomenon to sharp focus within a short timescale, using procedures that focus on the time-dependent variation within a single individual or unit. It can also complement other methods the researcher might wish to use, offering a different perspective on the same process.

The reader might recognize the term *idiographic* as a contrast to the *nomothetic* approach. Indeed, an idiographic approach aims to find what is unique in each individual, while a nomothetic approach looks for laws and generalizations that apply to a larger number of individuals. However, according to another topology by Rosenzweig (e.g. 1986), behavior should be explained from three, not two, complementary perspectives: nomothetic (psychological principles applicable to all or almost all individuals), demographic (statistical generalizations derived from a certain class of individuals) and idiodynamic. The idiodynamic perspective is concerned with markers of an *idioverse*, or a collection of events experienced by the individual phenomenologically (Rosenzweig & Hackney, 2004).

SAUL ROSENZWEIG (1986: 241–242, ORIGINAL EMPHASIS) ON THE HISTORY OF IDIODYNAMICS:

Fifty years ago Gordon Allport (1937), the well-known personality theorist, published a book, *Personality: A Psychological Interpretation*, in which he made a declaration of independence for personality theory. This declaration highlighted the distinction made earlier by the German philosopher Windelband (1894) between two classes of science: the *nomothetic*, including such disciplines as physics, chemistry, and biology, on the one hand, and the *idiographic*, among which Windelband included history, biography, and literature. The nomothetic sciences seek functional principles or laws in the form 'If a, then b,' for example, the principles of learning in psychology. The idiographic disciplines, however, attempt to account for particular or single events that transpire in history and that, though nonreplicable, are nevertheless the result of determinants which the investigator attempts to trace and establish...

Allport's stress on the idiographic (as contrasted with the nomothetic) was intended to underscore personal uniqueness, but his preoccupation with *traits*, rather than *events* (dynamic, behavioral reconstructions), fell short of what is here meant by idiodynamic. It should be clear that the idiodynamic differs from the idiographic by referring not to a statistical N of 1 (i.e., unique traits peculiar to one person) but to a universe of multiple events (the idioverse). A unique dynamic organization of events through time distinguishes one person from others in terms of the peculiar experiential history from which recurrent idiodynamic norms are derived. These norms, in conjunction with nomothetic principles and demographic generalizations, afford the necessary keys to understanding a given idioverse.

There are several distinct advantages to such an idiodynamic method (see also Velicer *et al.*, 2014). First, as we have suggested, procedures of data elicitation and analysis that focus on intra-individual variability can address novel research questions with different data, and may provide a different insight into that data. Second, this method can be applied in settings where more conventional between-subject research designs may be inappropriate or challenging to implement. Third, the idiodynamic method has important advantages for investigating patterns of change across time, can be used to determine how behavior of interest is generated and can addresses the relationship between variables over time. We explore these issues in more detail throughout this chapter.

VELICER, BABBIN AND PALUMBO (2014: 430) EXPLAIN THE COMPLEMENTARY NATURE OF INDIVIDUAL- AND GROUP-LEVEL APPROACHES TO RESEARCH IN CDST:

A strict adherence to either an idiographic or nomothetic approach may impair overall understanding of a psychological phenomenon. The two perspectives may not be separable, in that a unique individual is still a member of some population and is therefore a manifestation of that population.... Another way of looking at the continuum of idiographic–nomothetic conceptions holds that any observation can be considered in idiographic (unique) or nomothetic (general) terms. That is, no observation needs to be framed as inherently one or the other [and] the vantage points along the idiographic–nomothetic continuum are simultaneously important.

Research Questions

Through procedures that focus on temporal variation within a single individual or unit, the idiodynamic method allows the researcher to ask a number of interesting questions. Examples include:

* How do self-ratings (e.g. of motivation, anxiety and competence) change over the course of a task?

- How do self-ratings relate to other ratings (e.g. a researcher, a peer or an expert observer)?
- To what does the learner attribute these fluctuations (i.e. perceptions)?
- What factors (e.g. proficiency level, interlocutor) influence self-ratings and perceptions?
- Does the type of stimuli (e.g. audio only, video only or audio+video) have an effect on the learner's self-ratings or perceptions? In which tasks?
- What is the effect of training on self-ratings and perceptions (e.g. pragmatic strategy instruction)?
- How do self-ratings and perceptions relate to other physiological measures (e.g. heart rate, skin conductance, EEG and fMRI)?

As can be seen, questions that the idiodynamic method enables a researcher to investigate may be observational or experimental. In contrast to observational questions, in the experimental case the researcher deliberately manipulates certain factors, such as the status of the interlocutor and the difficulty of the task, to investigate their effect on different outcomes. These outcomes can be psychological, such as motivation, anxiety and willingness to communicate; they can also be linguistic, such as lexical choices, grammatical accuracy and fluency with language. Thus, the idiodynamic method provides the researcher with interesting real-time individual-level data that have the potential to explore new questions and offer new insights.

VELICER, BABBIN AND PALUMBO (2014: 427) ON THE IMPORTANCE OF MATCHING METHOD TO PURPOSE IN CDST RESEARCH:

In many cases, group-level analyses have the potential to give misleading answers. A key assumption with nomothetic methods is the additive constant, which assumes that each participant in a sample is equally influenced by an intervention. This assumption can obscure the problem rather than assisting in the solution. Because typically, no one is average, the derived conclusion may not describe the processes of any individual in the population. This is an important consideration, as the questions being asked by a researcher should determine the methodology being used.

Technical Features

In a nutshell, the idiodynamic method involves videotaping the participant and then showing them the video to solicit ratings about their own performance. The unique aspect in the idiodynamic method is that it allows the participant to provide ratings *for every second* of the task in a systematic manner using specialized software. One software program, Anion Variable Tester, is available for researchers free of charge and is easy to use.[1]

To be more concrete, there is a series of standard steps in an idiodynamic study:

- The participant engages in a task while being videotaped.
- Immediately after the task, the video is loaded into the software.
- The participant is then asked to watch the video and provide ratings on a specific variable (e.g. willingness to communicate) for every second of the task (quantitative data).
- Using stimulated recall (Gass & Mackey, 2000), the participant is finally asked to provide explanations for their ratings (qualitative data).

The software generates a graph and an Excel file of the ratings while the qualitative data may be transcribed by the researcher for further analyses. Depending on the purpose of the investigation, the researcher might perform a *horizontal analysis* by comparing patterns across different participants. Alternatively, the researcher might perform a *vertical analysis* focusing on patterns within one individual.

As an illustration, imagine that Mr Tim Cook, the current Apple CEO, responded to an ad recruiting participants for a study on anxiety from a CDST perspective, despite his busy schedule. The researchers videotaped him giving a public speech and then sat him at a computer screen so that he could rate his anxiety during that speech. The software, Anion Variable Tester, would look like the screenshot in Figure 17.1. Mr Cook would watch a few minutes of himself and, for every second, would click on either the Increase Anxiety or Decrease Anxiety buttons to rate how he was feeling at that moment.

At the end of this task, the software would generate a graph like that in Figure 17.2. Looking at the figure, we can see that Mr Cook initially showed high anxiety but then there was a sharp drop. Anxiety then spiked before dipping again. In the final stage, the ratings tended to move toward zero.

A quantitative researcher would most likely use the Excel sheet in Figure 17.3 for subsequent analyses (e.g. time series analysis; see Chapter 14). A qualitative researcher could apply stimulated recall for follow-up data elicitation to let Mr Cook explain these fluctuations. Mr Cook might explain that he was initially anxious about how the audience would react to his speech. During the course of the speech, however, he experienced two sudden dips in anxiety due to positive feedback responses, such as applause from the audience. Toward the end, his

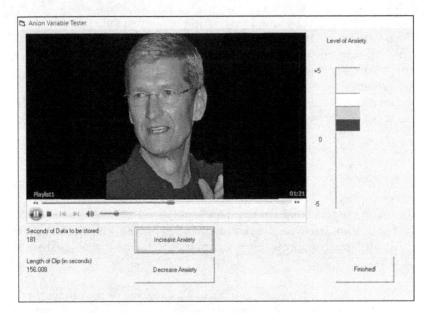

Figure 17.1 A screenshot of the Anion Variable Tester

anxiety gradually started to disappear because the controversial part of his speech was over.

It is not hard to see how this method provides unique CDST-compatible data. The idiodynamic method focuses on variability and change over time. The presence of a video functions as a cue to the participant so that complete reliance on memory can be avoided in data elicitation. At the same time, researchers should also be aware of potential biases in reporting on one's self. The amount of data that are generated can be enormous and messy, especially when a large sample of

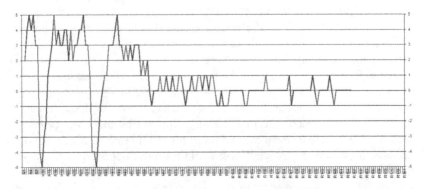

Figure 17.2 Hypothetical idiodynamic data generated by the Anion Variable Tester

◢	A	B	C	D	E	F
1	This program was generated by Anion Variable Tester v2.					
2	Created on 23-Sep for subject Tim Cook					
3						
4						
5						
6	Time	Anxiety				
7						
8	1	0				
9	2	2				
10	3	4				
11	4	5				
12	5	4				
13	6	5				
14	7	3				
15	8	3				
16	9	-4				
17	10	-5				
18	11	-3				
19	12	-2				
20	13	1				
21	14	2				
22	15	3				
23	16	5				
24	17	3				
25	18	4				
26	19	3				
27	20	3				
28	21	4				
29	22	4				
30	23	2				
31	24	4				
32	25	2				

Tim Cook's Anxiety ⊕

Ready

Figure 17.3 Excel sheet generated by the Anion Variable Tester

participants is used. Furthermore, these data may be highly idiosyncratic and contextualized, and therefore the researcher needs to consider how to link the findings to theory and practice.

PETER MACINTYRE (2012: 364–365) ON SOME QUALITIES OF THE IDIODYNAMIC METHOD IN COMPARISON TO OTHER METHODS:

Idiodynamics addresses questions about the patterns of change within an individual that cannot be addressed with cross-sectional, longitudinal, or qualitative-retrospective research designs. Cross-sectional studies look at individual differences within a sample. Statistical tools, such as ANOVA and correlation, treat the variability within groups or off the regression line (respectively) as error. But variability is the prime focus of the idiodynamic method, addressing research questions that are not appropriate for analysis with traditional correlation or ANOVA. In longitudinal studies that employ a test-retest approach, the intervening process is not studied directly as it unfolds; therefore the key drivers of change can be difficult to identify. Qualitative-retrospective studies can better address the drivers of change, but as the time span between events and the recalling of them increases, memory becomes more prone to a variety of biases. A long list of basic cognitive biases [has] been described that can affect qualitative-retrospective accounts, including forgetting information, absentmindedness, blocking specific memories, misattribution, suggestibility, retrospective biases, and persistence of intrusive thoughts (Schacter, 1999; see also Hilbert, 2012). In terms of accurately capturing an event, a short video beats a long memory almost every time.

Example Study

Boudreau *et al.* (2018) set out to examine the relationship between anxiety and enjoyment within an idiodynamic paradigm. Affect, and in particular discrete emotions such as anxiety, is well-suited to this investigative approach given the highly dynamic and situated nature of emotional phenomena. The researchers recruited 10 English native speakers learning French as a second language (L2). For the purpose of the study, they requested that the participants bring to the lab a photo of something they considered enjoyable.

When each participant arrived in the lab, they were asked to complete two tasks: a photo narrative task and an oral interview task (the order of these two tasks was counterbalanced). In the photo narrative task, the participant explained the photo in their L2 and why they thought it was enjoyable. In the oral interview task, the participant was asked a series of questions with increasing difficulty. They were asked to

- describe what they were wearing;
- discuss the education system in their home province in some detail;

- count to 100 by 10s;
- give directions from the lab to a local shopping center;
- discuss the role of parliament in the Canadian system of government.

The two tasks were videotaped and immediately loaded to the Anion Variable Tester software. The participant then watched the videos and rated their own anxiety and enjoyment separately (with the order counterbalanced).

In the following stage, a graph of the ratings was printed, and the participant was asked to explain the pattern and what caused the spikes and dips observed. The participant had the chance to explain their anxiety/enjoyment ratings and to what they attributed the stability and fluctuations in these ratings. This part was audio-recorded for later transcription.

In their analysis of the quantitative data generated, the researchers looked at the correlations between anxiety and enjoyment for each participant. They found that, in general, there was a negative relationship that tended to be medium to strong. However, when they looked more closely, they realized that this pattern was not consistent. In some segments within one individual, the correlation was sometimes approaching zero, and sometimes even positive. They also noted that, after a certain threshold, the impact of anxiety overrides enjoyment. In their article, the researchers quote some of the explanations that participants gave in an attempt to explain these patterns.

The researchers also gained some interesting methodological insights. Some participants reported feeling that the situation felt rather artificial, being videotaped in a lab setting. The researchers therefore recommended exploring the possibility of conducting idiodynamic studies in natural settings such as the classroom. The researchers, however, still emphasized the importance of immediate ratings and stimulated recall to take advantage of the participant's fresh memories.

Another insight the researchers obtained was the need to give the participants ample opportunity to practice using the software. Although the researchers explained how to use the software to each participant, some participants still seemed not to click as often as they were supposed to. The participant is expected to click the mouse every single second of the video, which might cause fatigue or boredom over time. As a possible solution, the researchers speculated whether using a larger time interval to collect ratings (e.g. every two seconds instead of one) would help ameliorate this issue. The current release of the software, Anion Variable Tester V2, requires providing ratings every second.

Annotated readings

MacIntyre, P.D. (2012) The idiodynamic method: A closer look at the dynamics of communication traits. *Communication Research Reports* 29 (4), 361–367. doi:10.1080/08824096.2012.723274

In this short article, MacIntyre – the originator of the idiodynamic method – gives a helpful overview of the various features of this method. He also explains its rationale in some detail as well as its connection to CDST.

MacIntyre, P.D. and Legatto, J.J. (2011) A dynamic system approach to willingness to communicate: Developing an idiodynamic method to capture rapidly changing affect. *Applied Linguistics* 32 (2), 149–171. doi:10.1093/applin/amq037

This is the seminal article using the idiodynamic method. The researchers examined the willingness to communicate of six female learners. They found that searching memory for vocabulary and language anxiety are important factors influencing willingness to communicate. They also showed how using one overall mean for each participant results in important individual-level variations being lost (i.e. the ergodicity problem).

Gregersen, T. and MacIntyre, P.D. (2017) Idiodynamics: An innovative method to build emotional intelligence through systematic self-assessment/reflection/critique. In T. Gregersen and P.D. MacIntyre (eds) *Innovative Practices in Language Teacher Education: Spanning the Spectrum from Intra- to Inter-Personal Professional Development* (pp. 33–53). Cham: Springer.

In this chapter, the authors present a more in-depth analyses of the idiodynamic method in the context of teacher emotional intelligence. The authors demonstrate how this method can be used as a tool by teacher trainers to uncover positive and negative thinking patterns in order to address them explicitly.

Gregersen, T., MacIntyre, P.D. and Meza, M.D. (2014) The motion of emotion: Idiodynamic case studies of learners' foreign language anxiety. *The Modern Language Journal* 98, 574–588. doi:10.1111/modl.12084

In this article, the researchers combined idiodynamic data with physiological data obtained from heart rate monitors – as well as self-reported survey data and qualitative interviews. The researchers reported different patterns of convergence and divergence among these data sources and tried to explain these findings.

Note

(1) At the time of writing, this software is freely available for download at http://faculty.cbu.ca/pmacintyre/.

References

Boudreau, C., MacIntyre, P. and Dewaele, J.-M. (2018) Enjoyment and anxiety in second language communication: An idiodynamic approach. *Studies in Second Language Learning and Teaching* 8 (1), 149–170. doi:10.14746/ssllt.2018.8.1.7

Chinn, C.A. and Sherin, B.L. (2014) Microgenetic methods. In R.K. Sawyer (ed.) *The Cambridge Handbook of the Learning Sciences* (pp. 171–190). Cambridge: Cambridge University Press.

Gass, S. and Mackey, A. (2000) *Stimulated Recall Methodology in Second Language Research*. Mahwah, NJ: Lawrence Erlbaum.

Larsen-Freeman, D. (2006) The emergence of complexity, fluency, and accuracy in the oral and written production of five Chinese learners of English. *Applied Linguistics* 27, 590–619.

Lowie, W.M. and Verspoor, M.H. (2019) Individual differences and the ergodicity problem. *Language Learning* 69 (s1), 184–206. doi:10.1111/lang.12324

MacIntyre, P.D. (2012) The idiodynamic method: A closer look at the dynamics of communication traits. *Communication Research Reports* 29 (4), 361–367. doi:10.1080/08 824096.2012.723274

Rosenzweig, S. (1986) Idiodynamics vis-à-vis psychology. *American Psychologist* 41 (3), 241–245. doi:10.1037/0003-066X.41.3.241

Rosenzweig, S. and Hackney, A. (2004) Idiodynamics and the idioverse. In W.E. Craighead and C.B. Nemeroff (eds) *The Concise Corsini Encyclopedia of Psychology and Behavioral Science* (3rd edn; pp. 456–458). New York/Chichester: Wiley.

Velicer, W., Babbin, S. and Palumbo, R. (2014) Idiographic applications: Issues of ergodicity and generalizability. In P. Molenaar, R. Lerner and K. Newell (eds) *Handbook of Developmental Systems Theory and Methodology* (pp. 425–441). New York: Guilford Press.

Part 4
The Future of CDST Methodology

18 Method Integration

Introduction

As we approach the end of this book, the most common-sense topic to address is perhaps the possibility of combining the different methods discussed so far. Part 2 of this book focused on qualitative methods while Part 3 dealt with quantitative methods. A straightforward answer could be to use what has come to be known as *mixed methods* (sometimes called *multi-method* research), where the researcher combines qualitative and quantitative methods in a single study. For many, it would make a lot of sense to argue that a combination of methods would bring the best of both worlds to overcome the inevitable limitations of any single method and naturally shed richer light on the complex phenomenon under investigation (see e.g. contributions in Hesse-Biber & Johnson, 2015). This also makes sense given what we have argued about complexity and dynamic systems theory's (CDST) transdisciplinary aims and its problem-oriented approach to scientific inquiry. However, on closer scrutiny things might not be as straightforward as they seem.

In practice, much of the published applied linguistics research purporting to use mixed methods (MM) follows a rather superficial approach. For example, it is by no means uncommon to find a large-scale, well-designed and meticulously conducted quantitative study followed by a brief qualitative component that simply lists some quotes from a short interview or from a couple of open-ended questions placed at the end of the main data elicitation instrument. Add to this the fact that most of this type of research uses the qualitative component primarily to demonstrate that the quantitative results are valid and that all the bases have been covered, so to speak. It is also common, though perhaps to a lesser extent, to see an ambitious qualitative study appended by a quick (and possibly dirty) quantitative component, again to show that the qualitative analyses were credible.

We have no doubt that many readers would agree that the foregoing research designs are not the most optimal. They are also likely far off the mark regarding how the respective methods were intended to be used originally. However, some methodologists have gone as far as saying that such situations have no remedy; qualitative and quantitative approaches *should not be mixed* at all, as they represent different and incommensurable worldviews. In contrast, other methodologists argue that methods should not simply be mixed superficially, with one tacked onto another as an afterthought, but *should be integrated* at a more fundamental level. Other researchers advocate Bayesian analysis, which is a quantitative approach that has a central qualitative element infused into it. These different positions are overviewed next.

The Problem with Mixed Methods

Some readers might be surprised that there is a handful of methodologists who challenge the idea of mixing qualitative and quantitative approaches. After all, the idea of MM has become a buzzword in recent years, with even dedicated peer-reviewed journals such as the *Journal of Mixed Methods Research* gaining prominence. In the field of applied linguistics, MM has also been discussed at length by methodologists, recommending it to established researchers and graduate students alike (Brown, 2014; Dörnyei, 2007; Mackey & Bryfonski, 2018; Riazi, 2017). At the same time, some misgivings have been expressed. For example, Dörnyei (2007: 46) acknowledges that when MM is endorsed, 'the reasoning or logic behind such an assumption is not always as readily expressed as is the sentiment itself'.

To extend our discussion on the topic in Chapter 3, such concerns about MM underlie a deeper philosophical mix-up. Generally speaking, there are two dominant but divergent worldviews: *objectivism* and *constructivism* (see Table 18.1). Objectivists believe that there is a reality out there, and our job as researchers is to try and understand it. It might be too complex, but we try our best to approach it. Some social constructivists, on the other hand, believe that knowledge is not out there for researchers to discover, but is instead created by 'epistemic authorities'. To quote Lincoln and Guba:

> The 'realities' taken to exist depend on a transaction between the knower and the 'to-be-known' in the particular context in which the encounter between them takes place. That transaction is necessarily highly subjective, mediated by the knower's prior experience and knowledge, by political and social status, by gender, by race, class, sexual orientation, nationality, by personal and cultural values, and by the knower's interpretation (construction) of the contextual surround. Knowledge is not 'discovered' but rather *created*; it exists only in the time/space framework in which it is generated. (Lincoln & Guba, 2013: 40, original emphasis)

This perspective, in its extreme, might lead one to the view that 'the Special Theory of Relativity is true because those in the scientific establishment who advocated it overcame the opposition from those who denied it' (Ladyman, 2007: 307). As discussed in more detail in Chapter 3, many complexivists embrace critical realism, according to which an objective reality does exist out there, though its complexity has historically tended to be underestimated theoretically and methodologically. Table 18.1 summarizes these two philosophical worldviews. It is important to note, though, that the flow in Table 18.1 describes broad tendencies and is not always as neat, since crossovers are possible especially at the level of methodology and methods.

Going back to the original topic, where does MM fit? Does it fall under one of these two paradigms, or does it have its own third paradigm? There does not seem to be a definitive answer to these questions. Some methodologists argue that MM does not represent a third philosophical position. They argue colorfully that, rather than representing the best of both worlds, most MM is simply (post-)positivism 'in drag', used as 'covers for the continuing hegemony of positivism' (Giddings, 2006: 195), and as 'a Trojan Horse for positivist enquiry' (Giddings & Grant, 2007: 52). Complicating the picture further, Creswell (2011) presents a list of 11

Table 18.1 An overview of the two main philosophical standpoints to research

Ontology (What is out there?)	Objectivism	Constructivism
	Existence is independent of observers	Existence is dependent on observers
Epistemology (How do we know what(ever) is out there?)	Post-positivism/critical realism	Interpretivism
	Truths are discovered by researchers	Truths are created by social actors
Methodology (What overall approach should we use?)	(Hypothetico-)deductive	Inductive
	From general to specific	From specific to general
Methods (What tools and techniques are available?)	Quantitative	Qualitative
	Empirical measurement	Subjective interpretation

controversies associated with MM research ranging from the legitimacy of the philosophical underpinnings of MM to the pragmatics of conducting an actual MM study. Such controversies might lead one to wonder whether MM is here to solve the qualitative–quantitative paradigm wars, or to add fuel to their fire.

AMEL AHMED AND RUDRA SIL (2009: 3) ON WHAT LIES BENEATH MIXING METHODS:

Our argument is straightforward: The claim that MMR [multi-method research] is inherently better than SMR [single-method research] is built on the faulty premise that one method can offer external validity for the findings of another. Different methods can at best corroborate each other's findings, but this does not yield a more compelling inference. We do not know more or know better as a result of triangulating different methods because different methods rest upon incommensurable epistemological foundations that even the most heroic attempts at translation cannot overcome. Though combining methods may and often does produce good scholarship, we find that MMR holds the same epistemological status as separate projects addressing the same question, and that SMR is no less likely to produce good scholarship.

On the other hand, some other methodologists advocate MM as advancing *pragmatic pluralism* and *eclecticism* that can help illuminate the underlying (especially causal) processes in the phenomena of interest (e.g. Teddlie & Tashakkori, 2010). But this view has not gone uncontested, either. A prototypical example of a sequential MM study is to conduct a large-N quantitative study that yields some generalizable relations among certain variables. However, because these findings may not shed light on the underlying causal processes, the MM researcher then selects a subsample for further qualitative analysis, which is then used to trace the potential causal pathways and perhaps suggest hypotheses for further research.

Many constructivists would object to this (mis)use of qualitative research, however. Qualitative research is *not* intended to offer falsifiable hypotheses for further empirical assessment or to refute claims. Instead, qualitative research aims to understand the context-bound and subjective reality created by the social actors themselves during interaction. To use it for hypothesis generation and subsequent hypothetico-deductive reasoning is little more than repurposing it to serve the goals of a rival worldview, which is why some scholars argue that MM is proffered as a masquerade for positivism.

Seawright (2016) gives an example that illustrates this problem. Coming from a political science background, Seawright reviews some research on the likelihood of a civil war in a mountainous area. He reports a coefficient of 0.219. He then wonders how qualitative analysis can explain this figure further. He cites Colombia as a case study and discusses the historical and context-bound factors that might not be relevant to other civil-war-prone states. After acknowledging the potential contribution of a mountainous landscape, he presents a qualitative counterargument:

> At the same time, the mountainous areas near the national capital at Bogotá have often been among the safest areas and the zones with strongest state presence in the country. Furthermore, mountain-free regions in the southeast and along the Caribbean coast have also served as important areas of refuge for anti- and non-state armed actors, thereby facilitating and prolonging the civil war. For instance, through the 1990s the FARC guerrillas had their primary bases in the jungle regions of southeastern Colombia. Thus, case-study consideration of Colombia would have to suggest that mountainous terrain plays a supporting causal role at some points and for certain actors in the Colombian conflict, but is not a relevant consideration at other points. Further research would likely illuminate how and why terrain matters for some aspects of Colombian political violence but not others. (Seawright, 2016: 6–7)

After presenting these two counterviews, he asks a reasonable question: 'How does this line of inquiry compare with the estimated coefficient of 0.219?' (Seawright, 2016: 7). Indeed, with a lucid description of a specific case that is characteristic of qualitative inquiry, how would the 0.219 figure help the qualitative researcher? This is not an unusual dilemma in qualitative inquiry. Different cases can have different unique features and circumstances, and for even the same case different constructivist investigators may come up with different interpretations and narratives. Qualitative findings are typically idiosyncratic to the case investigated, and there is no reason to expect such processes to generalize to other cases. For many qualitative researchers this is simply the norm, not a 'dilemma'.

For these reasons, a number of scholars do not hesitate to consider MM a futile endeavor. Ahmed and Sil (2012: 944) argue that 'What stands in the way of a more meaningful integration of "thick" narratives with "thin" formal models is the vast chasm between the ontologies undergirding a nomothetic model and idiographic narrative when it comes to the interpretation of social action'. Other researchers posit that 'qualitative and quantitative tools genuinely cannot collaborate in making a causal case' because 'in principle or in practice, qualitative evidence adds little to competent quantitative research' (Seawright, 2016: 20). Some others consider using MM to uncover causal processes an oxymoron as 'qualitative information cannot be adjoined in any meaningful way to quantitative data sets' (Beck, 2010: 499): 'For me, it is the general question that is of interest, and so it is unclear how the qualitative analysis provides additional leverage (beyond the idea that one should know and understand one's cases)' (Beck, 2006: 350).

The consequences do not stop here. Some methodologists additionally argue that MM has field-wide ramifications in that it can *subvert* methodological pluralism (Ahmed & Sil, 2009, 2012). With the rise of MM in applied linguistics, a ripple effect on the likelihood of publishing in top-tier journals, in the allocation of grants and awards and in the prospects of hiring and tenure is bound to happen. Researchers with knowledge of more methods would be privileged, but expertise in a particular method may be stigmatized. This may come at the expense of quality. Some readers might find the different qualitative and quantitative methods discussed in this book to be bewildering, though our book is by no means exhaustive of all possible methods for CDST research (see further resources in Chapter 19). If all these methods are to be taught as part of a graduate programme, time constraints would force emphasis on each to be spread thin, eventually producing a generation of jack-of-all-trades researchers who lack deep expertise. We would agree with Ahmed and Sil when they argue that,

> Where there is a pool of labor available, it is not at all clear what is gained by making all of the members of that pool make the same kind of investment in gaining the same array of skills. If anything, the gains to efficiency from more specialized training and from iterated applications of the same method are lost. (Ahmed & Sil, 2009: 5)

Another concern is the extent to which we can rely on self-report data. A growing literature is showing that individuals' explanations of their own behaviors tend to be naïve *post hoc* rationalizations innocently representing folk theories and cultural norms and expectations (see e.g. Al-Hoorie, 2015, in press; Kahneman & Tversky, 2000). Obviously, this is no problem within a constructivist paradigm whose primary target is how individuals make sense of and construe their own worlds. From post-positivist and critical realist perspectives, however, the validity and reliability of these accounts matter. This may be seen by some as making the contribution of self-report data a lower priority in understanding quantitative results, thus widening the gap between these two worldviews.

Within the applied linguistics field, Mirhosseini (2018: 473) surveys some of these concerns and highlights the tendency of applied linguistics research to simply ignore or bypass them. He argues that many applied linguists opt for 'quick fixes' of a 'naïve combination' of qualitative and quantitative procedures with little attention to the fundamental incompatibility of the two worldviews they represent. He also emphasizes that MM has not produced a convincing third worldview that is unique to it.

Instead, MM researchers still operate under the conventional objectivist or constructivist paradigms without addressing such deeper philosophical issues. As he put it, 'If there is an actual distinct epistemological foundation for mixed methods, it needs to be simply introduced in terms of the type of knowledge it defines. It does not sound convincing to knock on different doors to choose one' (Mirhosseini, 2018: 473). Many observers would agree with how Ahmed and Sil (2012) describe the status quo of MM: One method is used for the heavy lifting while the other for window dressing.

Integrative Mixed Methods

One solution proposed for the philosophical problems in MM is method integration. This topic has been discussed in depth in the literature with some book-length treatments of it (e.g. Seawright, 2016; Teddlie & Tashakkori, 2009). Some scholars advocating such integrative designs argue that 'triangulation' is not an appropriate approach. Originally, the metaphor of triangulation comes from geometry where the distance of an object is measured from two vantage points (Seawright, 2016: 4). When the two measurements match, we become more confident in the exact distance of that object. However, as previously explained, qualitative and quantitative approaches stem from different philosophical backgrounds and so it is not straightforward to make direct comparison of their results. Two methods might give very different results, and yet this does not necessarily mean that one is right and the other is wrong.

JASON SEAWRIGHT (2016: 152) ON THE LIMITATIONS OF QUALITATIVE–QUANTITATIVE TRIANGULATION:

Are case studies logically compatible enough with experiments to contribute in addressing these key issues of causal inference? One important argument to the contrary would focus on the contrast between experiments' standard emphasis on the sample average treatment effect with case studies' much greater attention to causation at the level of the individual case (Goertz and Mahoney 2012: Part 1). This is a compelling argument against any simple or direct comparison between the findings from an experimental and a case-study analysis of the same topic. Because of this fundamental difference, the two methods might produce seemingly opposite results without contradicting each other. For instance, an experiment might find no causal effect of a particular treatment on the outcome of interest, while a case study finds substantial evidence of a major effect. Both findings could be completely correct; the case study might simply focus on a case that is causally unusual in comparison with those studied by the experiment.

> To echo a recurring theme of this book, there is little to be gained
> from a triangulation-style comparison of overall causal effects between
> experiments and case studies.

Method integration is considered a hallmark of rigorous research.
Seawright (2016: 8) defines integrative designs as 'multi-method designs
in which two or more methods are carefully combined to support a
single, unified causal inference. With such a design, one method will
produce the final inference, and the other is used to design, test, refine, or
bolster the analysis producing that inference'. In other words, a primary
method will still do the heavy lifting, but the other is not just window
dressing. Put differently, the secondary method will buttress any weaknesses of the primary method *while* it is being applied (see also Mackey
& Bryfonski, 2018). In this way, the researcher will still operate within
their conventional framework but use the quantitative and qualitative
'tools' to improve their design. Constructivists, for instance, can use
quantitative analyses to further understand the subjective realities of
their participants:

> Perhaps away from the epistemological confusion, the claimed merits of
> mixed methods may be sought in constructivist and interpretive perspec-
> tives. Different methods of data collection and interpretation may be
> combined without the obligation to shift and confuse epistemological
> standpoints. The use of numerical and verbal data together for gain-
> ing profound understandings does not necessitate abandoning a con-
> structive epistemological position and forging or adopting a new one.
> (Mirhosseini, 2018: 475)

Similarly, a critical realist may use qualitative tools to bolster their
design. In contrast to triangulation, where the researcher uses more than
one method independently and compares results at the end, integrative
designs require that the primary method (e.g. quantitative) is refined
throughout by a secondary method (e.g. qualitative). Thus, 'in contrast
to the linear sequences or parallel designs typical of triangulation-based
research, integrative multi-method designs involve an indefinite cycle of
discovery and refinement' (Seawright, 2016: 10). This strikes us as a productive way to begin to transcend disciplinary silos and come at an issue
from different ways.

Seawright (2016) discusses some general integrative techniques that
many researchers may find useful:

(1) *Checking assumptions*: The term 'assumptions' is usually used to
refer to assumptions for a statistical test or model. However, assumptions have a much broader scope in research (Al-Hoorie & Vitta,

in press). Investigators make many assumptions in the course of their study. If the study involves giving participants a particular treatment (e.g. a classroom instructional method), the investigator assumes that the treatment has been received, taken up and processed in the way the investigator has intended it and for the whole duration of the study. This is discussed under the general rubric of *compliance*. The researcher can ascertain compliance by drawing from qualitative tools – not only interviews but also observation, diaries, etc. – depending on the nature of the study. It might be found that some participants have not used the treatment as intended and so they might have to be excluded or recoded as control participants, thus improving inference quality. Another important assumption goes by the name of the *stable unit treatment value assumption* (sometimes referred to with the unfriendly acronym SUTVA). This assumption requires that participants in different groups do not interact in ways that can affect the treatment given to each (e.g. different classes given different instructional interventions). This assumption is relatively easy to satisfy in the lab, but in field experiments spillover of treatment can easily happen, and would almost be expected in complex and dynamic settings. Qualitative investigation can be used to ensure satisfaction of this assumption, or at least to what extent it has been violated through student interaction outside class time. This investigation should be systematically integrated into the research design, not merely via adding another item about it to the survey.

(2) *Refining measurement*: Careful measurement is an important consideration in rigorous research, especially for critical realists. However, in many cases, perhaps more than the researcher might anticipate, the available measurement tools do not do justice to the complexity of the phenomenon under investigation. One possibility that has been used to address this issue is *experimental ethnography*. Here, instead of relying exclusively on quantitative measures to assess the variables in the study, the researcher also applies in-depth interviews and other qualitative methods before and after the experiment. These interviews give a richer insight of the feelings, emotions, cognitive processes, etc., that a standard survey could easily miss. The researcher might find qualitative changes before and after the treatments that are hard to capture numerically. Such qualitative instruments are integrated in the design of the experimental ethnography. Example Study 1 (see later in this chapter) gives an illustration of an experimental ethnography study.

(3) *Experimental realism*: This idea has to do with what is sometimes known as external validity and ecological validity. Do the results obtained in the study apply in real life? There are actually two parts to this question. The first, straightforward part has to do with the generalizability of the results. This is a relatively easy issue because

replicating this study in different contexts and with different participants would inform whether the initial findings apply to limited contexts only. A more complex question is whether the same processes and causal pathways apply outside the experiment as well. Do the participants think, make decisions and behave the same in real life as they do during the experiment? If not, then replication in a different context may not solve this problem. Of course, this is not to say that these experimental results are invalid, but that they lack experimental realism if they do not apply outside experimental conditions. One solution is to conduct a careful process tracing (see Chapter 5) or retrodictive qualitative modeling (see Chapter 8) and compare the results with those processes that the participants use under non-experimental conditions. Or the researcher could process-trace the thought processes of other non-experimental participants who are matched to the experimental participants in crucial demographic variables. To achieve this requires careful integration between the quantitative design and appropriate qualitative tools.

Thus, an experiment does not have to be a 'black box'. Qualitative tools should be integrated carefully to improve the research design and its eventual outcome. Nor should researchers distance themselves from the study for the sake of 'objectivity,' let alone relegate the work to a research assistant who is later asked to hand in numbers on a spreadsheet. The researcher should aim to obtain an intimate understanding of the complex phenomenon investigated. Achieving this is not limited by the three techniques previously described since different research questions require different and creative integrative designs (e.g. interactive, iterative and synergistic designs, see Nastasi et al. [2010]). For example, close observation of the complex phenomenon might reveal an opportunity for a regression-discontinuity design that can offer a unique viewpoint. Example Study 2 (see later in this chapter) describes a regression-discontinuity example.

In conclusion, there does not seem to be a consensus on a distinct philosophical standpoint for MM. Instead, researchers can still operate within their familiar paradigms while using different tools, qualitative and quantitative, to improve their designs and to understand complex phenomena better. We agree with Seawright (2016: 16) that limiting the contribution of a method (e.g. the belief that quantitative methods should be used to test the generalizability of qualitative results) is a persistent stereotype. These tools should be carefully integrated rather than using one as an appendix to the other. The latter approach may very well shed additional light on phenomena under investigation, but this will be missing the full potential of combining different methods.

Bayesian Methods

In 2011, psychologist Daryl Bem reported a series of nine studies conducted over a period of eight years supporting the existence of precognition, that the average individual can foresee unpredictable future events. These studies demonstrated that the participants were able to predict, at a statistically significant level, the sexually explicit stimuli that the computer would randomly generate. Bem (2011) also found that this 'time-reversing' phenomenon appeared most clearly in individuals high in sensation seeking (a facet of extroversion), leading him to offer an evolutionary explanation for it. Such results, according to Bem (2011: 423), 'challenge not only our classical conceptions of space and distance, as telepathy and clairvoyance do, but also those of time and causality'.

Much to the surprise of many observers, this paper passed a rigorous peer-review process and was accepted for publication in the prestigious *Journal of Personality and Social Psychology*. Although, in an editorial comment, Judd and Gawronski (2011: 406) described these results as 'extremely puzzling' since 'they turn our traditional understanding of causality on its head', the journal ironically desk-rejected failed replications, explaining that the journal publishes 'only the best original research' (see Aldhous, 2011).

Quite understandably, this study (re)ignited the controversy surrounding null hypothesis significance testing and whether the standards this approach prescribes for evidence are too low (e.g. Rouder & Morey, 2011; Wagenmakers *et al.*, 2011). These critiques offered a Bayesian perspective on how to interpret Bem's results. In this view, 'extraordinary claims require extraordinary evidence' (Wagenmakers *et al.*, 2011: 429). That is, although Bem's results managed to exceed the conventional 0.05 level, this is still not high enough to overcome our strong *prior belief* that such supernatural ability to foretell the future does not exist.

ANDREW GELMAN (2018: 21–22) ON THE HARMFUL EFFECTS NULL HYPOTHESIS SIGNIFICANCE TESTING (NHST) HAS HAD ON SCIENCE:

NHST has perhaps never been a very good idea, when studying small effects and complex interactions, it is particularly useless. Or, one might say, it has been a useful way for some people to get publications and publicity but not a useful way of performing replicable science... the current replication crisis in science arises in part from the ill effects of NHST being used to study small effects with noisy data. In such settings, apparent success comes easy but truly replicable results require a more serious connection between theory, measurement, and data.

In order to further illustrate this point, consider the opposite scenario. Imagine that a medical experiment had only five participants in each of its two conditions. After administering the experimental drug, two participants fell ill, one had to be hospitalized and one died. In this case, even though these results are unlikely to reach statistical significance (due to the small sample size), it would be common sense to terminate the experiment and conclude that the drug is unsafe. However, if we do not base this conclusion on statistical significance, then on what? The Bayesian reasoning in this situation would be that we have a very low prior belief that those young, healthy participants that were randomly selected would happen to fall ill or die suddenly after ingesting the drug for reasons unrelated to it. Because a coincidence of this sort is very unlikely, we are willing to accept this evidence, even if it does not reach the conventional 0.05 threshold. Similarly, when we have a strong prior belief that precognition is very unlikely, we would naturally require proportionately strong evidence to be convinced.

The foregoing scenarios offer a glimpse of a deeper clash between the two paradigm giants in statistical theory, *Bayesian* and *frequentist*, a clash that has been dated to two centuries ago (for reader-friendly introductions, see McGrayne [2011] and Salsburg [2001]). As previously explained, a unique feature of the Bayesian approach is that prior qualitative and subjective beliefs and knowledge of initial conditions can be incorporated in the statistical model, unlike null hypothesis significance testing in frequentist statistics; therefore, we do not have to start from zero every time we conduct an analysis. Bayesian analysis offers a formal account of the not unusual situation where researchers are sometimes skeptical of a result despite it being statistically significant, while at other times they readily accept a result that at first sight seems weak. These features are slowly attracting a growing number of second language development (SLD) researchers (Norouzian *et al.*, 2018; Ross & Mackey, 2015).

Another attractive feature is the rich and detailed information Bayesian statistics produce. In contrast to a simple binary significance outcome, and perhaps a single-effect size figure, Bayesian statistics can provide a *distribution* of the results, graphically showing the likelihood of each outcome. This outcome, rich as it is, can also be dynamically updated as more and more information is learned about the complex phenomenon under investigation. All this might imply that the results of Bayesian statistics would be obscure. Quite the contrary. Compared with *p*-values and confidence intervals, whose interpretations are not direct (see Al-Hoorie & Vitta, in press), Bayesian results are more intuitive and directly applicable. For example, frequentist *p*-value is concerned with the probability of the *data*, though we are typically more interested in the probability of our hypothesis (see also Chapter 16). Equally confusing is the interpretation of confidence intervals: 95% confidence intervals do not actually refer to the probability of the result of our study – though it is tempting to think so – but to the idea that if we were to repeat our study an infinite amount of times, we would obtain the population parameter 95% of the time. Our own study may or may not happen to be one of those 95% of the cases. This interpretation makes confidence intervals much less useful than they might be thought at first, with some critics going as far as describing them as 'scientifically useless' (Bolstad, 2007: 228).

VICKERS (2010: 61–62) ON THE WARPED INTERPRETATION OF P-VALUES:

So finally, after many hours of packing and loading, the bags are in the car, the children in their booster seats and the snack bag in easy reach, everyone is buckled in and my hand is on the ignition key. At which point my wife asks, 'Where is the camera?' Being a statistician, I instantly convert this question into two hypotheses: 'the camera is in the car' and 'the camera is still in the house.' Given that it is easier to pop back inside the house than to unload the car, I decide to test the second hypothesis. A few minutes later, I tell my wife that I have looked in all the places inside and couldn't find the camera. We conclude that 'it must be in the car somewhere' and head off on our road-trip.

There is something a little odd about this story: we concluded one thing (that the camera was in the car) because we couldn't find evidence to support something else (the camera was in the house). But as it happens, this is exactly what we do when we conduct a statistical test. First, we propose a null hypothesis, roughly speaking, that nothing interesting is going on… We then run our statistical analyses to obtain a p-value. The p-value is the probability that the data would be at least as extreme as those observed, if the null hypothesis were true, so if the p-value is low (say, less than 0.05) we say, 'These data would be unlikely if the null hypothesis were true, therefore it probably isn't.' As a result, we declare our result 'statistically significant,' reject the null hypothesis and conclude that we do indeed have an interesting phenomenon on our hands.

Bayesian analysis is useful not only for relatively simple questions, but it can also handle more complex problems. Any attempt to incorporate the large amount of available scholarship into one investigation would typically render it too complex to handle. This is why researchers tend to fall back on simple designs that advance knowledge in a piecemeal fashion. Probably the only option frequentist statistics offers to incorporate previous knowledge is using one-tailed hypotheses, and this is also still controversial (Freedman, 2008). On the other hand, Goldstein

(2006) illustrates how building a Bayesian 'belief net' can quantify and manage uncertainties in complex systems with high reliability. It allows researchers to synthesize information from diverse sources – for example when attempting to locate lost submarines and aircraft – by constantly updating prior beliefs, thus making it 'massively more efficient and flexible' to the extent that it is 'hard to imagine any other approach which could do so' (Goldstein, 2006: 405).

Framework for Dynamic Method Integration

Methodologists have proposed several typologies to conceptualize the relationship between qualitative and quantitative methods and how to combine them to maximize what researchers can learn from their designs (see Nastasi *et al.* [2010] for an overview). In this section, we build on these efforts and propose a framework for dynamic method integration that those doing transdisciplinary CDST research can adopt (see Table 18.2).

As can be seen in Table 18.2, there are three distinct levels: aim, unit and method. Starting with the aim, the researcher might try to explore a research question, or may attempt to test certain understandings or expectations whether observationally or (quasi-)experimentally. As explained in Chapter 3 in more detail, a critical realist perspective assumes that there does exist a reality out there to be known, though the most we can do is to try and approximate it due to its complexity. We made the case that when it comes to prediction in particular, although the complex social world does not lend itself to universals that can be applied across settings and populations, it is still possible to form some generalizations by comparison to other similar systems, under similar conditions and contexts, with similar outcomes (Uprichard, 2009). Therefore, there is no reason for critical realists to shy away from making predictions and then subjecting these predictions to the test.

Notice also that Table 18.2 uses the term 'falsificatory' rather than 'confirmatory'. This is because, no matter how detailed and accurate we

Table 18.2 Proposed framework for dynamic method integration

Aim	Unit of Analysis	Method
Exploratory	Individual	Qualitative

Aim	Unit of Analysis	Method
Falsificatory: observational and (quasi-) experimental	Group	Quantitative

Note: A given research question may be process oriented, outcome oriented or both.

think our knowledge is, it will turn out to be an incomplete depiction of reality and will eventually be disconfirmed through further rigorous research. Attempting to 'confirm' our knowledge is therefore inevitably bound to fail. For this reason, some philosophers argued that positive results cannot confirm a theory, but only corroborate it and make it empirically adequate (e.g. Popper, 1983, 2002/1934; van Fraassen, 1980). Expressions like 'confirm' and 'prove' are generally more appropriate when used in a mathematical sense and in deductive reasoning.

The double-headed arrow between exploratory and falsificatory indicates that critical realists should not limit themselves to either one if they would like to make their research maximally informative. Ideally, an integrative design should be characterized by a flexible switch between these two aims. If all that a falsificatory study could offer is just positive results supporting existing theory, this might as well be considered a failure. Such studies would not genuinely advance our understanding, and might imply that we already fully understand the complex phenomenon at hand. Although it might sound nonsensical to many readers that a positive result should mean we fully understand the topic in question, this is not what an observer would interpret from reading some recent applied linguistics literature. It is not uncommon to come across the celebratory tone that such-and-such a theory has been validated, confirmed or even proven by the results (see e.g. Al-Hoorie, 2018). Obviously, it is a contradiction to describe a theory as 'proven,' but then claim that we still do not have a full understanding – let alone suggest the need to falsify it. Adopting the exploratory–falsificatory approach proposed here should radically reorient researchers and their aims, making them actively seek negative, disconfirming results rather than celebrate positive ones. Consequently, a shift in perspective is expected to happen in relation to how researchers go about doing their research, interpreting their results and suggesting future directions for investigation.

The next level, unit of analysis, has to do with whether the analysis takes place at the individual or the group level. Group-based research is the norm in many areas of applied linguistics research, though individual-based research can also make a substantial and unique contribution (see Chapter 16). In fact, individual-based research may be more compatible with the assumptions of CDST as illustrated in various chapters of this book. Individual-based research allows the researcher to hold a close lens to development and change without resorting to averaging away individual idiosyncrasies. As we have suggested in Chapter 3, the notion that one level of data is superior to another may be a point of (mis)interpretation considering that a complex system is not restricted to representing an individual. If a group is the system chosen as the unit of analysis, or if it is any higher-level system than an individual, then it may well be that group-level data are more relevant. At the same time, Table 18.1 shows a double-headed arrow between the individual and the group, indicating that an integrative design should attempt to draw from both of these approaches. Individual-based research designs carry out meticulous analyses of single cases while group-based results point toward broader tendencies and how these results vary in the population.

The final level of the proposed framework is the method. Integrative designs draw from both qualitative and quantitative methods to advance knowledge in a particular area of investigation. It is a common misconception that macro-level analyses entail the use of quantitative analyses and the more individual level requires the use of qualitative data. CDST research supports no such claims and, as we suggest in Chapter 3, encourages the intelligent use and mixing of quantitative or qualitative methods appropriate for the phenomenon under investigation (see e.g. Chapter 10 for one such application). However, as explained in more detail earlier in this chapter, methods should be carefully integrated not just mixed. Both should support the research question in a unified manner. As we described earlier, the qualitative component could be used to check assumptions, refine measurements and examine experimental realism. This means that qualitative data should not be seen as a tool compatible only with constructivist or postmodernist philosophies (see e.g. Chapter 4).

Although our focus in the framework presented in Table 18.2 deals primarily with longitudinal data, it can also apply to cross-sectional data. We focus on longitudinal data simply because they are usually more CDST compatible. Still, longitudinal data can be of two types: outcome oriented and process oriented. *Outcome-oriented* research focuses on the outcomes or patterns that are reached at different points in time. An example might be the developmental trajectory of proficiency or attitudes over time. *Process-oriented* research focuses instead on the mechanisms that explain how an outcome is reached. An example would be the stages that proficiency or attitudes go through and what influences exist at each stage. Combining insights from process- and outcome-oriented research can enrich a research agenda (Gage & Needels, 1989).

To conclude this section, the framework proposed here calls attention to the need to dynamically integrate exploratory × falsificatory aims, individual × group analyses and qualitative × quantitative methods. Obviously, this is not to suggest that every study should have all six components. Instead, we would suggest that researchers try to incorporate the two aspects from at least one level. A study might have both exploratory and falsificatory aims, both individual and group analyses or both qualitative and quantitative methods. For example, if a study focuses on either an individual- or a group-based approach, it should ideally attempt to integrate either the exploratory–falsificatory level or the qualitative–quantitative level. Thus, a group-based experiment could utilize qualitative data, not just as an additional element appended to the end but as an essential component integrated into the study design. In fact, qualitative data could even be a primary tool of data collection in an experiment (see

Example Study 1). In contrast to a single study, a line of CDST research can and should exploit all six components in Table 18.2.

Example Study 1: Experimental Ethnographic Designs

As previously emphasized, qualitative data can be integrated in a meaningful manner within a quantitative design. Experimental ethnography is a method that does just that. It uses qualitative data as an essential data collection tool within a standard experimental design. This is why experimental ethnography has been described as a marriage between qualitative and quantitative research (Sherman & Strang, 2004). To quote Paluck (2010b: 60, original emphasis), 'experimentation—specifically field experimentation—can and should be more central to qualitative research... it is *not* inherently quantitative'.

Paluck (2010a) conducted a study utilizing experimental ethnography. The study was carried out in war-torn eastern Democratic Republic of Congo (through events that have come to be known as Africa's World War), in which militias continue to intimidate civilians through wartime atrocities and forced displacement. Paluck examined the effectiveness of an 'imagine-self technique' that encourages perspective-taking and imagining oneself as a member of different groups. The study was conducted through a weekly radio soap opera. Using a stratified sampling technique, the researcher randomly selected certain regions to broadcast this radio show (control group) and other regions to broadcast this show plus a subsequent talk show encouraging perspective-taking aimed at promoting intergroup tolerance.

The study included 842 participants who completed a questionnaire and participated in an interview and a test of helping behavior. In the helping behavior test, each participant was given a 2 kg bag of salt – a valuable commodity in that context – and was asked whether they were willing to donate some of that salt to a rival group. The researcher and her team recorded whether the participant agreed to donate, how much as well as their spontaneous comments about that decision. An interesting outcome of that study was the salience of grievances that were not captured by standard questionnaire items but that emerged from analysis of spontaneous comments. These comments were classified as negative (refusing to donate due to animosity), strategic (accepting to donate in the hope of stopping attacks, or refusing for fear of making enemies stronger) or positive (accepting to donate for religious or altruistic reasons). Some of the negative comments were too extreme to capture using standard questionnaire items. For example, some participants stated, 'They killed my mother/They make us poor' and 'I'd rather die than help them'. Had the researcher relied exclusively and rigidly on the Likert-type items in her study, as is the case in much experimental research, then selecting a 'strongly agree' option would not have revealed the salience of these grievances. Many emotions may be too complex to capture via a researcher-predefined set of response options. As Seawright (2016) put it,

> The idea here is to go beyond the most common measurement strategies for the outcome in social science experiments – survey questions or behavioral responses to situations – by using in-depth interviews and other qualitative approaches to provide insights into emotions, thought processes, and models of understanding, as well as to allow for surprising inductive discoveries of possible effects in these domains and others. (Seawright, 2016: 153)

Another curious finding in Paluck's study speaks to the complexities inherent in the application of interventions in real life. Contrary to expectation, the participants who received the imagine-self technique were actually *less* tolerant of outgroups in terms of their attitudes (both in the close-ended questionnaire and in the spontaneous comments) and in their donating behavior. Adding to the surprise, those who discussed the show with others, a strategy supposed to enhance the uptake of the intervention programme, showed the *lowest* tolerance.

Since these findings were contrary to theory and to many lab results, both constituting the basis of this intervention programme, Paluck tried to speculate about the reasons behind these surprising results. One potential explanation has to do with the type of participants. Most research supporting the theory underpinning the principles of this intervention programme is based on Western college students. This population might not be equivalent to the African population targeted in Paluck's study. In fact, according to Henrich *et al.* (2010), most research on human psychology and behavior published in top journals comes from what they call WEIRD societies: Western, Educated, Industrialized, Rich and Democratic. Henrich and colleagues argue that this is the least representative population for generalizing about humans. In many applied linguistics subdisciplines, though with some exceptions, a significant amount of research is similarly based on 'WEIRD' societies, thus possibly compromising its applicability to other contexts.

Another potential explanation is the complexity of real life. Even if researchers obtain favorable results under controlled conditions, this is no guarantee that the same results would be obtained under naturalistic conditions (cf. *experimental realism* discussed earlier). This underscores the indispensability of complementing lab experiments with field experiments, particularly experimental ethnographies. Additionally, this serves as a cautionary tale for certain thematic areas of research in applied linguistics (e.g. language learning motivation research) in which much of the practical advice given to stakeholders and practitioners is not based on field experiments but on observational, especially questionnaire-based designs (Al-Hoorie, 2018; Hiver & Al-Hoorie, 2020; Lamb, 2017).

'Without experimental research to support such pedagogical recommen-dations, this practice may be at best misleading, and at worst damaging to the field' (Al-Hoorie, 2018: 742).

Example Study 2: Regression Discontinuity Designs

Initially, we should be clear that regression discontinuity is *not* a sta-tistical test (as in multiple regression). Instead, it is a research *design* that can be used to uncover the causal role of an intervention when intentional experimental randomization is not feasible (Thistlethwaite & Campbell, 1960). This design involves comparing what happens before and after a cutoff point at which a treatment (e.g. a policy change) is enforced.

A concrete example might help clarify this abstract idea. Let's say that we would like to examine the effect of smoking on cancer. In an ideal world, researchers would assign some participants to an experimental group and instruct them to smoke daily, and other participants to a con-trol group and prohibit them from smoking even if they are so inclined. The researchers can then examine whether the experimental participants experience a higher rate of cancer incidence. This is in an ideal world. In the real world, however, ethical considerations prevent researchers from conducting such experiments, though ethical atrocities are not unheard of in the history of research methodology (e.g. the Tuskegee syphilis experiment; Reverby, 2009).

Consider this alternative scenario: imagine that economic sanctions were imposed on a country. As part of these sanctions, tobacco prod-ucts were no longer imported into that country. Researchers can now compare the cancer rate in the years before and after the sanctions, as smokers would suddenly cease smoking due to the unavailability of tobacco products. Imagine further that the monthly cancer deaths in the years before and after the sanctions were something similar to the plot in Figure 18.1. The vertical line down the middle is the time the sanc-tions were introduced. It is clear that there was a sudden and noticeable drop in death rates (see also Chapter 11 for instrumental variables).

Let us provide a brief example of how this has been used by research-ers. Angrist and Lavy (1999) used a regression discontinuity design to estimate the effect of class size on academic achievement. It is typically

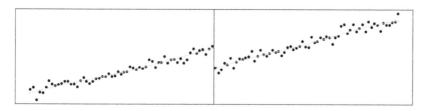

Figure 18.1 Hypothetical regression discontinuity data

hard to manipulate class size in actual schools to experimentally examine whether smaller classes lead to higher achievement. However, Angrist and Lavy located a region where the state law requires that classes have a maximum limit of 40 students. Once the number exceeds 40, the school would be required to split that class in half. Angrist and Lavy found this an opportunity to conduct a regression discontinuity analysis on classes with just under 40 and just over 40 (and so had to be split).

Angrist and Lavy's article contains some mathematical equations that might make it difficult to follow. However, their conclusions are clear. They found clear support for the hypothesis that smaller classes have a positive impact on reading and mathematics achievement for fifth graders, modest support for fourth graders and little support for third graders. What is relevant to the present discussion is how Angrist and Lavy integrated qualitative inquiry into their quantitative assessment. They closely examined the local context in order to find out the robustness of the regression discontinuity design. For example, they considered deliberate manipulation by parents to check the extent to which parents would transfer their children to other schools to escape large classes. Such 'strategic behavior' would threaten the internal validity of this design. The researchers also considered school sizes and the fact that urban areas tend to have larger schools overall. In addition, they considered possible selection bias within schools in cases where principals might deliberately group struggling students in smaller classes. They also scrutinized the local context to understand why the results for third graders were different. They reported that the testing conditions for this subgroup were different due to certain non-educational influences that affected the whole region at the time. Obviously, such careful qualitative analysis of the local context is essential to apply and justify this design. The same applies to the aforementioned hypothetical tobacco sanctions. At first, it might seem that it is a simple quantitative exercise: just compare the cancer rates before and after the sanctions. However, to convince the reader of the internal validity of their study, the researchers would need to closely examine the context in question. They would need to consider whether tobacco products continued to be available (e.g. through smuggling), whether smokers resorted to alternative (e.g. local) products, whether it was possible for some to cross the border to get their nicotine fix and many other possibilities that can threaten a clear interpretation of the results. Examining such issues requires good qualitative research integrated into the quantitative design.

It goes without saying that we are relatively unconcerned here with the substantive implications of the example studies we discuss (e.g. whether there is robust evidence that smaller classes are indeed better than larger ones). It is possible, in fact likely, that some scholars might disagree with some decisions and interpretations of these studies. Our concern is purely methodological, and we present these example studies in order to help the reader appreciate the method under discussion and to stimulate thinking about it.

Annotated readings

Hesse-Biber, S. and Johnson, R.B. (eds) (2015) *The Oxford Handbook of Multimethod and Mixed Method Research Inquiry*. Oxford: Oxford University Press.

Seawright, J. (2016) *Multi-Method Social Science: Combining Qualitative and Quantitative Tools*. Cambridge: Cambridge University Press.

Tashakkori A. and Teddlie, C. (eds) (2010) *SAGE Handbook of Mixed Methods in Social & Behavioral Research* (2nd edn). Los Angeles, CA: SAGE.

Teddlie, C. and Tashakkori, A. (2009) *Foundations of Mixed Methods Research: Integrating Quantitative and Qualitative Approaches in the Social and Behavioral Sciences*. Thousand Oaks, CA: SAGE.

These four books provide a wealth of information on mixed methods, the controversies surrounding them and optimal ways to integrate qualitative and quantitative methods.

Etz, A., Gronau, Q.F., Dablander, F., Edelsbrunner, P.A. and Baribault, B. (2018) How to become a Bayesian in eight easy steps: An annotated reading list. *Psychonomic Bulletin & Review* 25 (1), 219–234. doi:10.3758/s13423-017-1317-5

In this article, the authors made our job easier and presented an annotated list of readings on Bayesian statistics. This article comes as part of a special issue that contains some other useful articles on different aspects of Bayesian statistics.

Okasha, S. (2002) *Philosophy of Science: A Very Short Introduction*. Oxford: Oxford University Press.

O'Gorman, K. and MacIntosh, R. (2015) Mapping research methods. In K. O'Gorman and R. MacIntosh (eds) *Research Methods for Business & Management: A Guide to Writing Your Dissertation* (2nd edn; pp. 50–74). Oxford: Goodfellow.

Ladyman, J. (2007) Ontological, epistemological, and methodological positions. In T.A.F. Kuipers (ed.) *General Philosophy of Science: Focal Issues* (pp. 303–376). Amsterdam: North Holland.

It is also helpful for readers interested in CDST to be acquainted with the different philosophies of science. These three readings offer, in increasing level of detail, important introductions to the philosophy of science. All are reasonably accessible.

References

Ahmed, A. and Sil, R. (2009) Is multi-method research really 'better'? *Qualitative and Multi-Method Research* 7 (2), 2–6.

Ahmed, A. and Sil, R. (2012) When multi-method research subverts methodological pluralism—or, why we still need single-method research. *Perspectives on Politics* 10 (4), 935–953. doi:10.1017/S1537592712002836

Al-Hoorie, A.H. (2015) Human agency: Does the beach ball have free will? In Z. Dörnyei, P. MacIntyre and A. Henry (eds) *Motivational Dynamics in Language Learning* (pp. 55–72). Bristol: Multilingual Matters.

Al-Hoorie, A.H. (2018) The L2 Motivational Self System: A meta-analysis. *Studies in Second Language Learning and Teaching* 8 (4), 721–754. doi:10.14746/ssllt.2018.8.4.2

Al-Hoorie, A.H. (in press) Motivation and the unconscious. In M. Lamb, K. Csizér, A. Henry and S. Ryan (eds) *The Palgrave Handbook of Motivation for Language Learning*. Basingstoke: Palgrave Macmillan.

Al-Hoorie, A.H. and Vitta, J.P. (in press) The seven sins of L2 research: A review of 30 journals' statistical quality and their CiteScore, SJR, SNIP, JCR Impact Factors. *Language Teaching Research*. doi:10.1177/1362168818767191

Aldhous, P. (2011) Journal rejects studies contradicting precognition. *New Scientist*. See http://www.newscientist.com/article/dn20447-journal-rejects-studies-contradictin gprecognition.html (accessed 10 January 2018).

Angrist, J.D. and Lavy, V. (1999) Using Maimonides' rule to estimate the effect of class size on scholastic achievement. *The Quarterly Journal of Economics* 114 (2), 533–575. doi:10.1162/003355399556061

Beck, N. (2006) Is causal-process observation an oxymoron? *Political Analysis* 14 (3), 347–352. doi:10.1093/pan/mpj015

Beck, N. (2010) Causal process 'observation': Oxymoron or (fine) old wine. *Political Analysis* 18 (4), 499–505. doi:10.1093/pan/mpq023

Bem, D.J. (2011) Feeling the future: Experimental evidence for anomalous retroactive influences on cognition and affect. *Journal of Personality and Social Psychology* 100 (3), 407–425. doi:10.1037/a0021524

Bolstad, W.M. (2007) *Introduction to Bayesian Statistics* (2nd edn). Hoboken, NJ: Wiley.

Brown, J.D. (2014) *Mixed Methods Research for TESOL*. Edinburgh: Edinburgh University Press.

Creswell, J.W. (2011) Controversies in mixed methods research. In N.K. Denzin and Y.S. Lincoln (eds) *The SAGE Handbook of Qualitative Research* (4th edn; pp. 269–284). Thousand Oaks, CA: SAGE.

Dörnyei, Z. (2007) *Research Methods in Applied Linguistics: Quantitative, Qualitative, and Mixed Methodologies*. Oxford: Oxford University Press.

Freedman, L.S. (2008) An analysis of the controversy over classical one-sided tests. *Clinical Trials* 5 (6), 635–640. doi:10.1177/1740774508098590

Gage, N.L. and Needels, M.C. (1989) Process-product research on teaching: A review of criticisms. *The Elementary School Journal* 89 (3), 253–300. doi:10.1086/461577

Gelman, A. (2018) The failure of null hypothesis significance testing when studying incremental changes, and what to do about it. *Personality and Social Psychology Bulletin* 44 (1), 16–23. doi:10.1177/0146167217729162

Giddings, L.S. (2006) Mixed-methods research: Positivism dressed in drag? *Journal of Research in Nursing* 11 (3), 195–203. doi:10.1177/1744987106064635

Giddings, L.S. and Grant, B.M. (2007) A Trojan Horse for positivism? A critique of mixed methods research. *Advances in Nursing Science* 30 (1), 52–60.

Goldstein, M. (2006) Subjective Bayesian analysis: Principles and practice. *Bayesian Analysis* 1 (3), 403–420. doi:10.1214/06-BA116

Henrich, J., Heine, S.J. and Norenzayan, A. (2010) The weirdest people in the world? *Behavioral and Brain Sciences* 33 (2–3), 61–83. doi:10.1017/S0140525X0999152X

Hesse-Biber, S. and Johnson, R.B. (eds) (2015) *The Oxford Handbook of Multimethod and Mixed Method Research Inquiry*. Oxford: Oxford University Press.

Hiver, P. and Al-Hoorie, A.H. (2020) Re-examining the role of vision and imagery in L2 learners' motivation: A preregistered conceptual replication of You, Dörnyei, and Csizér (2016). *Language Learning* 70, 1–55. doi:10.1111/lang.12371

Judd, C.M. and Gawronski, B. (2011) Editorial comment. *Journal of Personality and Social Psychology* 100 (3), 406. doi:10.1037/0022789

Kahneman, D. and Tversky, A. (eds) (2000) *Choices, Values, and Frames*. New York: Cambridge University Press.

Ladyman, J. (2007) Ontological, epistemological, and methodological positions. In T.A.F. Kuipers (ed.) *General Philosophy of Science: Focal Issues* (pp. 303–376). Amsterdam: North Holland.

Lamb, M. (2017) The motivational dimension of language teaching. *Language Teaching* 50 (3), 301–346. doi:10.1017/S0261444817000088

Lincoln, Y.S. and Guba, E.G. (2013) *The Constructivist Credo*. Walnut Creek, CA: Left Coast Press.

Mackey, A. and Bryfonski, L. (2018) Mixed methodology. In A. Phakiti, P. De Costa, L. Plonsky and S. Starfield (eds) *The Palgrave Handbook of Applied Linguistics Research Methodology* (pp. 103–121). New York: Palgrave Macmillan.

McGrayne, S.B. (2011) *The Theory that Would Not Die: How Bayes' Rule Cracked the Enigma Code, Hunted Down Russian Submarines, and Emerged Triumphant from Two Centuries of Controversy*. London: Yale University Press.

Mirhosseini, S.-A. (2018) Mixed methods research in TESOL: Procedures combined or epistemology confused? *TESOL Quarterly* 52 (2), 468–478. doi:10.1002/tesq.427

Nastasi, B.K., Hitchcock, J.H. and Brown, L.M. (2010) An inclusive framework for conceptualizing mixed methods design typologies: Moving toward fully integrated synergistic research models. In A. Tashakkori and C. Teddlie (eds) *SAGE Handbook of Mixed Methods in Social & Behavioral Research* (2nd edn; pp. 305–338). Los Angeles, CA: SAGE.

Norouzian, R., de Miranda, M. and Plonsky, L. (2018) The Bayesian revolution in second language research: An applied approach. *Language Learning* 68 (4), 1032–1075. doi:doi:10.1111/lang.12310

Paluck, E.L. (2010a) Is it better not to talk? Group polarization, extended contact, and perspective taking in Eastern Democratic Republic of Congo. *Personality and Social Psychology Bulletin* 36 (9), 1170–1185. doi:10.1177/0146167210379868

Paluck, E.L. (2010b) The promising integration of qualitative methods and field experiments. *The Annals of the American Academy of Political and Social Science* 628 (1), 59–71. doi:10.1177/0002716209351510

Popper, K.R. (1983) *Realism and the Aim of Science*. New York: Routledge.

Popper, K.R. (2002/1934) *The Logic of Scientific Discovery*. London: Routledge.

Reverby, S.M. (2009) *Examining Tuskegee: The Infamous Syphilis Study and Its Legacy*. Chapel Hill, NC: University of North Carolina Press.

Riazi, A.M. (2017) *Mixed Methods Research in Language Teaching and Learning*. Sheffield: Equinox.

Ross, S.J. and Mackey, B. (2015) Bayesian approaches to imputation, hypothesis testing, and parameter estimation. *Language Learning* 65 (S1), 208–227. doi:10.1111/lang.12118

Rouder, J.N. and Morey, R.D. (2011) A Bayes factor meta-analysis of Bem's ESP claim. *Psychonomic Bulletin & Review* 18 (4), 682–689. doi:10.3758/s13423-011-0088-7

Salsburg, D. (2001) *The Lady Tasting Tea: How Statistics Revolutionized Science in the Twentieth Century*. New York: Freeman.

Seawright, J. (2016) *Multi-Method Social Science: Combining Qualitative and Quantitative Tools*. Cambridge: Cambridge University Press.

Sherman, L.W. and Strang, H. (2004) Experimental ethnography: The marriage of qualitative and quantitative research. *The Annals of the American Academy of Political and Social Science* 595 (1), 204–222. doi:10.1177/0002716204267481

Teddlie, C. and Tashakkori, A. (2009) *Foundations of Mixed Methods Research: Integrating Quantitative and Qualitative Approaches in the Social and Behavioral Sciences*. Thousand Oaks, CA: SAGE.

Teddlie, C. and Tashakkori, A. (2010) Overview of contemporary issues in mixed methods research. In A. Tashakkori and C. Teddlie (eds) *SAGE Handbook of Mixed Methods in Social & Behavioral Research* (2nd edn; pp. 1–41). Los Angeles, CA: SAGE.

Thistlethwaite, D.L. and Campbell, D.T. (1960) Regression-discontinuity analysis: An alternative to the ex post facto experiment. *Journal of Educational Psychology* 51 (6), 309–317. doi:10.1037/h0044319

Uprichard, E. (2009) Introducing cluster analysis: What can it teach us about the case? In D. Byrne and C.C. Ragin (eds) *The SAGE Handbook of Case-Based Methods* (pp. 132–147). New York: SAGE.

van Fraassen, B.C. (1980) *The Scientific Image*. Oxford: Oxford University Press.

Vickers, A. (2010) *What Is a p-Value Anyway? 34 Stories to Help You Actually Understand Statistics*. Boston, MA: Addison-Wesley.

Wagenmakers, E.-J., Wetzels, R., Borsboom, D. and van der Maas, H.L.J. (2011) Why psychologists must change the way they analyze their data: The case of psi: Comment on Bem (2011). *Journal of Personality and Social Psychology* 100 (3), 426–432. doi:10.1037/a0022790

19 Glossary and Further Resources for CDST Methodology

Introduction

This book has been concerned with designing and conducting research in ways that are sensitive to a complex and dynamic reality. In Part 1, we began with an overview of complexity and dynamic systems theory (CDST) and then explored its philosophy of science. This was intended to provide the background necessary to begin thinking and operating from a CDST frame of reference. However, many of the ideas reviewed in Chapters 2 and 3 rely on terminology that is unique to CDST and that conveys technical meanings. In this final brief chapter, we provide a glossary of CDST terminology for interested readers. While certain terms may have a non-CDST sense that is used by scholars in the field, here we clarify the CDST-specific meanings and uses of these terms to avoid ambiguity and maximize coherence. Terminology alone would also provide little guidance for doing research without the contextualizing information provided in those earlier chapters, and many of these entries are expanded on from their respective sections in Chapters 2 and 3. We have chosen to place these here, toward the end of the book, so as not to break up the flow of those chapters or front-load this technical language and risk overwhelming the reader. We envision the reader using this glossary as a resource in their reading, flipping back to it as necessary when looking for greater clarification. Throughout, we have intentionally provided multiple examples of the terms we use, and we have tried to carefully select and cite sources that would allow the interested reader to discover more on the topic should they enjoy the challenge of further, more technical reading. (An excellent supplement to the glossary in this chapter is found at www.complexityexplorer.org/explore/glossary.)

Finally, we end this chapter by summarizing various online and offline sources and databases related to CDST and CDST methodology. Our hope is that interested readers will continue their exploration of CDST and its contribution to applied linguistics research through these resources.

Glossary

Attractor (aka Attractor state)

An *attractor state* (n.) is a critical value, pattern, solution or outcome toward which a complex system settles down or approaches over time. *Attractor states* can be seen as a preferred state for a particular system, but they do not 'attract' in the everyday sense of the word. Instead, they are a way of describing the behavior of a system within pockets of stability and help observers understand what a system is doing as it reaches a dynamic equilibrium. Attractors can sustain behavior or generate change. (Chapter 2)

Attractor basin (aka Basin of attraction)

An *attractor basin* (n.) refers to the set of all initial conditions in time and in the environment that allow a complex system to reach a given attractor state. An *attractor basin* is the feature in state space that allows us to describe both the range of the attractor state's reach and the strength of an attractor state on the complex system. (See Chapter 2)

Autopoiesis

Autopoiesis (n.) refers to a self-referential property of a complex system that allows it to maintain and renew itself by regulating its composition and conserving its boundaries. Systems are said to be *autopoietic* (adj.) when they are capable of regenerating and maintaining their level of complexity independently of any other external objective (e.g. growth, development). (See Chapter 3)

Bifurcation

A *bifurcation* (n.) is a developmental change in the state space that occurs when a small adjustment to system parameters results in a major phase change or a qualitatively different outcome for a complex system. Systems *bifurcate* (v.) in ways that lead to greater equilibrium (i.e. period-halving bifurcations reduce the number of iterations necessary to reach equilibrium by half) or in ways that result in greater variability and complexity (i.e. period-doubling bifurcations double the number of such iterations needed). (See Chapter 2)

Co-adaptation

Co-adaptation (n.) refers to the co-regulatory process by which complex systems reorganize their internal working parts to adapt themselves to the problems posed by their surroundings or by other systems. Systems are said to be *co-adaptive* (adj.) when they evolve and attempt to optimize interactions with their surroundings and with other systems through time. (See Chapter 2)

Complex

Complex (adj.) describes a whole (e.g. a system) that is not analytically tractable from its components, and in combination has emergent capacities than are greater than the sum of its parts. *Complex* refers to the quality of existence as being interconnected, consisting of various parts formed in combination, united together and unknowable except as a whole. (See Chapter 2)

Complicated

Complicated (adj.) things, ideas or issues involve multiple elements that exist or occur together, and that are fundamentally knowable by breaking them down into their component parts. In contrast to what is complex, a complete and accurate picture of what is *complicated* can be taken from the attributes of its internal parts. (See Chapter 2)

Coupling

Coupling (n.) refers to the relationship that links the open boundaries between a complex system and the environment or another system. The presence of a *coupled* (adj.) relationship allows a transfer of energy, information or resources between a complex system and the environment or another system that can lead to adaptive patterns over time. (See Chapter 2)

Emergence

Emergence (n.) is a higher-order outcome in which a complex system shows qualitatively new behaviors or functions which cannot be described or explained by any constraints that define and control the complex system and its parts or from the interactions of its components. A pattern is said to be *emergent* (adj.) if it develops through time in a way that cannot be predicted or traced by relying on knowledge of the system and the order parameters that guide its existence. (See Chapter 2)

Equifinality

Equifinality (n.) refers to the principle in complex systems that a given outcome may be achieved with different initial conditions and via different trajectories. Two processes or models are said to be *equifinal* (adj.) if they lead a given system to the same stable state independently of any initial conditions and developmental contingencies. (See Chapter 3)

Ergodicity

Ergodicity (n.) refers to the characteristic of wholes to exhibit the same behavior and properties as their parts over time, and vice versa.

Systems and processes are said to be *ergodic* (adj.) when every sequence in time or sample in space is equally representative of the whole entity or developmental trajectory. (See Chapter 3)

Feedback

Feedback (n.) refers to the energy, information or resources from a complex system's output looping back as input and influencing change. *Positive feedback* is self-reinforcing feedback that amplifies a complex system's adaptive changes along a developmental path, thereby increasing returns over time. *Negative feedback* is self-maintaining feedback that dampens system change or adaptation to keep a complex system within a certain set of parameters that enable its stable functioning. (See Chapter 2)

Fractal

Fractals (n.) are a self-similar set of patterns that can be observed across all scales of the complex system. *Fractal* (adj.) describes patterns with identical dimensions or look-alike features that can be observed simultaneously across multiple scales (e.g. the global and the local).

Hard-assembled

Hard-assembled (adj.) mechanisms are processes for system adaptation that have a set process and are designed for a limited and specific outcome. These processes and mechanisms exist independent of the immediate context in which the complex system is nested, and are not flexible to change or alteration. *Hard-assembled* mechanisms apply across multiple contexts, are discovered independent to performance and exist offline in some form of inactive, absolute state. (See Chapter 2)

Hysteresis

Hysteresis (n.) refers to the phenomenon in which a complex system's current state is dependent on its temporal history. This is often observed as a dynamic lag between an input and an output or in the delay between instigating initial conditions of implementation and the emergence of system-wide effects. Systems are said to be *hysteretic* (adj.) when, like the ripples in a pond, effects at an initial time result in subsequent effects that exert some causal force on all successive iterations. (See Chapter 3)

Initial conditions

Initial conditions (n.) refers to the state of various complex system components, system dimensions and parameters, and environmental conditions at the point in time an observer begins observing that system's development. Because there is always continuity in system behavior and development, initial conditions are relative to the observer and are not 'initial' in a literal sense. (See Chapter 2)

Self-organization

Self-organization (n.) is a spontaneous or internally evolving process of coordinated restructuring and formation within a complex system that results in the appearance of a novel structure and functions. A process is said to be *self-organized* (adj.) if it proceeds without anyone purposely directing or engineering it into existence and leads to outcomes at a higher level (i.e. the system-wide level). Self-organization is a robust general process that leads to emergent outcomes. (See Chapter 2)

Self-organized criticality

Self-organized criticality (n.) refers to instances when a complex system reaches the critical point of transition between two discrete phases of stability or equilibrium – for example when a self-organized system reaches critical mass or critical velocity. This value is qualitatively different from other values in a state space, and the result of a system reaching self-organized criticality is often a dramatic change into a novel phase or attractor state. (See Chapter 2)

Soft-assembled

Soft-assembled (adj.) processes are a form of improvisational adaptations between multiple interacting components, freely combined from moment to moment on the basis of the context, task and developmental history of a system. These adaptations rely on principles for system change that come into existence and are realized only within the immediate context of a situation or task. *Soft-assembly* (n.) involves a particular adaptation of a complex system in its environment. It is contextually constrained, temporary, takes place in real time and involves only tools and structures that are currently available and necessary. (See Chapter 2)

State space

The *state space* (n.) is the N-dimensional landscape of total possible outcome configurations that a system can be found in at any given time. CDST uses this topographical metaphor to capture where dynamic behavior unfolds and which patterned outcomes can exist for a system. The *state space* provides a more or less comprehensive idea of all potential phenomenological outcomes for a complex system. (See Chapter 2)

Stochastic

Stochastic (adj.) processes are those that occur in a random (i.e. in the mathematical sense) and non-deterministic way through time, and exhibit a random probability distribution that cannot be predicted precisely. *Stochasticity* (n.) is a characteristic of complex systems, and results in probabilistic outcomes and behaviors, the opposite of deterministic outcomes. (See Chapter 3)

Further Sources and Resources

Online resources

Several excellent online sources exist for those interested in exploring the subject matter of CDST in a more in-depth way. In some ways, the best of these rival even book-length sources of technical information as they are much wider ranging in the information they feature and are curated by world-class experts in the complexity sciences.

- The Santa Fe Institute (SFI; https://www.santafe.edu/) is the premier center for the study of transdisciplinary topics in complexity science. The SFI was founded in 1984 as an independent, non-profit research center exploring the frontiers of complex systems science. As one of its prominent donors states on the SFI website: 'When I think about the world of science, when everything is going down the tubes and when ignorance is on the rise, if you could save one place that might start discursive thinking all over again, it would be the Santa Fe Institute'. Since its founding, the SFI has hosted scholars from around the world working on research projects and questions that span all disciplines and that are truly transdisciplinary in their focus on critical and seemingly intractable problems as they search for common patterns and principles. The SFI website provides information on:
  - Themes and projects under investigation.
  - Scholars and community partners working on these issues.
  - Publications and resources on complexity.
  - Scholarships and fellowships in the complexity sciences.
  - Summer schools and workshops.
- Complexity Explorer (https://www.complexityexplorer.org/home) is the Santa Fe Institute's center for educating the public on complexity science. This platform was launched through a grant from the John Templeton Foundation to the Santa Fe Institute in 2011, and in early 2013 the first course was launched with over 7000 enrolled students. The primary goal of Complexity Explorer is maximum diffusion and use of complexity science, and in order to accomplish this the website provides many of the tools and applications needed to become a complexity scholar. These include:
  - Massively open online courses.
  - Topical tutorials.
  - Resources and syllabi library.
  - Glossary.

- • Virtual labs.
- • Complexity challenges.
- • Working groups and shared interest groups.

   Readers who are interested in immersing themselves in complexity will find Complexity Explorer, as we ourselves have found, the closest thing to a one-stop learning center on the internet.
- • Map of the Complexity Sciences (http://www.art-sciencefactory.com/complexity-map_feb09.html) is a visual diagram of the transdisciplinary nature of complexity theory, created and curated by Brian Castellani. The 'map' can be read in a roughly chronological fashion and shows the progression of the complexity sciences on a decade-by-decade basis. Along this developmental trajectory, key scholarly themes and methods used across complexity science are placed at the rough points in time at which they became a major area of study (e.g. *Autopoiesis* appears in the late 1970s). Connected to each of these themes and methods are the scholars who either founded them or whose contribution to the complexity sciences best exemplifies work in that area (e.g. Humberto Maturana and Francisco Varela are associated with *Autopoiesis* on this map). The Map of the Complexity Sciences has gone through many revisions and continues to be updated by its creator.
- • Complexity Digest (https://comdig.unam.mx/) is the official news channel and community networking site for the Complex Systems Society, edited by Carlos Gershenson. This website features information on papers and books, events and conferences, as well as talks and podcasts taking place throughout the community (see also https://www.scoop.it/u/complexity-digest). The purpose of the Complex Systems Society itself, founded in 2004, is to assist and advise on problems of complex systems education and with the broader relations of complex systems to society, to foster interaction between complex systems scientists from different countries and establish a sense of identity among complexity scientists and to represent the complexity community at an international level. Its website (https://cssociety.org/home) also showcases some of the work from the regional organizations that make up its international membership, upcoming academic meetings and workshops on complex systems research, calls for papers on topics in complexity science and lists job openings in the field along with other miscellaneous information.
- • New England Complex Systems Institute (NECSI; https://necsi-global.org/) is an independent academic research and educational institution, slightly younger than the SFI, that houses students, postdoctoral fellows and faculty. Just a few of its stated aims are to reframe social problems as scientific ones and expand the boundaries of knowledge by increasing the role of complex systems science in society. In addition to its large in-house research team, NECSI

sponsors external faculty, students and affiliates from other universities, and hosts certificate programmes and seminars in complexity research, network modeling and data analytics. The NECSI website is a repository for research and educational opportunities in complex systems science. In addition to proceedings and encyclopedia-like entries on topical questions in complexity (e.g. Are complex societies governable? How can ethnic violence be solved?), these include such things as a video archive of seminars on subjects of interest in complexity research, and podcasts and informative talks. The scholarly work and informational resources range across topics and dilemmas in complexity research.

Journals and magazines

- *Complexity* is a peer-reviewed, online open-access journal founded in 1995 and affiliated in its earlier days with the Santa Fe Institute. Since 2017, the journal is published as part of a collaboration between the publishers Wiley and Hindawi (https://www.hindawi.com/journals/c omplexity/). *Complexity* reports important advances in the scientific study – in the broadest sense – of complex systems across a wide range of disciplines. Concepts that have been featured and published in the journal include the adaptability, robustness and resilience of complex systems; complex networks; criticality; evolution and emergent behavior; nonlinear dynamics; pattern formation; and self-organization. Papers can be found with a range of theoretical, methodological or practical foci. Issues of the journal published prior to 2017 are hosted on the Wiley Online Library (https://onlinelibrary.wi ley.com/journal/10990526).

- *Complicity: An International Journal of Complexity and Education* (https://journals.library.ualberta.ca/complicity/index.php/compli city) is a peer-reviewed, online open-access journal that publishes conceptual and empirical papers on all aspects of education that are informed by the idea of complexity whether these are technical, applied, philosophical or theoretical ways. This journal is affiliated with the Chaos and Complexity Theories Special Interest Group of the American Educational Research Association, and serves as the forum for related conference proceedings. At the time of writing, *Complicity* is being renamed the *International Journal of Complexity in Education* and transitioning to an updated platform (https://ijce.m ercy.edu/index.php/ijce/).

- *Emergence: Complexity and Organization* (https://journal.emergent publications.com/) is a peer-reviewed, online open-access journal on the organization and behavior of complex systems, particularly human organizations and social structures as complex systems. The mission of the journal is to bridge gaps between academic theory and professional practice, between the mathematics and the metaphors of complexity thinking and between formal idealizations and actual human orga- nizations. While its thematic focus is primarily on the development and management of human organizations, the broader purpose of this journal is to act as a venue for research on topics such as:

- Theoretical foundations of complex systems.
- Historical and philosophical aspects of complex systems.
- Data-driven approaches to complex systems.
- Non-linear dynamics.
- Self-organization, pattern formation and collective behavior.
- Structure and dynamics of complex networks.
- Sustainability and adaptability of complex systems.
- Complex systems and education.
- Applications across the humanities and social sciences.

- *Journal of Complexity* (https://www.sciencedirect.com/journal/j ournal-of-complexity) is the oldest peer-reviewed journal (founded in 1985) in complexity science. The journal is a technical forum for computational methods in complexity research, and because of this it features work that is much more mathematical in nature than other journals listed here. The *Journal of Complexity* also awards the annual Joseph E. Traub prize for achievements in information-based complexity. Some of the complexity topics featured in the journal include:
  - Computational stochastics.
  - Distributed and parallel computation.
  - High and infinite-dimensional problems.
  - Information-based complexity.
  - Noisy data.
  - System optimization.

Other peer-reviewed journals with a much heavier mathematical focus also exist. Just two examples are *Dynamical Systems: An Inter- national Journal* (https://www.tandfonline.com/toc/cdss20/current) and *SIAM Journal on Applied Dynamical Systems* (https://www.siam.or g/Publications/Journals/SIAM-Journal-on-Applied-Dynamical-Systems -SIADS). These journals serve as fora for communication across many different branches of nonlinear dynamical systems and are a platform to facilitate interaction between the mathematical theory of dynamical sys- tems and application in a variety of fields. Journals such as these feature highly technical information that many in the field of applied linguistics will probably find a high bar to understanding. Topics that readers can find in these journals include applications of:

- Non-linear differential equations.
- Bifurcation theory.

- Hamiltonian and Lagrangian dynamics.
- Hyperbolic dynamics.
- Ergodic theory.
- Topological and smooth dynamics.
- Random dynamical systems.
- Uncertainty quantification.

Books and anthologies

- Springer Series in *Understanding Complex Systems* (UCS) edited by J.A. Scott Kelso (https://www.springer.com/series/5394?details Page=titles) features over 120 titles that include monographs, lecture notes and selected edited contributions reporting on developments for understanding and realizing applications of complex systems in a wide variety of fields. The founders of this Springer Series explicitly intended UCS as a transdisciplinary platform to elaborate the concepts, methods and tools of complex systems at all levels of description and in all scientific fields. The series is designed to encourage novel applications of ideas from complex systems in various fields across the social, human and natural sciences. Titles in the series provide excellent exemplars of how commonalities and differences in the workings of complex systems can be researched and disseminated to a wide readership.
- Routledge *Complexity in Social Science* Series (CISS) edited by David Byrne, Brian Castellani and Emma Uprichard (https://www.routled ge.com/Complexity-in-Social-Science/book-series/CISS) is a book series that encourages social scientists to embrace a complex systems approach to studying the human and social world. Covering a broad range of topics from big data and time, globalization and health, cities and populations, policy and governance, sustainability and inequality, thinking and learning, and methodological applications, CISS is part of a scholarly initiative to expand complexity research across the disciplines as those disciplines continue to morph, data continue to diversify and responses to global social issues continue to challenge all involved. This series features various titles that propose a response to these challenges of complexity in the social sciences – with an emphasis on critical dialogue around, and application of these ideas in, a variety of social disciplines.
- The *Encyclopedia of Complexity and Systems Science* edited by Robert A. Meyers (https://www.springer.com/us/book/97803877588 86) is a 10-volume treasure trove of information compiled on every conceivable topic in the complexity sciences. This encyclopedia is *the* single most authoritative source for understanding and applying the basic tenets of complexity and systems theory as well as the tools and measures for analyzing complex systems. The editorial advisory

board and section editors include at least seven Nobel laureates and numerous winners of the Wolf Prize, the Fields Medal, the Turing Award, the Lasker Award and the IEEE Medal of Honor. We first stumbled on this encyclopedia while completing our PhDs at the University of Nottingham and knew at once that we would find no other treatment of complexity science that approached the depth and authority of these nearly 600 entries for answers to our deepest questions in CDST and CDST research.

- Finally, we have found it useful as researchers, and think it is advisable for others interested in CDST research, to develop some familiarity with how scholars in neighboring disciplines approach their research problems and what methods they use to do so. Here, we list several anthologies from other fields in social science that exemplify for interested readers the variety of CDST methods in action.

Bibliography

Allen, P., Maguire, S. and McKelvey, B. (eds) (2011) *The SAGE Handbook of Complexity and Management*. Thousand Oaks, CA: SAGE.

Byrne, D. and Ragin, C.C. (eds) (2009) *The SAGE Handbook of Case-Based Methods*. Thousand Oaks, CA: SAGE.

Diehl, M., Hooker, K. and Sliwinksy, M.J. (eds) (2015) *Handbook of Intraindividual Variability across the Life Span*. New York: Routledge.

Granott, N. and Parziale, J. (eds) (2002) *Microdevelopment: Transition Processes in Development and Learning*. Cambridge: Cambridge University Press.

Koopmans, M. and Stamovlasis, D. (eds) (2016) *Complex Dynamical Systems in Education: Concepts, Methods and Applications*. New York: Springer.

Molenaar, P.C.M., Lerner, R. and Newell, K. (eds) (2014) *Handbook of Developmental Systems Theory and Methodology*. New York: Guilford.

Newell, K. and Molenaar, P.C.M. (eds) (1998/2014) *Applications of Nonlinear Dynamics to Developmental Process Modeling*. New York: Psychology Press.

Valsiner, J., Molenaar, P.C.M., Lyra, M. and Chaudhary, N. (eds) (2009) *Dynamic Process Methodology in the Social and Developmental Sciences*. New York: Springer.

Index

CPSIA information can be obtained
at www.ICGtesting.com
Printed in the USA
BVHW090218270421
605935BV00010B/322